STUDIES IN THEORETICAL AND APPLIED ECONOMICS

General editor:
B. T. BAYLISS

THE ECONOMICS OF
PUBLIC ENTERPRISE

P. W. REED B.Sc.(Econ), MCIT
Head of Economics Branch, Civil Aviation Authority
Formerly, Lecturer in Economics, University of Reading

Distributed in the United States by
CRANE, RUSSAK & COMPANY, INC.
347 Madison Avenue
New York, New York 10017

THE BUTTERWORTH GROUP

ENGLAND
Butterworth & Co (Publishers) Ltd
London: 88 Kingsway, WC2B 6AB

AUSTRALIA
Butterworths Pty Ltd
Sydney: 586 Pacific Highway, NSW 2067
Melbourne: 343 Little Collins Street, 3000
Brisbane: 240 Queen Street, 4000

CANADA
Butterworth & Co (Canada) Ltd
Toronto: 14 Curity Avenue, 374

NEW ZEALAND
Butterworths of New Zealand Ltd
Wellington: 26–28 Waring Taylor Street, 1

SOUTH AFRICA
Butterworth & Co (South Africa) (Pty) Ltd
Durban: 152–154 Gale Street

First published in 1973

© P. W. Reed, 1973

ISBN 0 408 70452 7

Filmset, printed and bound in England by
Cox & Wyman Ltd., London, Fakenham and Reading

PREFACE

Interest in the systematic economic study of public enterprises is growing rapidly. One result of this is an increasing volume of literature on the subject, both academic and 'official'. As the sheer size of the reading task grows and the theoretical literature develops, so do the students' difficulties in mastering this important field.

The basic aim of this book is to provide a framework for study, linking theoretical and policy aspects. Needless to say, the task turned out to be more difficult than originally anticipated. For one thing, it would have been desirable to include some discussion of enterprises producing 'public' or 'quasi-public' goods. This had to be left out for space reasons.

Furthermore, the attempt to link theory and practice together led to difficulties of organisation. On the one hand, it would be possible to undertake a purely analytical treatment which would more or less turn into an exposition of those economic techniques relevant to the study of public enterprises; in effect, another welfare economics text. On the other, a 'tour' of the various public enterprises could have been undertaken. In the latter case, there would probably have been far more specific treatment of the various enterprises, bringing in historical data, factual information, political and social background, and so on.

The compromise solution adopted was to give the reader a basis of theory, then to move on to specific sectors and enterprises for illustrative examples, and to conclude with some general policy discussion. Such a scheme necessarily involves a certain amount of overlap and repetition but teaching experience suggests that this may not be a bad thing. The treatment may also be somewhat uneven in places both in form and difficulty: it is not easy to withstand the temptation to go through the manuscript again in order to insert all the qualifications to the theoretical arguments and to write about the wider non-economic contexts in which the enterprises should often be discussed.

Regrettably, theorists are often going to be disappointed—like the author—by the lack of rigour they will sometimes find. There are, how-ever, excellent books and articles which can help remedy this deficiency; many of them are given in the footnotes. It is precisely because so much of this material is difficult for the average second or third year student that I have engaged in simplification and attempted to explain the significance of such theory for practical problems. Such readers should have acquired enough knowledge of economics to tackle the book.

Some of the examples used may now seem somewhat 'dated' (that is, if classic studies ever do date!). In choosing such examples, I have been guided by practical knowledge of the sort of library difficulties that students frequently encounter.

Economists have traditionally focused a great deal of attention upon pricing decisions, and so we begin in this area of analysis. Our task is to take from micro-economic theory some basic concepts relevant to public enterprise problems. Inevitably, one must begin with two-dimensional abstractions. Nevertheless, these provide a useful starting point for the analysis of real-life situations, providing their limitations are remembered. As we work through the subject, attempts must be made to clothe such abstractions in the flesh and blood of industrial reality.

The close relationship between pricing and investment problems is emphasised. Indeed, in one case, we start 'the wrong way round', moving from an investment problem to a pricing rule. This particular sequence reflects the experience of economic practitioners who had to tackle the investment problem first and then work back to the pricing issue.

There follows some discussion of 'second best' problems. Here we have a good example of apparently abstruse theory which nevertheless has important implications for policy. In particular, the interactions between policies of public enterprises, and between those of public and private sectors, need to be examined. The pricing chapter concludes with an analysis of a complex form of pricing: multi-part tariff charging.

We go on to examine some of the issues associated with the investment decision. After dealing with some of the forecasting problems, an elementary exposition of appraisal techniques is undertaken. Here, an important influence has been knowledge of the difficulties experienced by many students in 'translating' algebraic formulations into simple arithmetic. This is attempted with the help of explanatory tables.

Having thus laid a basis of knowledge, discussion of the crucially important subject of choice of public sector discount rate may take place.

Much of the recent policy discussion of public enterprises has been concerned with the relevance of modern management techniques. A chapter is therefore devoted to some important dimensions of industrial decision-making not usually covered in the economist's treatment of pricing and investment.

First the principles of what has come to be known as 'corporate strategy' are considered. Taking the body of theory and practice developed by management writers and business undertakings, an attempt is made to consider the implications for the study of public enterprise.

This subject leads on to a consideration of marketing theory. Brief attention is then devoted to some concepts of management control. It is impossible to give an adequate survey of modern management theory and practice in such a small compass but the material should give assistance in understanding references to such concepts in the literature, particularly official reports.

Having established a conceptual framework, we are ready to start tackling the economic analysis of some specific industries or sectors. We begin with a chapter devoted largely to coal but containing also some discussion about the effects of introducing natural gas into an existing production and distribution system. The chapter ends with a description of the attempt to construct a policy model of the entire fuel and power economy. This model embraces the 'secondary' power sector also (electricity) but it was thought appropriate to include the material here on the grounds that it is precisely coal and natural gas that give rise to the most radical adjustment problems of the kind the model is designed to assist with.

Electricity supply and distribution raise some complex issues. After examination of the economics of an 'isolated' electric power generating station, the analysis is developed to take in the investment decision and the peak pricing problem. When we turn to the practical charging problem, we are compelled to undertake analysis on a network basis. The problem of choice between alternative techniques is tackled on such a basis. Finally, the possible contribution of linear programming to the solution of such problems is examined.

Then comes a treatment of railway economics. This chapter begins with a brief analysis of the operating problems of railways with special reference to freight. There follows a discussion of the basic categories employed in analysing the costs of railway services, which leads on to a consideration of problems of pricing and investment. The complications arising from network effects are again brought into the analysis.

The use of simulation models to tackle important policy problems is examined with some emphasis on the practical difficulties encountered. Finally, there is some discussion of a specific policy issue, that of stand-by capacity, to examine the contribution economic analysis may make to its resolution.

A chapter on the economics of roads begins with an analysis of road costs and revenues with special reference to recent policy discussion. Then comes a consideration of road investment criteria which embraces again the network problem. It is impossible to consider this subject without taking account of social costs and benefits and a section is accordingly devoted to this. Also included is some analysis of the very important question of the comparability of (consumers' surplus) rates of return on road investment with those in other sectors calculated on other bases.

Governments not infrequently change the organisational structure of public enterprises and also the legislative and fiscal framework within which they operate. A chapter is devoted to some of the more important recent developments, with particular reference to their economic logic.

The analysis begins with railways. Here there is a long tradition of regulation and the railways have several times experienced major reorganisation since being taken into public ownership. Several major themes are taken. The logic of the National Freight Corporation is then discussed. This leads on to an analysis of recent changes in the system of road haulage licensing.

We then move on to a consideration of recent changes in London Transport, the steel industry and the Post Office.

A concluding chapter deals with the general economic problems of the relationships of government and nationalised industries. Particular attention is devoted to the question of strategic control.

P.W.R.
University of Reading

ACKNOWLEDGEMENTS

I should like to thank Dr. B. T. Bayliss and Professor G. Maynard for reading and commenting upon large sections of the manuscript. Mr. S. Leeming gave some bibliographical assistance. Typing and secretarial assistance was rendered by Mrs. B. Wall.

Particular thanks are due to Mr. M. McQueen, who assisted me with the whole of the manuscript and, indeed, who provided me with first drafts on the subjects of 'second best', natural gas pricing and linear programming. Naturally, full responsibility for errors and omissions is mine alone.

I have had direct experience of, or close personal ties with, practically all the industries discussed in the book including a spell within a relevant part of the government economic service. Apart from accounting for my particular approach, this means that I am indebted to a large number of friends and former colleagues who have informed and stimulated my thinking over the years.

Extracts from various official publications are reproduced by kind permission of the Controller of Her Majesty's Stationery Office.

CONTENTS

CONTENTS

1

PRINCIPLES OF PRICING

From the economic point* of view, what principles should govern the pricing policy of public enterprises? The answer will, to a large extent, depend upon what those enterprises are being called upon to do. What are they in business *for*? What broad aims have they been set[1]?

Some possible approaches are:

1. Give no pricing directives. This might form part of a general 'non-interference' policy by the government or reflect a belief that other forms of control (economic, financial or administrative) are more important.
2. *Ad hoc* intervention. Set those prices which further certain short-term (often political) aims, e.g. charge low prices to 'export' industries or within 'depressed' regions.
3. 'Balance the books'. Put with a little more precision: taking one year with another do not, *at the least*, make a loss. It has been a popular misconception that the nationalised industries have been required simply to 'break even'.

* It is necessary to say this because a government's aims might be predominantly or even wholly non-economic in the sense used in this book. See Chapter 9 for further discussion of this point.

1. Basic discussion about this kind of question will be found in: FOSTER, C. D., *The Transport Problem*, Blackie, London and Glasgow (1963); GWILLIAM, K. M., *Transport and Public Policy*, Allen & Unwin, London (1964), and SHEPHERD, W. G., *Economic Performance under Public Ownership*, Yale University Press, New Haven (1965). Useful background material is provided by: SHANKS, M. (Ed.), *Lessons of Public Enterprise*, Cape, London (1963); THORNHILL, W., *The Nationalised Industries: An Introduction*, Nelson, London (1968), and TIVEY, L. J., *Nationalisation in British Industry*, Cape, London (1966).

I

On the whole, the nationalising Acts and government policy (at least until fairly recently) have been interpreted to emphasise approach No. 3. This does not give very clear guidance. In fact a pricing rule is only *implied*; basically this is a *financial* performance directive that merely hints at average cost pricing. It only 'hints' because the following questions have, for the most part, remained unanswered: How long is the time-span over which one must 'not make a loss'? What degree of cross-subsidisation is permissible? Who should benefit from that process? Who should lose?

All this is not very helpful. Is it possible to be more precise? First of all one can say that prices should reflect costs, and when we talk about the latter we have in mind the economists' notions of opportunity cost and escapability.

Secondly, it *is* possible to lay down, at least theoretically, fairly clear-cut rules. When the various possibilities are sorted out, we are left with three main contenders. These are: (1) to maximise profits, (2) to maximise consumers' surplus, and (3) to undertake marginal cost pricing. Let us examine them in turn.

PROFIT MAXIMISATION

Profit maximisation will be familiar as one of the textbook assumptions made in elementary economic analysis of the firm. The

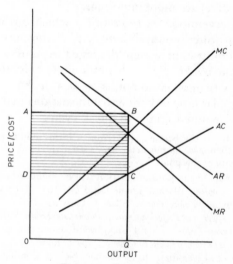

Figure 1.1. Profit maximisation

rule may be summarised by the formulation Marginal Revenue = Marginal Cost. It means simply that if the costs of producing the last unit of output are exactly the same as the additional revenue from selling that unit, the highest possible profit is made by fixing production at that particular level. If more output is produced, a loss will be made on the *additional* units produced; if less, the chance of further profitable production will be lost. *Figure 1.1* summarises the argument in diagrammatic form.

Use of the rule $MC = MR$ establishes output at OQ. The resulting price is OA and average cost OD. Total profits are defined by the rectangle $ABCD$ (shaded).

Imagine a series of such diagrams, each portraying costs and revenues for particular years in the future over the economic life of the plant. There are, it is true, difficulties in drawing accurately a series of such diagrams. It is necessary to forecast costs and, most difficult of all, revenues. The sets of curves will oscillate back and forth. But if the forecasting hurdle can be surmounted, the sizes of the rectangles $ABCD$ may be calculated over the succeeding years.

When this is done, each year's profit is discounted★ back to the base-year, and the discounted sums totalled. The resulting grand total may then be related to the initial capital investment. When expressed as a rate of return, which can be compared with returns obtainable from alternative investment opportunities, we have an investment criterion as well as a pricing rule.

There are many difficulties of interpretation facing the manager who attempts to put the $MC = MR$ rule into operation (as indeed there are with the application of any rule). Leaving aside such difficulties, we can set out some broad arguments for and against a policy of profit maximisation.

1. From the standpoint of welfare economics, to pursue profit maximisation policies could lead to a distortion in the pattern of resource allocation. The rationale of this is the same as for any other kind of enterprise, and has to do with the existence of monopolistic elements. Public enterprises generally have some degree of monopolistic power and a directive to maximise profits would inevitably lead to 'exploitation' of consumers. On the other hand, it is difficult to find any public enterprise, in Britain at least, with as much monopolistic power as may be implied by this argument. In the fuel and transport sectors, for example, competition is keen. With products such as steel, there is competition from foreign producers

---

★ The technicalities of discounting are discussed in Chapter 2.

and substitute materials. The freedom of action of management is severely circumscribed.

2. Profit maximisation might easily clash with statutory 'public obligations' and requirements to have 'consultation' with consumers. Consumer councils introduce an element of social control over the managers of public enterprises which, together with accountability to Parliament, will certainly act as a restraining force. This argument may be circumvented by talking of 'constrained profit maximisation'. There may be certain constraints to be regarded as 'absolute' but, within a residual commercial area, profits may be maximised. The railways now (after the 1968 Act) provide a good example of this.

3. The absence of reasonably precise rules about pricing has helped to lead to sizable financial deficits which have had to be covered by the taxpayer. Profit maximisation would prevent this. Indeed, it would lead to the generation of financial surpluses and, in accordance with its closely related role as an investment criterion, could lead to a much more sensitive adjustment to market forces. Although most welfare economists would probably not regard this as an ideal solution, they might prefer it to the 'book balancing' approach.

4. The generation of internal surpluses could provide funds for new investment. Perhaps, though, such funds would be creamed off by the Treasury either as a contribution to general taxation or to raise the finance to cover the social costs imposed on society by the operation of that industry. There is no obvious economic case for using public enterprises as a source of tax revenue over and above the general rate of company taxation. Such a possibility, however, is bound to look tempting to those with responsibility for revenue raising. The social cost argument looks attractive but, again, would provide a temptation.

The main difficulties in following the $MC = MR$ rule might well be political. Pressure for lower prices would be very difficult to combat if large financial surpluses were seen to be generated. There might also be a feeling, however inarticulate, that 'this is not what public enterprise is for'. A realistic appraisal must take account of such factors.

One point is, however, already clear. In choosing the exact rule adopted (if a rule needs to be adopted) social and *political* factors cannot be ignored; they shade into the economic arguments. Economists may demonstrate the consequences of following certain rules and may even state their own preferences if economic aims are held to be the most important ones. If, for example, it is decided by the government that resource allocation is the most important object of policy, the economist may then advise on how to bring this about.

There may be important aims of policy, however, which are quite outside the economist's terms of reference. Where this is so, political decisions have to be made.

CONSUMERS' SURPLUS MAXIMISATION

There are some types of publicly owned asset for which it is difficult, if not impossible, to establish a profit maximisation rule. Roads, for example, are provided 'free of charge' in the sense that users are not charged for their use as, when and where they use them. Construction and maintenance costs are met out of general taxation or periodic licence fees paid by users-in-general. (There is no 'earmarking' of revenue collected from this source for use only in the sector where it is collected. Such funds lose their identity in the general revenue pool.)

Profit maximisation without a charging mechanism is obviously a somewhat academic concept. This is not to say that charging is completely impracticable. Tolls may be employed and are levied on roads in some parts of the world. There is also the possibility of using various kinds of metering device. If such devices were introduced, prices could be set and the returns on capital invested calculated as outlined earlier. For the moment, we need not concern ourselves with the pricing problem as such. There is the important point, however, that the $MC = MR$ rule also provides an *investment* criterion. If that rule is inappropriate here, how may a return on the expenditure of public funds be calculated?

Could changes in the level of tax revenue be employed as a proxy? Some strange results could flow from this. For example, an important effect of constructing a new road link may be to lower fuel consumption per mile traversed. As tax element is a high proportion of the price of fuel, the return on the investment will be negative because revenue from such taxation will fall. Other traffic effects, such as reductions in vehicle fleets, may show similar financial results from the point of view of the authorities. Clearly, there is no guide to investment decision-making here either.

A quite different approach must be tried. One could attempt to assess the total net benefits to *users* enjoyed from the new road.

The criterion that has been developed to perform this task is consumers' surplus maximisation. Consumers' surplus is the difference between the maximum amount that consumers would be *prepared* to pay for a given output of a product (i.e. what would be recouped by the seller if he could employ perfect price discrimination) and the amount they *actually* pay at the ruling market price.

In the case of a road, there is no cost curve for the use of the road— at least so far as the individual user is concerned. (We must be very careful over definitions here. The road user obviously does incur costs by using the facility. There are the costs of operating the vehicle. Assuming maintenance costs to be insensitive to traffic volume, there exists, *in the absence of congestion,* no cost curve in respect of that particular stretch of road 'track'.) But there does exist a demand curve. If a new facility is constructed, there are various users who will obtain benefits they did not enjoy from the use of the routes they traversed before.

Some will obtain higher benefits than others. A number of motorists will unquestioningly switch from their former routes or make trips they would not have made if the new road did not exist. For others, the decision will be very much a marginal one. The demand curve is not merely 'notional'. Its existence would certainly be demonstrated if it were feasible to levy tolls. *Figure 1.2* illustrates such a demand curve.

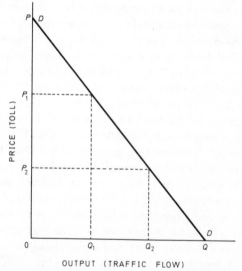

Figure 1.2. Possible charges on a toll road

The demand curve has conventional significance. If a toll OP_1 were charged OQ_1 number of vehicles would use the facility. If toll OP_2 were set OQ_2 number of vehicles would appear, and so on. The exact level of the profit maximising toll would, of course, depend upon price elasticity of demand at different points along the curve.

The total benefits to users provided by the new facility can thus be expressed by quantifying ('cashing up') the area of the triangle PQO. Practical techniques for doing this are described in Chapter 7.

Demand will grow over time as real incomes rise and private car ownership and use increase. Total user benefits will consequently increase. This may be represented by an outward shifting of the demand curve, as shown in *Figure 1.3*.

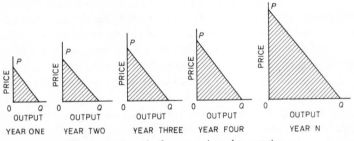

Figure 1.3. Growth of consumers' surplus over time

Having forecast future use of the road, it remains to select a period of time over which the calculations will be made ('time horizon'). With many types of industrial equipment, this is relatively easy: when will the machine reach the end of its physical life, or become so out of date in relation to competitive machines that it will 'pay' to replace? In the case of a road, a somewhat arbitrary period must be selected.

Future returns to consumers may then be discounted to base-year values and related to the capital costs of construction after deducting maintenance and any other current road costs (also discounted). The projects may then be ranked and those which show the highest consumers' surplus rate of return selected for construction.

So far, the appraisal has dealt only with the benefits to users of the new facility; there might be similar benefits to users of *already existing* facilities. The removal of traffic from them may mean a speeding up, and a reduction in the operating costs, of the remaining vehicles. This should be reflected in the benefit calculations. *Figure 1.4* illustrates the theoretical basis of the argument.

PRINCIPLES OF PRICING

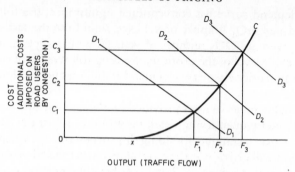

Figure 1.4. Effects of increase of demand for use of
a given road

This diagram also possesses cost curve C, which has appeared because the *existing* road system is experiencing some congestion: traffic cannot flow at the speed it would choose on an 'open' road, in unimpeded conditions. It therefore incurs costs *additional* to the operating costs associated with free flow conditions. Time is lost, fuel consumption rises and other costs increase when traffic flow exceeds Ox.

As 'capacity' fills up, the additional cost borne by each motorist rises. There comes a point where it rises very steeply. The amount of traffic using the road is determined by the flow (output) at which demand is in equilibrium with supply (the cost curve). With demand curve D_1, the cost to the user is OC_1 and the resulting flow OF_1. When demand has grown to D_2, the cost becomes OC_2 and flow OF_2; with D_3, OC_3 and OF_3. (The cost curve represents *average* costs and should not be confused with the marginal cost curve of road pricing theory.)

Now suppose that the completion of a new road facility that parallels the old causes a substantial amount of traffic diversion. The operators who continue to use the existing road will enjoy some benefit from the construction of the new facility. They, too, will be able to travel faster, more smoothly and at lower cost. The effect may be traced out as in *Figure 1.5*.

The first effect is a radical swing in the demand curve from D_3 to D_4. It is assumed here that it is 'marginal' users who stand to benefit the most by using the alternative facility. Those users already enjoying a large consumers' surplus are rather less likely to switch.

Before the opening of the alternative facility, demand is summarised by D_3, average cost incurred by each user is OC_3 and flow is

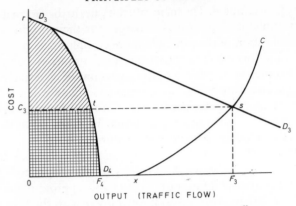

Figure 1.5. Changes in benefits accruing to traffic on a given road due to construction of alternative facility

OF_3. Afterwards, demand changes as shown by D_4 and additional costs imposed by congestion sink to zero. Flow becomes OF_4.

These particular users were originally sharing in a consumers' surplus defined on the diagram by the triangle rsC_3. They will continue to enjoy that part of it delineated by rtC_3.

Now that additional user cost has diminished to zero, the whole of the area rF_4O has become consumers' surplus. That part of it (rtC_3) shaded diagonally was already being received; the part shown cross-hatched (C_3tF_4O) is additional net benefit, and should be counted in as part of the return on the alternative road facility. Consumers' surplus no longer enjoyed on this road is at least regained on the new road (or else travellers would not change their routes).

It may seem from this that consumers' surplus maximisation has strictly limited applicability as a 'criterion of last resort'. Is it a tool of economic decision-making to be employed only when a more 'normal' calculus is technically impracticable?

The first point to note is that the 'abnormal' areas of the economy, those in which there exists no practicable charging mechanism, may be rather large. In fact, they may be so large that the employment of a different investment calculus in them compared to what is employed elsewhere in the public sector (and other sectors) may lead to a distortion in the flow of resources. At first sight, the returns on an investment project measured thus may seem to be far higher than those measured by the application of some other criterion.

A possible solution might lie in the application of the consumers' surplus criterion to *all* kinds of public enterprises. This could certainly be attempted. The main difficulty lies in the fact that many types of public enterprise make charges for their products. This makes application of the principle more complicated.

One could formulate the criterion, for example, as 'consumers' surplus maximisation subject to the constraint of covering private costs'★. *Figure 1.6* illustrates this. Output and price are derived from the point of intersection of the Average Cost and Average Revenue curves. (Strictly speaking output should be based upon the rule $MC = AR$ in order to maximise consumers' surplus, and price upon $AC = AR$ in order to meet the financial constraint. Such a 'solution' would, however, lead to physical shortages and $AC = AR$ for both price and output is a reasonable approximation. The reader may care to work this out for himself with the help of the diagram.) So we may neatly summarise the criterion as $AC = AR$.

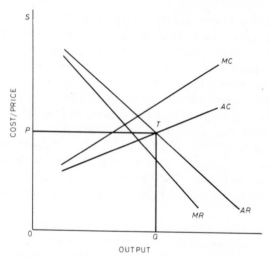

Figure 1.6. The consumers' surplus criterion applied to an enterprise constrained to cover private costs in full

Output is OQ and price OP, with consumers enjoying surplus STP. It is this surplus that is relevant when considering the investment decision. As with roads, the shape of those 'triangles' over the lifespan of the investment would have to be forecast, and the benefits discounted and related to initial project cost.

Some possible ambiguity attaches to the notion of consumers. Who, exactly, *are* the consumers? They are not 'consumers-in-

★ This formulation has been developed by FOSTER, op. cit., pp. 117–150.

general' in the sense that most of us, sooner or later, will make use of publicly owned transport facilities or the products of nationalised power industries. Consumers are consumers only when actually consuming that specific good or service.

Moreover, all consumers are treated 'equally'; there must be no preferential treatment for special groups and no cross-subsidisation of certain products or services★.

On the principle that charges must reflect the specific costs of providing specific services, there may, therefore, be a great variety of charges. It will be apparent that the $AC = AR$ rule as interpreted here has little in common with the 'book balancing' policy often pursued by public enterprise.

What can one say about profits? There is nothing in the criterion to say that profits should not be retained and interest paid (the latter most probably on fixed interest stock). Risk premia (explained in Chapter 2) may certainly be applied when calculating the returns from investments. There is no argument against a certain amount of self-financing. In all these matters, the same practical problems arise as with the interpretation of any other kind of criterion.

Perhaps the most difficult problems of application arise from the existence of joint costs†. These problems, however, are common to most criteria and rules. With joint costs, it will often, perhaps always, make no sense simply to divide up, and share out, the total over the services making use of a joint facility. All one can say is that *at least* the marginal costs of using a joint facility should be covered.

★ Cross-subsidisation is the operation of a service at a financial deficit where the losses are made up by surpluses generated by another service. Although financial is not necessarily the same as economic, as we shall see later, the danger is that the deficit-making service will be artificially kept alive where it should be closed down or contracted. On the other hand, use of the surplus-making service is artificially reduced.

† Joint costs are incurred or, to put it another way, joint products produced when two or more products are made by a single process: one cannot make the one without also producing the other. Indeed, it may not even be possible to vary the proportions in which the different commodities are produced. For example, if a farmer produces a given amount of wheat, he must also produce a related amount of straw. One can distinguish *common* from joint costs. Common costs may be incurred by producing several commodities together but they may be 'escaped from' if one of these goods is no longer made. Railway track shows examples of both categories. Remove trains requiring high quality track and signalling and certain costs may be saved. They were simply incurred 'in common' with other trains. This removal process may be undertaken with all kinds of traffic but, ultimately, there remains an irreducible, basic track cost that cannot be attributed to specific trains. This is a *joint* cost. (*See* Chapter 6 for a development of this theme.)

There is no doubt that a consistent criterion can be worked out. Perhaps the main difficulties are practical rather than theoretical. First there is the difficulty of measuring consumers' surplus. This must necessarily be indirect by looking at the benefits, measured first of all in physical terms, and then assessing how much consumers would have been prepared to pay to enjoy these physical benefits.

In the second place, there is the question of comparability with other sectors or industries, mentioned earlier. This is taken up in Chapter 7.

It will be observed that much of the foregoing discussion of a pricing rule has referred to the use of consumers' surplus maximisation as an investment criterion. This was because its practical usefulness as an investment criterion was realised first and the implications as a pricing rule were developed later. Use as an investment criterion, however, does not necessarily *dictate* use as a pricing rule. Indeed, it may well be that consumers' surplus rates of return upon investments may be calculated where profit maximising charges are raised. Practical circumstances may well dictate some strange (from the textbook point of view) combination of pricing and investment rules.

THE MAXIMISATION OF SOCIAL SURPLUS

In some situations, various kinds of constraint may make difficult the employment of any of these criteria or even any form of 'cost-covering'. An enterprise of this kind (perhaps a new urban transport facility) may fall into such a category, as depicted in *Figure 1.7.*

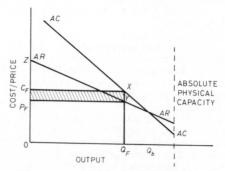

Figure. 1.7. Demand and cost relationships
for an urban transport facility

The facility, let us suppose, requires an immense amount of investment. That investment is 'lumpy' in the sense that it is difficult to 'tailor' capacity to traffic; there are important indivisibilities.

In this case, the AR curve only intersects the AC curve at output OQ_b, which is only just short of absolute physical capacity. One contributory factor could be the existence of high peaks, i.e. the concentration of demand into a few brief periods of the day. If demand in the off-peak hours could be expanded, the diagram could be redrawn to show the two curves intersecting further to the left of the diagram on account of an upward shift of the AR curve.

How may price and output decisions be determined? Commonly, price is fixed by external factors such as the need to adhere to a fares structure geared to a whole complex of routes and facilities in addition to this one. Let us call this fares level OP_F. The setting of such a fare causes output OQ_F to be demanded. At this level of demand, the undertaking will incur average costs of OC_F and there will be a financial loss of $C_F X Y P_F$ (shaded).

This procedure, whatever may be said for it on other grounds, offers little help to the investment decision-maker. Introduction of the notion of consumers' surplus can help matters. This is measured by the area $Z Y P_F$. If consumers' surplus is greater than the financial loss ($C_F X Y P_F$) there are positive returns accruing to such an investment. These may be discounted, totalled, related to the investment and used as a calculus for deciding whether or not to construct. Various benefits accruing to consumers of other transport services may be added on.

The reader should ponder the situations where the AR curve, starting from the left of the diagram below the AC curve, never intersects that curve. Could one still make out a social surplus maximisation case for investment in the facility? If so, what would one conclude about pricing policy?

MARGINAL COST PRICING

Marginal cost pricing has a completely different genesis. The reasoning here starts from the recognition that a profit maximisation rule does not bring about optimal resource allocation in a state of less-than-perfect competition. It is argued that such optimality can be achieved by adopting the price/output rule $AR = MC$.

As shown in *Figure 1.8*, with profit maximisation ($MC = MR$)

there is some possible additional output which can be produced at *less* than the prevailing price. In the situation depicted, it would be produced at a profit, but not at the *maximum* profit. Resources are lying unused when prospective buyers would be prepared to pay at least the opportunity cost of making them available. They should be made available to anyone prepared to pay a price that covers these marginal costs of production. As *Figure 1.8* shows, the $AR = MC$ rule often involves a lower price and a higher level of production than the $MR = MC$ one.

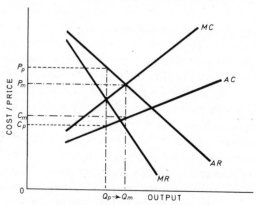

Figure 1.8. *Profit maximisation and resource allocation*

OP_p = Price (with profit maximisation)
OC_p = Cost (with profit maximisation)
OQ_p = Output (with profit maximisation)
OP_m = Price (with MC pricing)
OC_m = Cost (with MC pricing)
OQ_m = Output (with MC pricing)

With the adoption of $AR = MC$, rather than $MC = MR$, output would be higher (OQ_m rather than OQ_p) and price lower (OP_m rather than OP_p).

SHORT-RUN MARGINAL COST PRICING

There has been controversy about whether marginal cost pricing should be based upon short-run or long-run marginal costs[2]. This

2. *See* FOSTER, op. cit., Appendix 1, 'A note on Marginal Cost Pricing', and WALTERS, A. A., 'The Cost of Using Roads', *Finance & Development*, Vol. 6, No. 1, pp. 16–22 (1969).

problem, though, is not peculiar to this particular form of pricing. Decision-makers contemplating investment opportunities undertake their calculations on a long-run basis; they require sufficient net revenue to recoup the original capital outlay plus (at least) a minimum acceptable rate of return. Suppose, however, that the demand forecasts are not realised and that long-run costs, including the required return on capital, cannot be recouped. Then, on the principle that 'any contribution to fixed costs is better than nothing', production will continue if *at least* short-run costs can be covered. (This bald statement depends upon various assumptions such as that the capital equipment has little or no value in alternative uses. But, as a general proposition, it can stand.)

Much will depend upon the level of capacity utilisation of the facility to be installed. Suppose we have a situation like that illustrated in *Figure 1.9*.

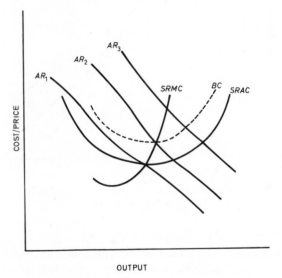

Figure 1.9. *Short-run marginal cost pricing*

The *SRAC* and *SRMC* curves in the diagram have conventional significance. *BC* (the conventional book-keeping costs of the accountant which reflect the historic costs of the original investment) are derived by 'adding on' 'fixed' or 'capacity' costs. We assume that such fixed costs are sunk for ever into this enterprise and that the equipment has no value in alternative use. AR_1, AR_2 and AR_3 represent three different demand situations.

On the basis of the $AR = MC$ rule, $AR_1 = SRMC$ will generate a financial loss; $AR_2 = SRMC$ a break-even; and $AR_3 = SRMC$ an accounting surplus. The reader should verify this from the diagram.

Now consider the case of an asset that consists of a great lump of indivisible fixed costs, like the one illustrated in *Figure 1.7*. Assume again that the structure of demand is such that it is difficult to attain anything like 'full' capacity working. The situation depicted in *Figure 1.10* may therefore apply.

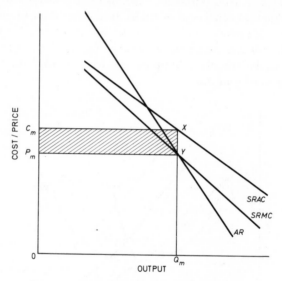

Figure 1.10. Financial implications of marginal cost pricing: a short-run example

It will be observed that output is OQ_m ($AR = SRMC$) and price OP_m. As costs are OC_m, there is a financial deficit as shown by the shaded rectangle, C_mXYP_m. Furthermore, this 'deficit' is a short-run financial loss; no contribution is being made towards capacity costs.

Should the short-run application of the principle be discarded here? The answer is no. The relevant costs are those which will be inescapably incurred if additional units of product are demanded. Until 'capacity' is fully taken up, those costs are represented by the $SRMC$ of *Figure 1.10*. If long-run marginal costs were charged or some other variant of long-run costs, certain consumers would take less of that product than if price were based on $SRMC$. Resources would thus lie unused, even though consumers were ready and willing to pay for any additional costs incurred in putting them to use.

Far from discarding it as a basis for charging, therefore, one might say that *SRMC* is the only logical basis for marginal cost pricing.

What, then, is the significance of long-run marginal cost charging? *LRMC* becomes relevant when it is equal to, or below, *SRMC*. *LRMC* charging is appropriate when there is no 'spare' capacity and where an increase in demand might make necessary a further instalment of capital investment. The costs of that instalment, in such a case, must be reflected in the charge to the consumer.

LONG–RUN MARGINAL COST PRICING

Long-run marginal cost charging can also lead to financial deficits, however. When one examines a conventional textbook diagram showing the relationship of short-run to long-run costs, it is usually (and necessarily for theoretical purposes) assumed that a choice is possible between different sizes of plant. All the sets of short-run curves in the classic 'envelope' diagram are *alternative* sizes of capacity. In real life, one rarely has such a choice if talking about the capacity of the whole industry. Capacity has been installed in the past; it is *there*! Moreover, much of that capacity may operate at relatively high cost levels and embody old-fashioned technology. Bygones are bygones, and there may be little that can be done about it. The problem is one of installing *incremental* capacity. One is faced with a situation of the kind illustrated in *Figure 1.11*, where each successive plant installed, as one moves to the right of the diagram, is more efficient than its predecessor.

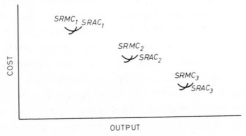

Figure 1.11. Families of short-run cost curves

LRMC pricing must be based, in such circumstances, upon the total costs of the marginal unit (more precisely upon the *SRMC* of the marginal unit subject to total costs of that unit being recovered, i.e. average costs★). The marginal unit here will be the latest, lowest cost increment to productive capacity. *LRMC* pricing, i.e. the basing of the price on the costs of that most efficient unit, inevitably means a financial loss for existing, higher-cost units. At the prevailing price level, the old capacity cannot meet its historic financial commitments, as demonstrated in *Figure 1.12*

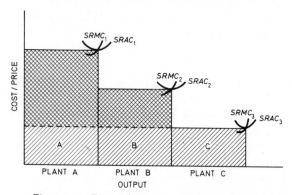

Figure 1.12. Financial consequences of LRMC pricing

The lowest point in the *SRAC* curve has been used as a basis for converting the cost/output data into columns of unit costs. Plant C has the lowest costs and these serve as the basis for the price charged. Plants A and B must, therefore, work at a financial loss. The size of this is indicated by the cross-hatched areas of columns A and B.

We can go further. If price covers the escapable costs of existing plants A and B, they will be physically retained, although accountants will probably re-write their book values. If this is not possible, they will be scrapped and replaced by additional plants of type C.

Theory apart, there are pragmatic reasons for advocating such a pricing policy. If it is true that the incremental capacity represents the most efficient available technique, it is in the interests of consumers-in-general that the low prices now possible should be generalised throughout the industry. In the example of *Figure 1.12*, the prices charged by productive units A and B will come down, perhaps to the extent that only short-run costs can be covered. In any event, the book value of the assets will have to be 'written

★ A demonstration of this principle is given in Chapter 5.

down'. If the new price levels do not even allow continuance in operation on this new financial basis, replacement will occur. Either way, consumers will gain.

MARGINAL COST PRICING: SOME THEORETICAL CONSIDERATIONS

Consumers of that commodity will no doubt be happy. Is it necessarily true, however, that society as a whole will gain? Financial deficits of public enterprises have to be made up somehow and there will consequently be income distribution effects—perhaps important ones. Certain consumers will pay more and others less for a given purchase-mix. These changes may extend right through commodity and factor markets. Is such subsidisation not infringing the basic principle that economic efficiency is improved if, *and only if*, some people are made better off but *nobody* is made worse off?

The answer is: not necessarily. There has been discussion about principles of 'compensation' that would allow the interpersonal comparison difficulty to be overcome (i.e. the difficulty of even attempting to measure or compare the utilities enjoyed by different persons). It has been argued that, if compensation were assumed, one could still draw conclusions about resource allocation even though income distribution effects occurred.

What is required is a mechanism to allow 'gainers' to compensate 'losers' so that there will be an *overall* increase in welfare. It has been argued that there is no need actually to make compensation payments, although this has been the subject of dispute. The only requirement is that compensation *could* be paid and that, after such 'notional' payments, some people would still be better off.

If the argument is accepted, it is possible to state 'marginal conditions' for maximising welfare ('welfare' may be defined as the maximisation of national product, subject to a given distribution of income). The classic formulation consists of the so-called Pareto* conditions[3]. There are several sets of such conditions relating to production, exchange and investment/savings. One of them for example stipulates that the rate at which factors can be substituted for each other at the margin, holding amount constant, must be identical in all spheres of production.

This Pareto system does not claim to provide one unique set of

* After the economist who formulated them.
3. For the Pareto conditions and discussion of them *see*: LITTLE, I. M. D., *A Critique of Welfare Economics*, Oxford University Press, London, Ch. VIII and IX (1956).

conditions that ensures maximum welfare. To do this would entail an interpersonal comparison of different distributions of income. What the system does is to specify an infinite number of possible optima, assuming income distribution as given. The number of such optima, therefore, depends upon the number of possible distributions of income.

From this it follows that the marginal conditions provide a means for finding a relative maximum though not an absolute one. (An absolute optimum would depend upon one's political judgement about the optimal income distribution.) A pricing rule that harmonises with the Pareto system, one based upon marginal costs of production, will, it is argued, yield greater welfare than one that does not meet the marginal conditions.

What help does such analysis give to the basic problem of making up the financial deficits arising from marginal cost pricing whilst doing the least allocative damage?

Let us test three main possibilities[4]:

1. Make prices proportional to marginal costs. The trouble here is that care must also be taken not to violate the marginal conditions in relation to factors of production. Their price also must be increased by a similar mark-up on the marginal costs of the product. But, if that happens, *marginal* costs of final products will have increased in proportion and, once again, $P = MC$. We are back where we started from.

2. The Hotelling solution (named after the eminent economist). This is a lump sum tax, which eats into producers' or consumers' surpluses and therefore does not violate the marginal conditions. Unfortunately such a tax (inheritance and rent on land are possible sources) would probably not provide sufficient revenue. Income tax would be needed as a supplement. Income tax, however, falls on factors of production and therefore violates the marginal conditions of production. Furthermore, the tax is not necessarily collected from people who receive the benefit from the subsidy. The interpersonal comparison problem is still, therefore, very much present for those remaining unconvinced by the compensation arguments.

3. Price discrimination. Although this might be a workable system, many writers have stressed its complexity. The revenue to make up financial deficits would have to come from the people

4. *See* RUGGLES, N. (1949), 'Recent Developments in the Theory of Marginal Cost Pricing', *Public Enterprise: Selected Readings*, Ed. R. Turvey, Penguin, Harmondsworth, pp. 11–43 (1968).

consuming the relevant products and no one else, if the marginal conditions were not to be violated.

THE THEORY OF 'SECOND BEST'

One may note in this context the development of the theory of 'second best' which has important implications for the pricing policy of public enterprise. Basically, this is an argument against the allocative validity of marginal cost pricing because of the effect of market imperfections.

The starting point is the introduction of a constraint into a general equilibrium system which prevents the attainment of one of the Pareto marginal conditions. Such a constraint may be, for example, the existence of external economies or diseconomies of production. The condition that more of certain products can be produced without affecting the production of anything else may thus be infringed.

In that case, it may be argued, optimal resource allocation can be attained only by departing from *all* the other Paretian conditions. And what can be said about the changes necessary to 'correct' (if that is the right word) for the imposition of the original constraint? It has been argued that *nothing* can be said about the direction or the magnitude of the 'necessary' changes[5].

It follows that, *a priori*, one cannot judge how near different situations are to optimality when various conditions are not attained. One cannot even say that a situation where *some* of the conditions are fulfilled is superior (or even only likely to be) to one in which fewer are fulfilled.

After all, the following possibilities are not remote where public enterprises are concerned:

1. Social 'overhead' capital is characteristically 'lumpy'. There may be no smooth transition to a point where price equals marginal costs. Often, there will be a choice between an output where MC is greater than price and another where it is smaller than price.

2. A public enterprise may be so large that, given its demand for

---

5. LANCASTER, R. K., and LIPSEY, R. G., 'The General Theory of Second Best', *Review of Economic Studies*, Vol. 24(1), No. 63, pp. 11–32 (1956). Readers of this book might find such an article tough reading. A clear verbal exposition is to be found, for example, in: MEYER, J. R., KAIN, J. F., and WOHL, M., 'Pricing, Subsidies, Market Structure and Regulatory Constitution', *The Urban Transportation Problem*, Harvard University Press, Cambridge, Mass., pp. 334–341 (1965).

factors of production, a perfectly elastic supply of those factors at a constant price level certainly cannot be assumed. An increase in the enterprise's activities may have a marked effect upon factor prices.

3. An enterprise may be in the situation that an increase in output, given marginal cost pricing, will lead to a disproportionately large decrease in prices. All consumers of the product using it as an input will benefit. They will, in all probability, increase their demand for the products, benefiting all other producers whose goods are complementary to the output of that product. The demand for goods which are substitutes for such products will consequently go down.

In all these cases, there is no approximation to the smooth, harmonious marginal adjustments of theory.

An important policy conclusion flows out of this reasoning. Suppose that the rules designed to lead to a welfare optimum were accepted in respect of one or a group of public enterprises. These rules, it must now be emphasised, would only lead the economy towards such an optimum if applied *universally*. To apply such rules in only one sector might move the economy further *away from* an optimum position. That is, a blind adherence to the $MC = P$ output/price rule might well lower the allocative efficiency of the economy. It could easily lead to a more than justified increase in demand for the output of the public sector; or the opposite.

At first glance, the consequences for welfare economics perhaps seem to be unfortunate: assume one additional constraint, and the whole Paretian system would appear to disintegrate. Recent discussion, however, has tended to minimise the damage. It has been argued, for example, that traditional theory was merely saying that a constrained welfare maximum entails necessary conditions. 'Second best' theory points out that, if additional constraints are imposed, the necessary conditions for such a maximum are more complex. Obviously, optimum conditions strictly relevant only to the simple case of a single constraint are no help here.

Thus one arrives at a rather pessimistic conclusion. In the absence of universal optimisation, nothing can be said. Neither is there any prospect of obtaining the enormous amounts of information required to derive quantitatively exact second-best solutions.

Perhaps, however, one can still say *something* useful in certain situations, starting from the familiar optimum rules, even though they are not universally complied with. Let us suppose, for example, that the constrained sectors are relatively small compared with the unconstrained ones. Let us assume also that the price/marginal cost discrepancies of the 'free' sectors are large compared to those of the constrained. In that case the more confidence one can have that matters can be improved by optimisation in 'free' sectors alone than by 'doing nothing'. Indeed, matters could be improved by adopting the price/marginal cost rule in the constrained sector[6].

Coming down to a practical policy problem, how confident could one be in recommending a movement towards MC pricing in a specific public enterprise? This would depend upon the extent to which the rest of the economy—particularly that part of it competing with the enterprise for resources and consumer markets —did not embrace the marginal conditions. ('Approximating the competitive norm' might be another way of putting it.) Also relevant would be the cross-elasticities of demand between that enterprise and the other sectors, i.e. to what extent are the competing sectors close alternatives or complements?

'Second best' theory is a developing field of analysis. It would seem to be prudent to be cautious in making claims of allocative efficiency on behalf of marginal cost pricing. Caution, however, is not the same as abandonment.

Note that, so far, the discussion has been confined to private costs and resources. At a later stage the analysis must be widened to include categories external to the enterprise: social costs and benefits.

Sometimes referred to as externalities, social costs and benefits are not reflected in the internal financial statements of agents or organisations that cause such effects to be experienced. For example, the fume and noise nuisance inflicted upon society by some transport operators will not be reflected in their profit and loss accounts. Neither will the traffic congestion they may impose upon other operators. Such issues are discussed in Chapter 7.

MULTI-PART TARIFFS

The multi-part tariff has much importance in the charging practice of some kinds of public enterprise. With a two-part tariff, to take the simplest example, the consumer is called upon to pay two

6. This argument is developed in MISHAN, E. J., 'Second Thoughts on Second Best', *Oxford Economic Papers*, Vol. 14, No. 3, pp. 205–217 (1962). Recent discussion of these subjects is provided by NATH, S. K., *A Re-appraisal of Welfare Economics*, Routledge & Kegan Paul, London (1969) and DOBB, M., *Welfare Economics and the Economics of Socialism*, Cambridge University Press, London (1969).

separate charges. A charge that is fixed for some specified period is combined with another that varies according to actual consumption of the product. There are several kinds of variation on this theme. For example, *all* charges may be directly related to consumption but succeeding 'blocks' of consumption priced at different rates.

The following tariffs, summarised in *Table 1.1*, are taken from a recent gas bill received by the author. The first tariff is named the Credit Block. It consists* of a low standing charge (per quarter) and

Table 1.1   EXAMPLES OF MULTI-PART TARIFFS

Tariff	Standing charge per quarter	Price per 100 cubic feet		
Credit Block	50p	First	200	100s of	6·55p
		Next	2 200	cu. ft.	5·10p
		Next	17 600	per	4·25p
		Next	20 000	quarter	3·55p
		All over 40 000		at	3·10p
Standard Two Part	£2·60	All gas used per 100 cubic feet			4·25p
Special Two Part	£3·90	All gas used per 100 cubic feet			3·55p
Commercial Heating	£13·00	All gas used per 100 cubic feet			3·55p

diminishing rates for the consumption of successive blocks. No less than five of the latter are distinguished. This is, in effect, a six-part tariff.

Then follow the two-part tariffs: the Standard Two Part, the Special Two Part and the Commercial Heating. The difference between the Standard and the Special Tariffs, it will be observed, is that consumers are offered a relatively high standing charge combined with a relatively low running charge; or vice versa. The most notable feature of the Commercial Heating tariff is the relatively high standing charge.

There are many reasons for the introduction of such pricing systems[7]. Six of the most important may be:

* The present tense is used in this practical illustration but these particular tariff levels are now superseded.

7. LEWIS, W. A., 'The Two-Part Tariff', *Overhead Costs*, Allen & Unwin, London (1949). This book is still the best source for the type of issues discussed here and some of those later on.

1. In complex industries requiring a great deal of capital equipment in various forms—centralised production plants, elaborate physical distribution networks, sophisticated control mechanisms —it is difficult to ensure that charges accurately reflect costs. Different consumers have different requirements, and thus incur various levels of installation and metering costs. A multi–part tariff is capable of reflecting this diversity.

2. Following on from this, multi–part tariffs may be used as a tool of cost attribution where there are regular fluctuations of demand, i.e. peaking. One possible, though slightly novel, application might be to charge a big share of fixed costs to peak users (plus whatever running costs they cause to be incurred), whereas off-peak users might be charged a relatively small share in addition to running costs. This, it might be calculated, would have the probable effect of inducing peak users to cut down their consumption and also to promote more consumption in the off-peak.

3. The reasons outlined above are concerned with price *differentiation*, i.e. making tariffs that reflect costs incurred in supplying particular consumers or groups of consumers. But multi-part tariffs can also be employed as a form of price *discrimination*, i.e. charging on the basis of what 'that traffic will bear' according to respective demand elasticities. In particular, consumers may be charged different fixed tariffs.

4. In given conditions of demand, it may be possible to extract more revenue from each individual consumer than with a unitary pricing system.

5. There is uncertainty in installing large amounts of capital equipment on behalf of individual consumers. That equipment may not be used as much as originally planned. A pricing system based wholly on consumption might fail to recoup the supplier's costs. If an element to cover capacity costs were included as a standing charge, the user would have a strong inducement to make maximum use of the facility.

6. Commercial thinking in the electricity industry has traditionally attached weight to the 'promotional' advantages of multi-part tariffs. Commonly, a fixed charge has been set for a period based upon the greatest *rate* of supply the customer would ever take. This would reflect the maximum demands ever made upon fixed equipment. Low charges for current taken would, it was hoped, encourage demand to grow because decisions to consume more electricity would often be taken on the basis of the 'marginal' rate.

Once the general outlines of a technique of economic analysis or commercial practice are established, they are gradually refined and elaborated to take account of changing circumstances. With the evolution of the electricity industry, for example, the necessity for price differentiation becomes greater. In particular, peak charging practice has become very sophisticated as will be seen later.

Perhaps it is easiest to begin elaboration with price discrimination. It is useful to begin with a situation in which unitary charging is employed, as in *Figure 1.13*.

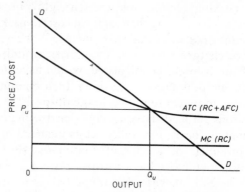

Figure 1.13. Demand and supply of electricity with unitary charging

Let us suppose that the diagram represents the demand for and supply of electricity on a given system. The demand curve, D–D, is quite conventional. The marginal cost curve reflects the costs of running the system with the given capacity, MC ($= RC$)*. The average total cost curve is constructed by adding capacity (or fixed) costs to running costs and is designated ATC ($= RC + AFC$).

Assuming that ATC is defined to include a 'normal' rate of return on capital, it can be taken to represent the supply curve of the system. The 'equilibrium' price will be OP_u, with quantity OQ_u of electricity being consumed.

Suppose now that we experiment with a two-part charging system as in *Figure 1.14*.

The variable part of the tariff is based on marginal costs (defined as before). The appropriate charge is OP_t^1 and the quantity consumed OQ_t^1. (This is, of course, derived from the point at which the D–D and MC curves intersect.)

---

* An analysis to justify this formulation is presented later on, in Chapter 5.

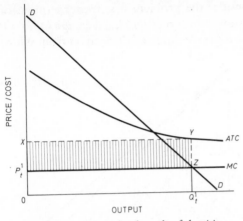

Figure 1.14. Demand and supply of electricity
with two-part charging

Now for the part of the tariff designed to recoup capacity costs. The amount of revenue to be recovered is delineated by the vertically shaded rectangle $XYZP_t^1$ of *Figure 1.14*. This represents the total costs (including rate of return on capital) incurred by a plant required to produce that output not covered when price OP_t^1 is charged. Those costs must now be recovered out of consumers' surplus. At output OQ_t^1 and price OP_t^1, this is the area shaded horizontally in *Figure 1.15*, i.e. MZP_t^1.

The problem, therefore, is to 'scoop out' of the consumers' surplus amounts at least equal to capacity costs, i.e. an amount that equals $XYZP_t^1$ in *Figure 1.14*.

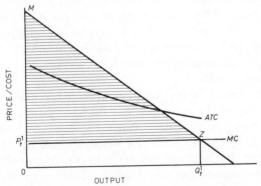

Figure 1.15. Marginal cost pricing and consumers'
surplus

Let us consider the problem first from the point of view of a solitary consumer. In *Figure 1.16* fixed charge $OP_t^2 - OP_t^1$ has been set, but there is a wide range of alternatives from which to choose.

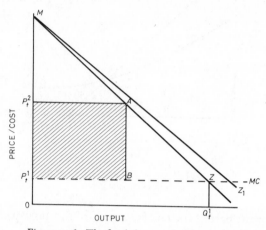

Figure 1.16. The fixed element of a two-part tariff

The 'fixed' tariff having been established, the undertaking no doubt hope that the consumer's eyes will be trained firmly upon consumption *at the margin*. The fixed charge is 'lost for ever', at least during the charging period or until the consumer decides whether or not to retain the service, wholly or in part.

From the point of view of the supplier there might well exist a virtuous circle. Demand may increase on the basis of the variable tariff (shown in *Figure 1.16* as a shift to MZ_1) and eventually this 'short-run' expansion will be converted into a 'long-run' expansion. Then it will become possible to raise the fixed charge. This increase can be justified as a reflection of the additional capital equipment needed to cater for that increased demand. This is the thought process underlying the electricity manager's notion of 'promotional' tariffs.

It has also been held that although average revenue per unit will fall as consumption goes up (because the fixed part of the tariff can only be adjusted periodically), demand 'valleys' will be filled up in the process. Electricity loads, for example, may have originated with lighting, but low marginal prices have encouraged the expansion of consumption for, say, domestic electrical appliances. Such evening-out of the load makes possible more intensive use of given capital stock.

So far we have assumed that each consumer in a given market is called upon to pay the same tariff. In practice this will not necessarily be the case. Small consumers will not usually be called upon to pay the same fixed charge as large ones; if they are they will be legitimately able to complain of being discriminated against (on the grounds that their demand for electricity does not cause the same amount of capacity costs to be incurred as that of the larger consumers; on the other hand, it should cost less to serve larger consumers *per unit supplied*). The fixed charge may be scaled proportionately or a totally different tariff system may be employed.

The possibilities of price discrimination will depend upon the existence of the usual conditions, i.e. the possibility of insulating the different consumers from each other, and upon the shape of their individual demand curves.

The first condition is perhaps self-evident. If the consumers not being discriminated against (i.e. the ones not called upon to pay a proportionately high contribution to fixed costs) were to exchange information with the others it would be difficult to follow the practice. There would be strong pressure for the lower fixed charge to be generalised to all consumers.

If such insulation were possible, the amount of the fixed charge would depend upon the shape of individual consumers' demand curves. A consumer whose demand curve was highly inelastic along most of its length would pay a relatively large contribution; a consumer whose demand curve had the opposite characteristics would pay a relatively small one.

We must pause here for reflection. Is it really possible to extract from consumers a higher *average* charge by using a complicated rather than a simple pricing system? Everything depends upon the behaviour of the consumers. It was suggested earlier that they might take consumption decisions on the basis of marginal prices. If, on the other hand, the customers watch the *total* bill rather than the marginal price, the demand curve facing the firm will be substantially the same regardless of the charging system used. In other words, income elasticity of demand becomes highly relevant.

An implicit assumption in much of this is a zero, or at least very low, income elasticity of demand. The two-part tariff is commercially superior where it enables the firm to sell more at any given average price than it would if average and marginal prices were to coincide.

It will now be apparent that the six reasons given for the introduction of multi-part tariff systems are sometimes interdependent.

In particular, we have seen that reasons 2, 3, 4 and 6 are often inter-related. Let us now consider reasons 1 and 5.

Reason 1 was the case where costs were incurred specifically in relation to a given customer's supply: the costs of carrying the current to his premises, the wiring and fitting, the installation of metering devices, and of reading and maintaining them and keeping his accounts. Such costs do not vary directly with current consumed. There is nothing to be gained, and much to be lost in costing precision, by lumping them together with capacity costs, i.e. generation and distribution in general.

From the point of view of resource allocation, charges should reflect those installation costs, and nothing else. In an imperfect market, however, this will not necessarily come about. The two elasticities discussed earlier are once again relevant. By manipulating the charge, it may be possible to cut into consumer's surplus; in certain circumstances it might even 'pay' to grant free installation if it would lead to a substantial increase in demand at the margin*.

Reason 5 was the desire of entrepreneurs to minimise their risks. If a large amount of highly durable fixed equipment is required there is the danger of being unable to recover the capital invested. How can the entrepreneur protect himself? The best way may be to require each consumer to pay, perhaps in advance, a share of the capital costs. If, in the aggregate, consumers pay the total costs of the fixed installations, the risk will evaporate. If that is an overstatement, at least the undertaking will have a breathing space in which to re-equip itself with more modern techniques.

A good example may be taken from modern railway operations. Much railway freight traffic originates and/or terminates in private sidings, i.e. railway tracks and loading facilities owned by railway consignors or receivers. The railways constantly face the risk that customers may divert traffic to other forms of transport. The provision of a siding is, in that case, an unacceptable risk. The 'fixed' charge thus takes the form of the rail user paying directly for the facilities, even to the extent of the railways not being involved at all financially; from their point of view the siding is provided 'free'. The principle might even be extended to rolling stock.

When really large installations are involved, this fixed element assumes great importance. Modern 'Merry-go-round' trains carry-

---

* At one time it was common to base the fixed charge on some such basis as rateable value. Some would argue that this was quite an arbitrary method but it could also be regarded as a form of discrimination. (*See* LEWIS, op. cit., p. 54, for more discussion of this point.)

ing coal from mines to electric power generating stations require elaborate loading and unloading facilities at each terminal. In a case like this, the actual division of the costs is a matter of high-level negotiation. What is more, any such agreement is bound to be embodied in a long-term contract, thus giving the providers the necessary freedom from risk.

THE MULTI-PART TARIFF AND MARGINAL COST PRICING

Before leaving this subject, it may be useful to examine briefly the relationship between multi-part tariff charging and the marginal cost pricing of the preceding section. We have seen that the variable charge is based upon the marginal cost of additional output and that, *given certain assumptions about the income elasticity of demand for the product*, the output of the commodity is determined by marginal conditions.

This resemblance to marginal cost pricing may lead one to conclude that multi-part tariff pricing may be a solution to the problem of how to recoup total costs when marginal cost pricing is employed in an industry with increasing returns to scale. The marginal conditions would be satisfied by the variable charge. Furthermore, enough consumers' surplus could be gathered in by the fixed charge to ensure that the industry would not suffer financial losses.

Let us examine this contention with the aid of *Figure 1.17*.

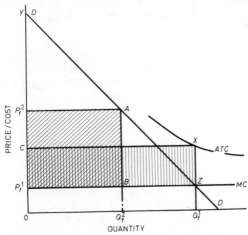

Figure 1.17. *Two-part tariff charging and marginal cost pricing*

Applying the rule $P = MC$, we arrive at output OQ_t^1 and price OP_t^1. Average cost at that output is, however, OC and there is a financial deficit measured by the shaded rectangle $CXZP_t^1$. The fixed part of the tariff would attempt to recoup those losses from the consumers' surplus (YZP_t^1).

Some form of discrimination would be essential to make the two systems compatible. Consumers at or near the margin would have to be charged a fixed tariff of zero or near-zero. By the same token, it would be intra-marginal consumers who would be burdened with the whole of the fixed element. Moreover, it would have to be those whose income elasticity of demand for the product was zero. In our example, we might assume that consumers of up to OQ_t^2 are charged OP_t^2, the receipts (over and above MC) being represented by $P_t^2 ABP_t^1$. Consumers of from OQ_t^2 to OQ_t^1 are charged price OP_t^1. It can be seen from the diagram that if $P_t^2 ABP_t^1 \geqslant CXZP_t^1$, there are no financial losses.

These conditions would appear to be extremely difficult (if not impossible) to identify and to translate into charging practice. Theoretically, nevertheless, multi-part charging is one way of reconciling 'commercial' behaviour with marginal cost pricing where the latter policy would ordinarily lead to financial losses.

FURTHER READING (additional to references in text). A survey of the industries discussed is provided by: REID, G. L., and ALLEN, K., *Nationalised Industries*, Penguin, Harmondsworth (1970).

More advanced theoretical work is provided by: MILLWARD, R., *Public Expenditure Economics*, McGraw-Hill, London (1971); TURVEY, R., *Optimal Pricing and Investment in Electricity Supply*, Allen & Unwin, London (1968), and TURVEY, R., *Economic Analysis and Public Enterprises*, Allen & Unwin, London (1971).

2

INVESTMENT
DECISION-MAKING

There are, perhaps, two fundamental groups of problems associated with the investment decision: the forecasting of costs and benefits, and the establishment and application of appropriate rates of discount.

THE FORECASTING OF COSTS AND BENEFITS

The further one proceeds into the future, the more difficult it becomes to make accurate forecasts of costs and benefits. On the cost side, there is the problem of forecasting the prices of factor inputs. Labour costs, for example, will almost certainly rise in real terms. They will probably not rise at a uniform rate in all sectors. What is important is the *relative* price of labour and capital. This will have an important influence on the choice of technique, i.e. the precise combination of productive factors.

The problems are no less serious on the demand side. To some extent, they may be dealt with by making explicit allowance for 'risk' and 'uncertainty'. A risky situation may be defined as one in which one can make a fair shot at the probability distribution of possible outcomes. Uncertainty, on the other hand, is where there is no prospect of obtaining such a distribution.

It is vitally important to make explicit the risk and uncertainty assumptions made in relation to public sector investments. Upon examination, it may be found that there is a choice (a 'trade-off') between a high return, on the average, with a substantial amount of unforecastable variability between different projects and a lower average return with less variability. The particular mix of projects chosen will depend a great deal upon the objectives of the undertaking.

A public enterprise, for example, may have as its first objective the achievement of a certain (minimum) financial performance. It may, accordingly, be appropriate to follow a conservative policy; projects showing lower but safer returns would then be favoured. An alternative policy might require a less detailed attention to financial performance and greater weight to be placed on other objectives such as labour employment generation or 'import saving'. In such a case, a greater element of riskiness might willingly be accepted.

Much may depend on the relative importance of an individual project in the total programme of the sponsoring enterprise or of the relevant government department. (This point is emphasised where public finance is to be drawn upon.) It may be considered that fluctuations in demand for the output of individual projects may cancel themselves out over the collection of projects. Clearly this kind of conclusion is more likely to be reached if most individual projects are relatively small.

Possible approaches would be to:

1. Adopt a deliberately conservative attitude in calculating costs and benefits, and to fight hard against overconfidence in project evaluation. The authorities vetting such projects might impose penalties by increasing the costs and lowering the benefits, to take account of forecasting errors.
2. Add a premium to the discount rate (i.e. add a few percentage points on to the minimum acceptable rate). Like the penalties attached to costs and benefits, this will vary directly with the lack of confidence in the estimates.
3. Make conservative estimates of the life of projects. This will, of course, be highly relevant in situations of rapid technical progress.

One defect of a conservative approach is simply that is *is* conservative. Risky schemes may be ruled out as a matter of course but, clearly, a proportion of them will be worth undertaking. A more systematic analysis of the risk involved might be undertaken. All the specialists involved with an investment scheme could be asked to develop a probability distribution for each key element in the capital budgeting exercise. A simulation model could then be used to test the sensitivity of the possible variations in each element upon the rate of return for the project.

The output of such an exercise would be a distribution of possible returns with a probability attached to each. Management would still need to judge whether to go ahead with the scheme. But economics, while providing assistance to such judgement, can provide no substitute for it.

There is much more to the problem, however, than assessing the degree of risk and uncertainty from the vantage point of the public entrepreneur and social financier; one cannot be certain exactly how *future* generations will value the benefits of a long-term scheme. With large urban redevelopment schemes, for example, it is conceivable that wealthier—and perhaps wiser—future generations will value environmental quality far more highly than the present one. They may be prepared to pay far more to limit noise and fumes or, indeed, to get rid of them altogether.

Equally, solutions proposed now may be thoroughly obsolete by the time they are fully implemented. An example (perhaps controversial) is the failure to adapt urban development schemes to the needs of private motoring.

The use of a discounting procedure helps to cut down the size of such potential mistakes. By discounting benefits (and costs) accruing in the distant future more heavily than those nearer to the present, some flexibility of decision is given to those future generations. They are less likely to be saddled with obsolete assets. They will have a choice: either to keep broadly the asset structure they have inherited or alternatively to adopt some radically different approach.

From this point of view, therefore, a discounting procedure is crucially important. Before discussing the principles involved in choosing a discount rate, however, let us remind ourselves of the basic techniques of investment appraisal[1]. We begin with the Net Present Value method.

1. For an exposition of the technique of investment appraisal *see*: NATIONAL ECONOMIC DEVELOPMENT COUNCIL, *Investment Appraisal*, H.M.S.O., London (1969); BAUMOL, W. J., *Economic Theory and Operations Analysis*, 2nd edn, Prentice-Hall, New Jersey, Ch. 19 (1965), and MERRETT, A. J., and SYKES, A., *The Finance and Analysis of Capital Projects*, Longmans, London (1963). An enormous source-book (almost an encyclopaedia) of information is provided by: WESTON, J. FRED, and BRIGHAM, E. F., *Managerial Finance*, Holt, Rinehart and Winston, New York (1966).

TECHNIQUES OF APPRAISAL: NET PRESENT VALUE

Algebraically, Net Present Value may be expressed as:

$$\frac{b_1}{(1+r)} + \frac{b_2}{(1+r)^2} + \frac{b_3}{(1+r)^3} + \ldots \frac{b_n}{(1+r)^n} \geqslant C$$

where $b_1, b_2, b_3, \ldots b_n$ are benefits (net of operating costs) forecast for the years 1, 2, 3, . . . n (depreciation and interest are excluded), r is the rate of discount adopted and C is the initial capital cost of the project.

The decision to invest will be taken when discounted benefits are equal to or greater than costs.

Table 2.1 NET PRESENT VALUE. DISCOUNT RATE = 8%

Year	Capital outlay	Net returns	Discount factor	Discounted returns
(1)	(2)	(3)	(4)	(5)
0	£1 million (A)	—	—	—
1	—	£250 000	0·926	£231 500
2	—	£350 000	0·857	£299 950
3	—	£250 000	0·794	£198 500
4	—	£200 000	0·735	£147 000
5	—	£100 000	0·681	£ 68 100
			Net Present Value:	£945 050(B)

Table 2.1 translates this algebra into simple arithmetic. The capital outlay and the net returns for a project with an assumed life of five years costing £1 million are set out.

Column (1) gives the year of the project's life; year 0 is the base year in which the investment is taking place but has not yet produced any return. In this case, we have a 'once-and-for-all' capital expenditure but, in real life, such outlays could recur in one form or another throughout the life of the asset. Consequently, like the 'net return' of column (3), they would be discounted. The net returns here are the operating surpluses left after deducting short-run costs from total annual revenue. They consequently exclude (this is an obvious point but it ought to be made) depreciation and interest. Depreciation does not arise because capital outlay has been treated as a 'lump' in column (2). Interest is accounted for by the discount factor of column (4).

These discount factors are the product of a simple arithmetical process. Let us take year 3's results as an example. We begin with the expression $b_3/(1+r)^3$. For practical calculations it is usual to derive first the expression $1/(1+r)^3$ and apply the resulting discount factor to the net benefits.

So we have $1/(1·08)^3$ with an 8% rate of discount. This gives us 0·794 (to three places of decimals, that is; it may be advisable to work to, say, six places). We enter this factor in column (4). It only then remains to multiply b_3 (£250 000) by this factor to arrive at the annual discounted returns (column 5).

Discounted returns are then summed to give total Net Present Value. With this project, it will be observed that total discounted returns come to £945 050, a sum that falls short of initial capital outlay. In other words, the project does not secure an 8% rate of return. (There are tax complications but these are not strictly relevant to the exposition. They are consequently ignored.)

Let us test the project again, as in *Table 2.2*, with a 5% discount

Table 2.2   NET PRESENT VALUE. DISCOUNT RATE = 5%

Year	Capital outlay	Net returns	Discount factor	Discounted returns
(1)	(2)	(3)	(4)	(5)
0	£1 million (A)	—	—	—
1	—	£250 000	0·952	£238 000
2	—	£350 000	0·907	£317 450
3	—	£250 000	0·864	£216 000
4	—	£200 000	0·823	£164 600
5	—	£100 000	0·784	£ 78 400
				£1 014 450 (B)

rate. The project does now meet this test, i.e. it provides at least a 5% rate of return.

So far we have been analysing the project in terms of its Net Present Value. The discount rate is *given* (i.e. the minimum rate of return that the project must earn to be acceptable is decided in advance). The two boxes in the table are compared and if the sum in Box B is higher than that in Box A the project has passed its first test.

It has only passed its first test because there might be a shortage of capital (a 'budgetary constraint') that makes it impossible to carry out all projects giving a satisfactory rate of return. Take the example shown in *Table 2.2*, which is very much a borderline case. This project, which just scrapes through the test, might easily be a casualty in such a situation.

COST/BENEFIT RATIOS

Because Net Present Value thus provides a test of 'minimum acceptability', it needs to be supplemented by a further principle where there are insufficient funds to undertake all projects passing the discount rate test. One method of dealing with this is to make use of a shadow price of capital, and is discussed later. Another method is to use a cost/benefit ratio.

As it is the supply of capital that is constrained (i.e. scarce), it is capital cost that is relevant as denominator (column 2, Box A). Benefits are net benefits (column 5). The cost/benefit ratio is therefore (using the figure of *Table 2.2*) 1 : 1·01. This ratio may then be compared with ratios of other projects, with different capital requirements, and ranked in order of profitability. In conditions of budgetary restraint, a 'cut-off' ratio may be applied to ration out funds between competing projects. For example, a cost/benefit ratio of 1 : 1·25 may be demanded before going ahead with a scheme.

TECHNIQUES OF APPRAISAL: INTERNAL RATE OF RETURN

The relationship of N.P.V. to internal rate of return (I.R.R.) is not very complicated.

The project in *Table 2.2* shows a return of at least 5%. We know this because we applied a test discount factor of 5% and received back more than our capital outlay. Suppose we were to manipulate the discount rate until the present value of total discounted return was *exactly* the same as the capital outlay. It will be apparent that the rate to do this will be somewhere between 5 and 6%. This rate would be the I.R.R.

DIFFICULTIES OF APPLICATION

A difficulty of application concerns projects that are mutually exclusive, i.e. if you invest in one of them then there is no point in investing in the other. This problem could arise where there is a choice between techniques (e.g. nuclear or conventional electric power generating stations), different levels of capacity provision (e.g. various possible transport networks ranging from simple and inexpensive to elaborate and costly) and alternative timings (e.g. invest now or at some later date when costs and returns may be different).

With N.P.V. it is simply a question of selecting the option with the highest N.P.V. With I.R.R., however, one cannot simply choose the variant with the highest return. In the absence of a budgetary constraint, any project securing a return greater than the prevailing test rate of discount should be undertaken. One project will probably require more capital than the other.

The *additional* capital outlay for the most expensive project should be compared with the additional returns (if they exist) and the rate of return upon this marginal variation worked out. If the rate of return upon the latter project is equal to, or greater than, the test rate of discount, that variant should be taken.

Why should this be so? Unless the rate of return upon the incremental project is greater than the test discount rate, it would pay to engage in the lower-cost project. The capital thus released could be invested in another project whose return is greater than the test rate.

CHOICE OF DISCOUNT RATE

How should the discount rate be chosen[2]? Traditional theory suggests a *single* interest rate that equates the marginal time preference of savers with the marginal productivity of capital in investment. People are faced with the choice: consume now, or consume later. Consuming later means saving now. If people are to postpone consumption they must be persuaded to do so by the payment of interest. The higher the rate of interest the more people will postpone consumption; the lower the rate of interest, the more they will consume in the present.

Entrepreneurs will make use of resources freed by the postponement of consumption if they can find a profitable use for them. They will compare the marginal rate of return on investment with the

2. A very full discussion is contained in: HENDERSON, P. D. (1965), 'Investment Criteria for Public Enterprises', *Public Enterprise: Selected Readings*, Ed. R. Turvey, Penguin, Harmondsworth, pp. 86–169 (1968). This entire chapter owes a great deal to Henderson's work.

rate of interest payable on borrowed funds. The more capital is invested, so will marginal return tend to diminish. As more investment funds are called forth at the expense of consumption, so will the rate of interest required to tempt marginal savers be pushed up. And so the two rates will come into equilibrium.

The interest rate may change for several reasons. Consumers' time preference may change markedly either way. Investment opportunities may increase in number and profitability. These phenomena are closely interrelated. A low rate of consumption, for example, would increase the amount of potentially investible funds; it would also limit investment opportunities, thus also affecting the demand for funds. Both effects would tend to depress the interest rate.

The analysis depends upon the assumption of perfect competition. Only on that assumption will such an equilibrium rate of interest inform private savers/investors how to maximise their welfare over time.

Much more than the conventional 'perfect knowledge' assumption is required however. Individual savers must know the shapes of their incomes and wants profiles over time. They must also have precise information on the future prices of all the commodities they are likely to be interested in. As their future income will depend on the savings and investment decisions of society as a whole, is it realistic to assume that the individual can obtain the necessary information for redistributing his income through time?

Similarly, will entrepreneurs be able to obtain sufficient information about the marginal rate of return on capital investments in each conceivable option? To what extent can they allow for the way in which revenue streams inevitably depend on investment decisions of other entrepreneurs? Remember, there will be investment decisions that have not been taken when individuals are working out their 'optimum' division of consumption and saving.

Suppose, however, that a perfect market interest rate *could* guide investors so as to maximise their welfare over time. Would that interest rate produce *socially* optimal investment decisions? This is doubtful. To produce a social optimum, an interest rate that equated the social productivity of investment with a socially determined savings schedule would be necessary.

What is the reasoning behind this? It is simply that the private rate of return on capital does not necessarily reflect the social productivity of capital. The gains to society from installing a certain project may be far greater, or indeed far smaller, than those to the private investor. We shall look at this possibility in a little more detail later on.

So much for the theory. It is hardly surprising that one does not find such a unique interest rate in real life. Apart from the stringent assumptions made in the theory, there are institutional factors which help to prevent the emergence of such a rate. There is a whole array of interest rates. A problem therefore faces the public enterprise decision-maker: which is the relevant interest rate for his purpose? Indeed, are any of the market rates relevant or is there some 'synthetic' rate that should be taken?

We are not concerned here with the *actual* rate of interest that public enterprises should pay on borrowings from the government. Such interest payments have no function other than a financial one, although they do set a practical lower limit to the overall rate of return that a public enterprise must aim to secure.

A test rate of discount that has no relationship at all to the servicing of capital provided by the government may be applied to investment projects. Such interest payments may be regarded as a device for *sharing out* the gross surpluses of public enterprise; and no more.

THE OPPORTUNITY COST DISCOUNT RATE

One approach might be to look at the 'prevailing' rate of return elsewhere in the economy, taking into account the risk and uncertainty associated with different projects. Investment in the public sector might displace an equivalent amount of investment in the non-public sector. What will be the return if those resources are invested in the most likely alternative use? The rate of return from that alternative investment has been foregone. It is reasonable to expect that the public sector investment should give at least that rate of return. Ideally, one would identify the private sector project thus displaced and require the public project to obtain at least that return.

In practice, however, this means that the public enterprise decision-maker should look at the marginal rate of return (i.e. the minimum acceptable) in the private sector. After making appropriate adjustment for risk and/or uncertainty, that rate would be adopted when discounting projects. Before this can be done, it is necessary to make adjustments for the different tax treatment of the private sector, including the effect of company taxation and investment stimuli.

This approach still involves the sifting through of a variety of rates. For one thing, a wide range of evaluation techniques is employed in private industry and not all of them have the same economic respectability as the two illustrated earlier on. Sometimes forecasting of costs and receipts may be somewhat rough and ready. Furthermore, risk and uncertainty may not be explicitly allowed for but reflected by adjusting project estimates on the basis of 'judgement and experience'.

More fundamental objections than this could be raised. It has already been argued that the social return from an investment will usually exceed the private return to investors. Consequently, private demand schedules for investment funds would not reflect the *social* productivity of capital (or the lack of social productivity if there were, for example, important external disbenefits); neither would the private market rate of return on marginal investment.

Increasing attention is being paid to the evaluation of social costs and benefits but, particularly in the private sector, many of these are still excluded as a matter of course or are too elusive. The fundamental problem is: should a discount rate taking no account of such social returns (or losses) be employed in the public sector?

So far, it has been assumed that public investment would displace private. Is this necessarily true? Might it not happen that other government expenditure should be displaced? Consider, for example, a situation in which the state is providing large sums of money on revenue account for a publicly owned railway system to make up operating deficits; it is also financing capital investment. It could happen that, within a budgetary constraint, investment might be increased at the expense of revenue advances. The system might be slimmed by shedding relatively unprofitable services while investment is increased in order to cater for 'growth' traffics.

There is a further possibility: public expenditure might displace private consumption. Again, the mechanism is relatively straightforward. It involves the raising of funds for public investment by means of a tax on private consumption.

It would appear, therefore, that there is no *a priori* reason to assume that public sector projects will displace private investment at the margin rather than private consumption or government current expenditure. This is a question for the facts. (Whether the facts can ever be accurately known 'ex ante' is another matter.)

These are some of the more important difficulties of interpretation or practicability associated with the opportunity cost approach. One must now ask whether the *concept* of an opportunity cost discount rate is acceptable. Should a government, when adopting rate of discount, be influenced by the activities of profit-making entrepreneurs? Are there more fundamental considerations?

SOCIAL TIME PREFERENCE

Consider the possibility of government support for the development of a brilliantly effective new chemical fertiliser. Apply the fertiliser and crop yields are immediately trebled. Appraisal of the investment (in support) on the basis of O.C. shows a very high return indeed, even when all conceivable social costs are brought into the calculation. There is just one worry: any land thus treated will, forty years hence, become completely barren, sterile and, indeed, poisonous to all forms of life. According to the best available scientific advice, it can never be used for agricultural or recreational purposes again after that period has elapsed. No matter: those effects will be 'discounted away'.

Perhaps this is a slightly unreal example. One can think, however, of many types of public investment decision where such long-term effects are very important. Land reclamation and protection schemes of the type carried out in the Netherlands may make an extremely poor showing if evaluated in the conventional manner. So might a large-scale urban redevelopment scheme.

In such cases, the O.C. approach may appear to give absurd results*. Something is required to supplement or even replace it. That 'something' is a judgement about the value placed on future rather than present consumption. The judgement may be made in two possible ways:

1. The government may decide. It may feel that, as guardian of the interests of future generations, it 'knows best' or can interpret the true desires of society. Such interpretation would no doubt be influenced by the prevailing political climate.
2. If given a choice, the present generation might consciously make a bigger sacrifice of consumption than its behaviour in the market would suggest. But it would probably only agree to do this *collectively*, i.e. *each individual would have to be convinced that each one of his fellows was doing exactly the same.*

* Because, at a rate of (say) 10%, the net benefits accruing over a long period will rarely offset initial capital costs even if those benefits are astronomically large in the *very long run*.

In the case of (2), it is not easy to visualise the mechanism suitable for testing society's wishes on such issues. Alternative (1) might seem to be the only workable one. Governments are in fact, explicitly or implicitly, making decisions of this kind all the time.

IMPLICATIONS OF SOCIAL TIME PREFERENCE DISCOUNT RATE

Universal adoption of an S.T.P. test rate of discount would inevitably mean that capital rationing would become necessary; in making various long-range schemes viable, many hitherto non-viable short-range schemes would be admitted. Thus, at the end of the day, nothing substantial would really have been achieved. (Actually, this bold statement is not quite true. The use of a radically different discount rate would have effects upon the *ranking* of schemes. It would also change the balance between capital-intensive and non-capital-intensive projects. The reader should again test this point with the help of simple tables such as those presented in this chapter.)

If it is desired to 'provide for future generations' in certain spheres, it would seem that the adoption of S.T.P. is feasible only in the public sector or in some subsidised area of the non-public sector. In the latter, profit-maximising businessmen would presumably require to have the gap between a 'commercially acceptable' rate of return and an S.T.P. return bridged by payments from the public purse before they would agree to go ahead with such investments. The projects to be evaluated on an S.T.P. basis would need to be very carefully defined; one can imagine the queue of special interests claiming to 'represent future generations'.

It would be necessary to 'wall-off' a sector in which the S.T.P. approach would be accepted. The exact definition of this sphere would provide a tough problem.

Even if this course be adopted, two difficulties remain. The first might be regarded ás a dynamic version of the 'second best' problem. To apply different kinds of investment rules in different sectors might lead to strange results. 'Strangeness' does not necessarily equal allocative inefficiency. Evaluation of the results flowing from such a policy, however, might well be far beyond the present capability of economics.

The second difficulty relates to forecasting, as discussed earlier. The further ahead one attempts to forecast into the future the less likelihood there is of accuracy. Is it certain that future generations will agree with the values placed on benefits from such schemes by the present generation? Is there not a possibility that current solutions for long-term problems may be obsolete by the time they are finally implemented? Once again, economics alone cannot solve the problem although economists can set out the consequences of alternative policies. The need is for broad political judgements.

If this sounds to be a vague conclusion, it should be emphasised that governments are taking such decisions all the time, albeit implicitly. The Soviet government took such a decision in the 1930s. The British government implicitly applied S.T.P. to the economics of the nuclear power programme. Any injection of economic rationality into such decision-making processes can make an important contribution even if the main result is simply to make the assumption used *explicit*.

Other kinds of influence are the pressure of aggregate demand, the current state of the balance of payments and monetary policies of foreign governments. These factors compound the difficulty of establishing the relationship between market-determined interest rates and social time preference. They do this because current interest rates are not simply the expression of people's or governments' preference for present as opposed to future consumption but are also a weapon of monetary policy. Thus a government facing a serious balance of payments deficit which cannot be financed from reserves has few policy options if devaluation is ruled out. One option would be to finance the deficit by raising Bank Rate, thus attracting an inflow of short-term funds. Conversely, the lowering of Bank Rate may be used as a signal that an expansion of aggregate demand is on the agenda.

Is there, then, nothing at all specific that can be said about social time preference? Can one even declare for a positive rate? (Theoretically, there is no compelling reason to prevent a negative rate from being employed. The reader should attempt to work out the implications of this for himself.) There are three main arguments for a positive rate:

1. The future is subject to risk and uncertainty which are bound to increase the further one travels into the future.
2. Positive time preference is logical because all human beings will die sometime. Consumption in the future should be discounted by the probability of an individual receiving it. Such a probability could be worked out for society from a knowledge of age distribution and the actuarial possibilities of

survival at each age. (This does not take account of the future generations' problem, but it would be unreal to expect present generations to take a purely altruistic view of the interests of future generations as opposed to their own.)

3. As real income per head increases, each absolute addition will yield successively smaller increases in economic welfare. Consequently a given future increase in consumption is worth less than an equal present increase.

Against these points, it might be argued that:

1. As succeeding generations will be wealthier, the consequences to them of wrong investment decisions being taken now will not be so severe. This might neutralise, or at least soften, argument 1.
2. Civilisation as we know it could hardly have developed if past societies had fully accepted argument 2.
3. As real income per head increases, the desire for consumption goods might *increase* more than proportionately. Each absolute addition to real income might yield successively larger increases in economic welfare. Here we are in a tricky field, and it is difficult to make any firm statement about such inter-generational comparisons.

Different sets of assumptions may produce a range of rates. All one can do is compute such a range. This is bound to be quite wide. Any set of assumptions is bound to be controversial; few will agree upon the underlying value judgements—or even, perhaps, upon the facts.

All kinds of arguments can be produced to support particular rates between a wide range of values. It can perhaps be said that the S.T.P. rate will be significantly lower than the O.C. rate. It has been suggested that a rate consistent with the value judgements of present-day British governments might be around 3–4% (Henderson, 1965). This kind of conclusion can be drawn from studying various decisions taken by government (e.g. the nuclear power example discussed in Chapter 5).

SOCIAL TIME PREFERENCE WITH SOCIAL OPPORTUNITY COST

S.T.P.-with-S.O.C. is another approach that has been suggested. It involves the building into cost/benefit calculations of an estimate of the opportunity cost as distinct from the money cost of a given project.

Table 2.3 illustrates the method. The same figures of net returns (column 3) are used as in *Table 2.1*. It will be recalled that the original proposal, involving a capital outlay of £1 million, failed to satisfy the test of an 8% test rate of discount.

Table 2.3 NET PRESENT VALUE SOCIAL TIME PREFERENCE. DISCOUNT RATE = 2%

Year	Capital outlay	Net returns	Discount factor	Discounted returns
(1)	(2)	(3)	(4)	(5)
0	£1·5 million (A) (Shadow price 'money' cost = £1 million)	—	—	—
1	—	£250 000	0·980	£245 000
2	—	£350 000	0·961	£336 350
3	—	£250 000	0·942	£235 500
4	—	£200 000	0·924	£184 800
5	—	£100 000	0·906	£ 90 600
				£1 092 250(B)

The same capital outlay is taken here but, instead of £1 million, a 'shadow' price of £1·5 million is taken for purposes of the calculation. This is the 'social opportunity cost' part of the method. It will be observed that a discount rate of 2% is then applied to the net returns.

Total discounted returns come to £1 092 250. This sum falls short of the 'shadow price' of the capital invested by a considerable margin; the investment is not viable.

What is the point of such an apparently complex procedure? First, projects can be ranked according to S.T.P. (i.e. the low discount rate relatively favours longer-term schemes), but capital may still be 'rationed' by a shadow price representing the opportunity cost of capital. This acts as a minimum benefit/cost ratio. Such a shadow price could be varied with changes in the macro-economic climate.

Secondly, one can go further by taking into account the opportunity cost of a specific project rather than that of public sector projects globally. Take the example of a scheme to be implemented in an area of high unemployment. With such a scheme, the shadow price of capital might be taken as less than unity (i.e. with the example of *Table 2.3*, we might take a 'shadow price' of £0·75 million). In a region of overstrained resources, the 'shadow price' of *Table 2.3* might be deemed appropriate. (An alternative approach in this particular case could be to use a shadow price of labour in working out net returns.)

The setting of a generally applied shadow price bristles with problems. The difficulty of saying what kind of expenditure is displaced, discussed above in relation to O.C., has not disappeared. There is now the additional problem of saying 'how much'. With both these problems there is a dynamic aspect. The true opportunity cost of a project is not adequately measured by the present value of what it currently displaces; the effects in later periods must also be taken into account. Furthermore, the macro-effects of all displaced categories of expenditure, past and future, must be assessed.

Similarly with a specific project in a particular region the difficulty still remains, arising from the inevitable time lag in installing a large project. In the five to seven years taken to build, say, an electric power generating station, the whole economic circumstances may have changed. The appropriate 'shadow price' may then be entirely different. Moreover, if a large number of such schemes are programmed, their combined impact may raise the problems discussed in the previous paragraph.

Clearly, it is far from easy to arrive at an optimal discount rate— if such an 'optimum' exists. For the present, at least, official policy is to adopt the O.C. approach. To be more precise, the *average* rate of return in the private sector is taken (based upon observed rates of profit) and not the marginal rate of return. The economic significance of doing this is not at all clear. There is, however, the advantage that some kind of explicit rule is provided that the civil servants and managers of the public sector can follow. A basis for economic discussion thus exists.

3

OBJECTIVES, PLANNING AND MANAGERIAL CONTROL

Modern industrial economies are in process of rapid evolutionary change. That process, moreover, is rarely smooth and harmonious: it shows frictions, discontinuities and variations of pace. Realistic analysis must take account of these evolutionary factors.

The analytical tools discussed so far, indispensable though they are, cannot by themselves be used to explain every dimension of industrial behaviour. An economic system ensuring optimal resource allocation at *every given moment* of time may well result from following the prescriptions of welfare economists. It may, however, be inferior in terms of economic growth to one that rarely, if ever, achieves such optimality. Indeed, such failure to achieve static optimality might be a necessary condition for the long-run performance. Micro-analysis of any specific part of an economy may throw valuable light upon that specific part of an economy; it can rarely, if ever, do more.

The total reality is much more than the sum of individual pieces of analysis. An important—if not *the* most important—part of such total reality is what Schumpeter[1] called the Perennial Gale of Creative Destruction: the constant birth and execution of commodities, technologies and organisations. Change is the essence of reality. Whatever 'monopolistic' devices a firm or industry may erect to provide some element of protection and security in a cold, hostile and uncertain world, these will ultimately be to no avail.

1. Indispensable reading here is SCHUMPETER, J. A., *Capitalism, Socialism and Democracy*, Allen & Unwin, London (1943). *See* particularly Chapters V to VIII.

49

Organisations, if they wish to survive, must anticipate the course of economic change. To react passively to change is dangerous; to ignore it, fatal. This is what the subject matter of this chapter is all about.

Modern management theory has developed a systematic approach to the long-term development of organisations. Investment appraisal and other economic techniques, it may be argued, do not provide suitable equipment to grapple with 'perspective' problems.

As an example, the economist's basic principle 'examine the widest possible range of options' does not offer guidance on *how* to select that range. Investment opportunities have to be *perceived* and related to a general idea of organisational development within a dynamic environment.

Furthermore, many factors are extremely difficult to quantify in terms of investment appraisal. These intangibles may include such items as 'public goodwill' or a 'favourable labour relations record'. They cannot simply be purchased like a new machine or a supply of raw materials (although different policies may involve different outlays). Policies in these areas have to be developed over long periods of time.

What an organisation (or, rather, those who own or control it) must do is to clarify what exactly it is trying to achieve. To say 'profit maximisation', for example, is insufficient[2]. Are we talking about short-run or long-run profit maximisation? To what extent is a firm prepared to trade-off profit maximisation, however defined, against its favourable public image? or against overall risk to the survival of the firm? or against the greater organisational security that might come with expansion?

Long-term planning (or what is referred to by various other names such as Corporate Strategy*) is the name given to this attempt to establish a systematic approach to the subject[3].

---

2. For a discussion of the objectives of the modern corporation as seen by some modern economists *see*: DRUCKER, P., *The Practice of Management*, Heinemann, London (1955); GALBRAITH, J. K., *The New Industrial State*, Penguin/Hamish Hamilton, Harmondsworth (1967), and MARRIS, R., *The Economic Theory of 'Managerial' Capitalism*, Macmillan, London (1967).

3. *See*: ANSOFF, H. I., *Corporate Strategy*, Pelican, Harmondsworth (1965), and ANSOFF, H. I. (Ed.), *Business Strategy*, Pelican, Harmondsworth, particularly Ansoff's 'Toward a Strategic Theory of the Firm', pp. 11–40 (1969).

* The reader should be prepared to find variations in terminology in the course of his reading.

OBJECTIVES

The process must begin with the establishment of objectives. These are, perhaps, best explained by an example. Suppose that those who control an organisation have decided that their objective is to 'survive' indefinitely, at a certain level of output and employment. The organisation is currently in a healthy financial position, using as a yardstick rate of return upon capital invested. Market research, however, has shown that several product lines lack potential for future development: in five to ten years' time the markets which they serve may be severely contracting. These products are responsible for a large proportion of the firm's output. The outlook for future profitability is therefore somewhat bleak.

What can take the place of the threatened products? Are there any potential successors? These might seem to have little prospect of mass sales *at the moment*. Consequently they are dubious candidates for investment funds *just now*. Future prospects may, however, be very attractive in terms of profitability. This might be true even if the products currently exist only as concepts.

An organisation in such a situation might define its objective ('survival') a little more precisely as a 'target' rate of return in, say, ten to fifteen years' time. It will plan ahead by choosing now that combination of products and markets necessary to achieve the objective by the end of *that future period*.

An objective could, therefore, be defined in terms of rate of return on investment within some future period. The setting of a precise figure (or a range) to quantify the performance desired is defined as a 'goal'. In a profit-maximising firm, for example, a figure of 20% might be taken as a goal, with perhaps a 'threshold return' (i.e. the minimum acceptable rate of return) of 15%. (These figures are purely illustrative.)

The non-quantifiable objectives of the organisation cannot, by definition, give rise to such precise goals. They must often, however, play just as important a role in the working out of the organisation's strategy. Verbal statements of policy might therefore be formulated.

STRATEGY

Having established objectives and set goals, the next stage is to work out a strategy. This is a summary of *how* the goals set for the organisation as a whole, and for each individual sector or activity, are to be achieved. In a complex organisation with a large number of interacting component parts, major feasibility studies may often be required to weigh up possible alternative strategies. Often the number of factors that can vary and interact may be such that the use of mathematical models is essential. Only after this stage will specific investment projects emerge. These investment projects may then be evaluated using the appraisal techniques discussed in the preceding chapter.

In working out a strategy, a firm may tackle the job under headings such as the following:

1. Scope in existing product markets. What is the strength of the competitive challenge, existing or potential? Will these markets continue to exist in the same form? Will they contract, expand, become more sophisticated?
2. Prospects for development of new or improved products. Are there entirely new markets waiting to be developed? Should the firm, with its new product potential, aim to fill such gaps? Should traditional industries within which the firm has not hitherto been represented be invaded? Is there a case for growth through diversification that is not 'product-based', i.e. via acquisition on purely organisation/financial criteria?
3. The basic strengths of the firm (and, by implication, its weaknesses). Does it possess a strong management team? What is the state of its research competence? Very different conclusions will be drawn here as between, say, an organisation with a strong background of marketing ephemeral consumer goods and one whose strength is 'high technology'.
4. Synergy implications. Sometimes referred to as the '2 + 2 = 5 effect', this is the notion that some combinations of products can provide a greater return from a given expenditure of resources than others, i.e. the combined return will be differentially greater than that of the sum of individual returns. When thinking about new product development or the acquisition of other organisations, the prospects for joint use of plant, research facilities, management skills, etc., are vital considerations.
5. Non-economic implications. Are they consistent with a public image of technological dynamism? or of concern for environmental effects? What possible strategic developments—under 1 to 5—are compatible with the 'intangible' objectives? Will

they lead to rationalisation of productive facilities, labour redundancies and, consequently, clashes with trade unions?

Such headings make some of the more important components of a strategy. A series of problems is brought up by the particular answers arrived at under each heading. For example: how should the type of growth aimed at be timed? What are the financial, administrative and operating strategies required to achieve these objectives?

The answers to these problems sum up to a plan, a term sometimes used rather loosely. Here it is no more than a plan of action flowing out of the strategic requirements of an organisation. The plan embraces not only investment projects but also the associated organisational, pricing, marketing and other changes[4].

OBJECTIVES AND PLANNING IN PUBLIC ENTERPRISE

Let us now attempt a schematic summary of all this as it applies to a public enterprise. *Figure 3.1* illustrates the processes in flow chart form. (References are made in what follows to the appropriate box numbers in the diagram.)

The process begins with the formulation of objectives and the setting of goals (box 4). Questions about the purpose of the organisation are highly relevant*. The management of a public enterprise, at least in the form that we generally know it in Britain, is much more constrained in its actions than that of a private firm[5].

Such industries have been established by Act of Parliament. These Nationalising Acts (box 1) usually define the scope of activity of the enterprise. The British Railways Board, for example, have a general duty to provide railway services in Great Britain

4. For a detailed example of the process *see*: LONG, R. A., 'Corporate Planning in Railways', *Institute of Transport Journal*, Vol. 33, No. 2, pp. 45–53, 63 (1969). THORNHILL, W., *The Nationalised Industries: An Introduction*, Nelson, London (1968) and TIVEY, L. J., *Nationalisation in British Industry*, Cape, London (1966) provide good discussion of this subject. A recent summary is provided by SIR RONALD EDWARDS, *Nationalised Industries: a Commentary*, Stamp Memorial Lecture republished by Electricity Council, London (1967).

5. *See* THORNHILL and TIVEY, op. cit.

* The different streams of thought contributing to the idea of public enterprises should be noted. Much of the thinking did not emphasise economic objectives at all. These views still find important expression and cannot be ignored.

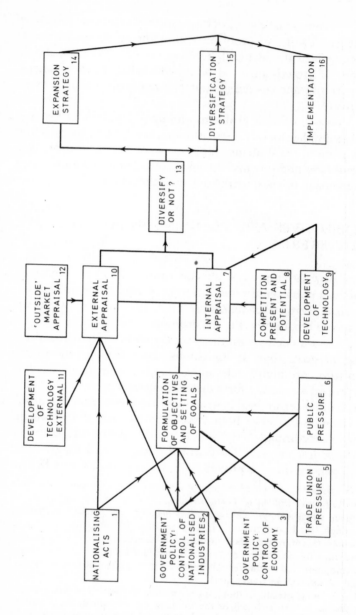

Figure 3.1. The long-term planning process in a public enterprise

with due regard to efficiency, economy and safety of operation (Transport Act, 1962) and are required to observe certain financial constraints (Acts of 1962 and 1968).

Furthermore, certain relationships with other bodies are defined by statute. The British Railways Board and the National Freight Corporation have a duty to co-operate with one another in the exercise and performance of their respective functions so as to secure the proper discharge of the Corporation's duty[6a]: '. . . to provide, or secure or promote the provision of, properly integrated services for the carriage of goods within Great Britain by road and rail; and to secure that, in the provision of those services, goods are carried by rail whenever such carriage is efficient and economic'[6b] (the Transport Act of 1968).

Even such a relatively unimportant matter as allowing railway workshops to manufacture for an 'outside' market has to be brought about by legislation. (This again, was a provision of the 1968 Act.)

Neither should it be overlooked that sponsoring government departments have their own statutory responsibilities in relation to the industries concerned.

Such statutory constraints are supplemented by the development of government policy regarding control of nationalised industries (box 2). This heading takes in the setting of financial targets, the establishment of test rates of discount, policy towards vetting of specific projects, intervention for social purposes, and so on. The cross-arrow from box 6, Public Pressure, will be noted. In matters such as railway closure, government is bound to be sensitive to public pressure for continuance of services. Such issues are discussed later.

In addition, there is an important influence stemming from government macro-economic policy (box 3). Examples of the kinds of influence exerted might be changes in the test discount rate or the 'adjustment' of investment programmes as part of a general cut in expenditure.

These influences substantially diminish the freedom of action of the management of a public enterprise in the formulation of object-ives. They are represented by the arrows converging on box 4.

Such influences, however, do not add up to an adequate and complete set of objectives. It is, perhaps, more appropriate to regard them simply as constraints, and no more than that.

6a. Transport Act, 1968 (Ch. 73, Part I, 2(a)).
6b. Transport Act, 1968 (Ch. 73, Part I, 1(a), (i) and (ii)).

Let us take the British Railways Board as an example and assume, for the sake of illustration, that the management has set itself (or has been set) goals of organisational survival (as a threshold, i.e. minimum). It is assumed that the government will require a 10% return on capital. Furthermore the long-term maintenance of a gross rate of return on total capital invested of at least 5% points better than this is sought in order to 'play safe'. In other words, a goal of 15% may be adopted for internal planning purposes.

A further, apparently non-quantifiable goal may be the 'progressive improvement of the railway's public image'. Imagine that this has been translated into:

1. Maintenance of the system and the services running upon it to the maximum possible extent compatible with the (overriding) goal of the 10% minimum return on total capital.
2. Ensuring that the existing management will be succeeded by a new generation of managers capable of achieving at least the same efficiency performance in the business environment of the future.
3. Passenger fares should increase at a rate no faster than that of prices in general (either for competitive or perhaps for public relations reasons).
4. The earnings and conditions of the labour force employed should improve at least as fast as those in the economy in general.
5. The development of an image of technical progressiveness: 'space age' technology and comfort.

These goals and the objectives they reflect, may be modified by pressure from trade unions (box 5) and the general public (box 6). The importance of these two factors in any real-life context cannot be overstressed.

Pressure from trade unions is not necessarily confined to matters of wages and conditions. For example, clashes of interest are probable where the labour force is reduced and productive units relocated in order to meet financial goals. A management may well decide to forgo the full cost reduction benefits of such rationalisation in order to maintain good labour relations. Sometimes the response of employees will be anticipated, and taken into account. Obviously, the more distant the time period under contemplation, the more important the role of such anticipation.

Just as formal machinery exists to enable the management of

public enterprise to negotiate and consult with employees, so there usually also exists machinery for consulting users. (These are often named Consumer Councils★.) Such bodies may be used to transmit all kinds of grievances about services to the management. Once again, it is not immediate issues that are of concern: the reaction of the travelling public to, say, a drastic reduction of the route mileage of the railway system is obviously an important factor in setting objectives.

The job of formulating a strategy will probably begin with the Internal Appraisal (box 7). This should be a fearless, objective analysis of the future prospects (over, say, the next decade) of the organisation within its *present* markets and with its *existing* products. 'Present' and 'existing' are relative terms, for the essence of such an approach is a recognition that everything is in a state of flux. The terms are used here to mark off spheres of interest that are historically familiar to the enterprise from those that would constitute new territory. With railways, the internal appraisal would review the markets for passenger and freight transport and the competitive strengths and weaknesses of the railways within those markets. It would be necessary to undertake forecasting exercises. Taking freight, for example, trends in national product, industrial location, nature of product (e.g. bulk/weight ratios), market characteristics '('lead' times, reliability, packaging, etc., requirements) would have to be carefully studied.

Global market estimation is insufficient by itself. Account must be taken of the development of the competitive strength of other forms of transport. There needs to be a cool appraisal, for example, of the possibility of higher permitted vehicle-carrying capacities on the roads, increases in negotiated road scheduling speeds, and so on. Any organisation, in performing this task, might do well to take a deliberately pessimistic view of what the opposition is capable of (box 8), so as to be geared to meet the toughest possible challenge. Moreover, totally new forms of transport may develop (tracked hovercraft) that will pose serious competitive threats to orthodox rail transport (box 9).

It should be noted that there is far more to study here than the evolution of 'hardware'. New forms of traction introduce such

★ It is outside the scope of this book to go into questions of constitution, organisation and function of these bodies. Much of the literature dealing with such councils seems to conclude that they have had little influence. This writer's own experience, of the Transport Users' Consultative Committee (before its powers were truncated by the 1962 Transport Act), does not support this conclusion.

problems as noise, fumes and visual intrusion. A realistic appraisal needs to forecast government response to such problems. Hence the cross-arrow linking boxes 2 and 10.

The importance of the next stage (the External Appraisal, box 10) is crucial. Earlier, the objective of survival was put forward as one possible objective, but this could have been supplemented by growth of the organisation and/or entry into growth sectors. These latter objectives may carry a great deal of weight with an organisation that is facing a contraction of traditional markets.

In this context, the role of the stages mentioned in box 11 (Development of Technology: External) and box 12 (Outside Market Appraisal) are obvious. These processes have been developed to a fine art by various kinds of company in North America grouped under the heading 'conglomerate'. Having assessed internal and external possibilities, they have answered the question 'Diversify or Not?' (box 13) in the affirmative. A programme of acquisition has then often taken these organisations very far from their original starting points.

Moving along the arrows to boxes 14 or 15, Expansion or Diversification Strategy, we arrive at decision about product selection and development, market penetration tactics, and so on. When we arrive at the Implementation stage (box 16), we then encounter some of the traditional concerns of the economist: investment criteria and pricing policy.

THE EVALUATION OF LONG-TERM PLANS

The evaluation of a plan must start with the question: how well does it cope with the problem of changing reality? Ranges of different outcomes are possible and an important consideration is the extent to which *alternative* strategies have been considered. Suppose that the environment does not evolve in the way it was thought likely to do so; there should be sufficient built-in *flexibility* to allow for such possibilities.

Take a hypothetical example. A railway management may consider that the long-run (15–20 years hence) warranted system size is, say, 10 000 route miles. This capacity projection is perhaps based, some may argue, upon a slightly optimistic view of the performance capabilities of competitive modes of transport. An alternative projection may lead to the conclusion that a 5000 route mile system is the viable one. This will, of course, have serious implications for all parts of the business. On the other hand, it is conceivable that management will be somewhat conservative in assessing their own technical and economic potential as well as that of competitors. Perhaps environmental factors will have far greater long-run importance than now appears likely, and that this will be a powerful factor working in favour of railways. Route mile *expansion* might well be taken as an option.

To re-state the principle: the widest practicable range of alternatives must be considered at each stage of the process and the maximum possible flexibility sought for.

One very interesting problem of evaluation is how to measure the economic gains, or losses, from allowing public enterprises to diversify. The classic argument, from the point of view of society, for allowing such diversification is that the dynamism of an outstanding management may be infused into areas where it can do a great deal to raise efficiency levels. In the U.S.A., for example, aerospace firms have invaded 'traditional' industries such as shipbuilding, bringing with them advanced technology and managerial professionalism.

With private sector firms, traditional arguments about 'control of monopolies' have been rehearsed in this context. Public enterprises, as we have seen, find it statutorily very difficult to expand by diversification. The policy issue arises: should they be allowed to do so? From the economic point of view, there is certainly a case for this, providing:

1. Such expansion is a faithful reflection of managerial efficiency (i.e. cross-subsidisation is not possible) plus economic strength and not merely an exercise in public spending; and
2. That there is social satisfaction with the various control and accountability mechanisms imposed upon public enterprises.

Recent developments have emphasised the role of long-term planning in public enterprises. There is no doubt that this sphere of activity will become even more important in the future.

Some fundamentally important questions arise regarding the organisational structure of public enterprises. Unfortunately, it is difficult to lay down many general principles that will make real-life sense. One fundamental aim of policy might, however, be to constrict public sector managers as little as possible by statute[7], and

7. In this context, note particularly the quotation from LORD BEECHING in EDWARDS, op. cit., p. 10.

to emphasise instead economic/financial control levers. Beyond that, one cannot say too much.

Certain common themes do emerge, though, in much of recent management thinking and these themes have been influential in helping to shape some recent structural reforms[8]. 'Public service' is tending to be replaced by 'marketing orientation'. Traditional notions of 'staff and line', a hierarchical command structure with control exercised administratively from the centre, are giving way to policies aimed at securing decentralisation, flexibility and individual responsibility.

The following are examples of some of the more important concepts.

THE CONCEPT OF MARKETING

Individual components of the long-term plan need to be based upon careful surveys of market potential. These surveys will embrace not only price relationships but also factors relatively diffi-cult to quantify such as quality of service elasticities, i.e. measures of the response of demand to changes in, for example, comfort, speed, frequency. Marketing tactics may then be based upon the inter-relations between the supply possibilities and market demand, the latter expressed in different 'currencies' (i.e. price and the different aspects of service quality). Results must be examined to gauge effectiveness[9]. This is far removed from the simple process of supplying a market for a homogeneous commodity, the price of which is set by impersonal forces over which the individual firm has little or no control.

Marketing technique implies a highly selective approach. A specific group of consumers is identified, a product 'tailored' to their requirements and a selling effort aimed directly at them. Similarly, on the supply side, the product is reshaped, or designed anew, to serve this particular market.

Let us stay with railways. Here is a commodity that is apparently homogeneous: the simple production of 'capacity-ton-miles' or 'seat-miles'. Yet this is a dramatic oversimplification; in fact it

8. See MINISTRY OF TRANSPORT, *Railway Policy* (Cmnd. 3439), H.M.S.O., London (1967), and *Transport in London* (Cmnd. 3686), H.M.S.O., London (1968).
9. For exposition of the quantitative techniques employed in marketing *see*: GREEN, P. E., and FRANK, R. E., *A Manager's Guide to Marketing Research*, Wiley, New York (1967).

could hardly be further from the truth. Indeed, modern railway managements increasingly tend to differentiate their product in order to serve specific markets. A hypothetical example is constructed here.

Railway services face severe competition in certain markets from private cars. With economic growth, the number of cars existing, the proportion of car-owning householders and the volume of car trips made, all tend to increase. Car ownership tends to be most highly concentrated in certain socio-economic strata of the population.

The first task is to examine the trip-making characteristics of the most affluent groups. The logic here is that detailed research might well show that certain service qualities such as speed, convenience, comfort and freedom from car-driving strain are rated very highly by such potential customers. If rail could match, or improve upon, the service quality provided by the private car, inroads could be made into this market. Such a service would probably need to be priced at a high level to ensure profitability, but these travellers exhibit choice-making behaviour that indicates a low weighting placed upon cost as opposed to the factors mentioned above.

Now the traffic must be defined more exactly. Let us suppose that it turns out to be holiday trip flows of higher income group families along certain corridors that are served already by rail. Business travellers might form an important minority group. The idea emerges of car-carrier trains which are designed to offer precisely that combination of price and quality that the market calls for. Cars would be carried on one part of the train and their passengers on another. Perhaps sleeping accommodation would also be provided.

Let us now suppose that a decision is taken to introduce such a service but to concentrate only upon those routes where there is a substantial traffic potential. The investment return is kept very much in mind here. The problem of pricing is discussed in a later chapter and here it is assumed that the charge made is constrained by the need to make at least the minimum acceptable rate of return. There are, however, substantial problems in addition to that of price-setting.

These relate to physical design of the service in such a way that the required service quality is provided. Important headings here would be terminal design, rolling stock, reservation system, catering and other on-train facilities. Here again, survey methods would be crucially important in finding out the preferences of consumers.

It might well be, for example, that the standard of heating or air-conditioning on the trains or the state of lavatories at terminals could have an immensely important effect upon consumer choice.

Having identified the potential demand and worked out the nature of the physical service required, it remains to complete the marketing task. Here, let us suppose, the railway management decide to launch a specific image (as, indeed, they have done in Britain with their 'Motorail' concept). This would probably involve a national advertising campaign perhaps concentrated upon the 'decision-making period' for this type of traffic (perhaps December to February for holiday trips). Although national in geographical scope, the campaign would be concentrated upon potential users.

Publicity might be closely geared to the image it is desired to develop[10]. The staff concerned might, for example, be equipped with special uniforms to help develop that image.

Pricing policy, subject to the overall constraint of securing the minimum acceptable rate of return, will be harmonised with the marketing concept employed. 'Luxury' travel and 'Family Plans' might, for instance, offer means of differentiation and/or discrimination* between sub-markets. Peak/off-peak price differentiation to even-out demand, coupled with physical control of advance reservations as a rationing device, is not inconsistent with such a policy. Indeed, marketing effort may sometimes be directed to expanding off-peak traffic[10a].

Techniques such as this are commonly used by all kinds of commercial enterprise. Are they out of place in the context of a public enterprise? Certainly, where there has been a long tradition of public service, management has sometimes found it difficult to adjust to a market-oriented approach. The answer is surely that marketing techniques are essential if a public enterprise is to thrive in a commercial environment.

10. On the image projection aspects of marketing, there is no better or more readable source than MCGINNISS, J., *The Selling of the President*, Penguin, Harmondsworth (1970).

10a. The broad pricing rules of Chapter 1 have to be adapted to fit into the dynamic context outlined here. *See*: BURSK, E. C., and CHAPMAN, J. F., *Modern Marketing Strategy*, Mentor, New York (1964), particularly Ch. 16 and 17.

* Differentiation = price variation based upon difference in the cost of providing facilities.

  Discrimination = price variation based upon differences in price/quality of service demand elasticities.

Once set up, an organisation does not 'run itself'. Management is a highly skilled job. It would be quite futile to talk about securing allocative gains from, say, introducing marginal cost pricing policies if an organisation could dramatically lower entire cost arrays simply by improving management quality. Briefly mentioned now are some of the concepts that have been evolved to secure the efficient day-to-day running of enterprises[11].

MANAGEMENT BY (SHORT-RUN) OBJECTIVES

Objectives and goals may be broken down until they confront segments of an organisation, or even individuals. Indeed, the principle may be interpreted in the sense of short-term performance standards, i.e. within a given current period of time. In effect, an organisation may be decentralised into a collection of financially self-contained units, transactions between them perhaps even taking place in cash terms. Certain important functions such as control of capital expenditure may still be reserved for the centre.

Once a particular manager, or administrative unit, has been set a certain performance target, he can be left alone to get on with his job. Actual performance, compared with 'planned', will help evaluate his efficiency. Higher management need then only intervene 'by exception'.

Many managers and administrators perform tasks the outputs of which cannot readily be quantified. Nevertheless, there is a tendency to attempt the quantification of short-run objectives in such situations. An administrator responsible for claims and damages, for example, might be set a 'target' of not exceeding X number of claims and not paying out more than £Y in damages within a given budgetary period. To the extent that the targets are exceeded, the administrator is not performing well; and vice versa.

Difficulties arise with the too-mechanical use of such indicators. With labour relations, for example, an objective may be set of keeping staff turnover down to a certain level. But the factors responsible for high turnover rates may be outside the control of the personnel specialist. Furthermore, turnover may be kept low

11. *See*: DAVIES, D., and MCCARTHY, C., *An Introduction to Technological Economics*, Wiley, London (1967). This book deals with decision-making at different levels in a way that will be familiar to economists, and contains much useful material relevant to the whole of this chapter. On this subject, *see also*: DRUCKER, op. cit.

(or industrial disputes avoided) by always 'giving in' to union/employee pressures.

BUDGETARY CONTROL

With a budgetary control system, costs (and sometimes revenues) are forecast for significant activities in a business. Actual cost performance may then be compared with budget estimates. Deviations from budget can be investigated and, when the causes come to light, managerial action undertaken.

Various levels of management may simply be required to operate the budget or, perhaps, improve upon the forecast performance. Thus the system may provide the basis for management by objectives.

Controversy exists about the extent to which budgets should be allowed to vary with changes in circumstances. It is held that managerial control is weakened if a budget can be varied too easily; on the other hand, a completely inflexible budget can become somewhat academic.

PROFIT CENTRES

In many large organisations, responsibility for selling may be divorced from that of incurring costs. Imagine a railway system that is divided up into 'districts'. District A is geographically small but 'originates' a lot of traffic. Its receipts are therefore high; costs incurred low, for a very large proportion of these are inflicted upon other districts throughout the network. There will be a probability that District A will aim to maximise revenue rather than, say, profits.

A solution might be to charge the whole of network costs incurred by the traffic from District A to that district, i.e. to draw up a profit and loss account. Traditional budget centres (e.g. there may be a track maintenance budget for the system as a whole, which is not directly related to traffic revenue) are thus replaced by profit centres. This idea may be developed to the extent of having internal markets with the different districts 'buying' and 'selling' railway haulage to and from each other.

The close relationship between these concepts will be apparent.

The kind of thinking reflected here leads to a certain philosophy of organisation. Members of a management board, it follows, should not have detailed executive responsibility for particular functions. They should be free to concentrate as far as possible on long-term planning and other policy questions.

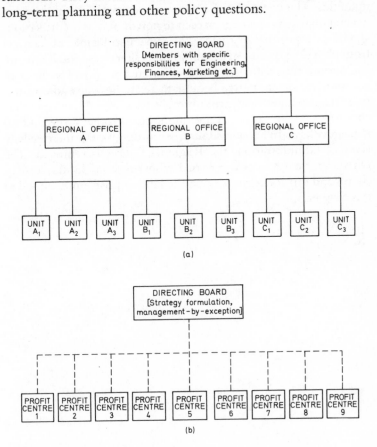

Figure 3.2. *Alternative forms of organisation, (a) traditional,*
(b) management by objectives

Figure 3.2 illustrates schematically some of the basic differences between the traditional forms of organisation and those discussed above: (a), a Directing Board, composed largely of members with functional responsibilities such as engineering or finance, exerts administrative control over Regional Offices. Those offices may, in turn, reflect the functional responsibilities of the Directing Board as may their relationships with the operating units reporting to them. Such units may carry the principle to such lengths that they have specialists concentrating upon their function alone with no manager responsible for the attainment of unit-wide targets.

This is an extreme example; there have been many variations upon this. The line and staff concept, for example, would involve general managers in charge of each region or unit, with the various specialists reporting to them. The general principle of 'control from above' by means of administrative directives would remain.

Contrast this with the forms illustrated in (b). The lines of communication are dotted because there are now few administrative directives; performance at profit centres is evaluated by reference to success or failure in meeting profit or other targets. Local managers have full responsibility. Accordingly, the intermediate layer of administration, the Regional Office, is removed. The Directing Board is now released from most of its day-to-day chores and can concentrate upon the kind of problem discussed in this chapter.

4

COAL, GAS AND THEIR ROLE
IN THE ECONOMY

THE COAL INDUSTRY

The coal-mining industries of many countries face some difficult
economic problems. In Britain, a hitherto technically backward
industry has been modernised but, during that process, there has
been a big change in the demand for coal products.

Traditional markets have been lost due to changes in the kind of
fuel used by once important customers, e.g. the substitution of
diesel and electric traction for steam power on the railways.
Remaining markets have been invaded by new competitors: fuel
oil, natural gas and nuclear energy. Problems of expansion have
given way to problems of decline.

There exist complex and important social factors that must be
taken into account. Economic analysis is essential in helping to
determine what the exact role of the industry should be and how
that role may be most painlessly achieved.

The industry in Britain has now been in public ownership for
about a quarter of a century. Apart from an insignificant amount
produced under licence*, the National Coal Board have a monopoly of production. Having monopoly rights to coal production
is, of course, very different from being a monopoly fuel producer;
the various fuel markets are, in some senses, highly competitive.

* The Licensing Authority is the National Coal Board itself, created by the
Coal Industry Nationalisation Act, 1946 (9 and 10 Geo. VI, c. 59, s.1(1)). The
references to duties cited in the next few paragraphs are taken from this source.

The Board has been charged with such duties as:

1. Mining coal in Great Britain.
2. Securing the efficient development of the coal-mining industry.
3. Making supplies of coal available, of such qualities and sizes, in such quantities and at such prices, as may seem to them (i.e. the N.C.B.) best calculated to further the public interest in all respects, including the avoidance of any undue or unreasonable preference or advantage.

Furthermore, the Board must ensure that its revenues '. . . shall not be less than sufficient for meeting all their outgoings properly chargeable to revenue account on an average of good and bad years'.

Such statutory duties are capable of varying interpretation when establishing objectives, and measuring the performance of the industry.

Important influences on the policy of the N.C.B. during the first decade of its existence (broadly speaking, between the late 1940s and late 1950s) were:

1. Priority to *quantity* of production, i.e. a policy of *output* maximisation which inevitably meant a substantial amount of coal produced at a financial loss. This policy has been superseded during the last decade when the major problem has arisen of economic adjustment to a declining market for coal.
2. 'Priority to the home market'. At certain times, the Board have imported high-cost foreign coal and sold it at a lower domestic price. The resulting losses were made up by cross-subsidisation.
3. Labour shortage. Determined attempts were made to make mining careers more attractive. More recently, the problem has become one of how to deal with redundant labour resulting from colliery closures.
4. Reconstruction. The pre-nationalisation industry was fragmented into many too-small pits, a high proportion of them technically backward compared with best foreign practice[1].

1. MINISTRY OF FUEL, *Report of Technical Advisory Committee on Coal Mining*, H.M.S.O., London (1945); often referred to as the 'Reid Report'.

5. Government agreement to changes in prices[1a].

The combined result of these influences has been to place the Board in a 'kind of half world' in which they are neither wholly a public service, nor wholly a commercial undertaking. Criticisms, for example, about not always behaving like a commercial firm are irrelevant[1b]. Output maximisation in such a context was bound to lead to the undertaking of projects that would later appear to be uneconomic according to 'normal' criteria, i.e. a high policy weighting was implicitly attached to short-run increases in output. This policy undoubtedly diverted investment funds from higher-yielding, yet longer-term investments.

Coal-mining has traditionally been a highly labour-intensive industry, with labour costs making up perhaps three-quarters of the total. (This is now changing with the advent of new types of mechanisation: remote-control coal face equipment, the replacement of pit-ponies by electric underground haulage, and so on[2].)

Natural factors assume great importance. Thickness of seam is an example. Broadly the same investment has to be incurred to work different kinds of coal seam; obviously, the thicker the seam, the larger the amount of output for a given investment in shafts, tunnels, communications and coal-cutting machinery. The same point applies to the quality of the coal, i.e. its heat-giving properties and freedom from unwanted impurities. Hazards such as faulting, flooding and gassing are often quite unpredictable in their occurrence.

Historically, the most accessible seams (usually those outcropping or nearest to the surface) have been worked first. Those deposits progressively less accessible and attractive in terms of seam thickness and quality have followed on. As the industry matures, underground distances tend to become greater and shafts often have to

1a. An example of such an influence has been the existence of a 'Gentleman's Agreement' to discuss proposed price increases with the Ministry of Power. There has also been the possibility of being required to submit proposals to scrutiny by two Coal Consumers' Councils and/or the National Board for Prices and Incomes. See: SELECT COMMITTEE ON NATIONALISED INDUSTRIES, 'Pricing Policy', Ministerial Control of the Nationalised Industries, Vol. III, H.M.S.O., London, Appendix 41 (Memorandum by the National Coal Board), pp. 226–229 (1968).

1b. SELECT COMMITTEE ON NATIONALISED INDUSTRIES, National Coal Board, H.M.S.O., London, para. 9, p. vii (1958).

2. See: NATIONAL COAL BOARD, Annual Reports and Accounts, H.M.S.O., London. Apart from interesting cost and other data, these documents contain up-to-date information about developments in all aspects of the industry.

be deepened at great cost. One can therefore speak of a historical tendency to increasing costs. These historically increasing costs must be countered by greater capital and labour productivity.

One of the arguments for the establishment of the National Coal Board was the need to look at such problems as seam and coalfield development from an *industry*-wide point of view[3]. With hundreds of separate owners, this was difficult to achieve. The danger of sub-optimisation, both in operation and with investment, is obvious. As a result of ownership boundaries[3a] and various kinds of market sharing, uneconomic units were maintained in existence and rationalisation thus frustrated.

One of the fruits of public ownership was a 'Plan for Coal' which outlined a long-term programme of capital investment, productivity improvement and cost-reduction based upon an industry-eye view[3b].

THE COST STRUCTURE OF MINING

It is not easy to apply conventional analytical categories to the cost structure of an individual mine. For one thing, the frequent variation in the type and quality of product from individual mines must be taken into account. Indeed, there are really a number of distinct products. Abstracting away from such difficulties, it has sometimes been assumed that the AC and MC of an individual mine are constant, after an initial fall, to the point of maximum capacity working.

'Individual mine' and 'capacity' are difficult concepts to grapple with in the context of mining. A system of underground workings may have several shafts to serve it; these shafts may successively be abandoned, as the workings move on, to be replaced by others. Thus it was possible, until recently, to come across mines which were nominally 100–200 years old.

Capacity partly depends upon the amount of shift working, but also upon the size of the investment in access workings.

3. See: ALLEN, G. C., *British Industries and their Organisation*, 5th edn, Longmans, Harlow, particularly Ch. III, section VI (1970).

3a. Perhaps the classic summary of the case for nationalisation of the coal industry is: TAWNEY, R. M. (1919), 'The Nationalisation of the Coal Industry', reprinted in *The Radical Tradition*, Allen & Unwin, London, pp. 118–137 (1964).

3b. See: NATIONAL COAL BOARD, *Plan for Coal*, London (1950). Although now mainly of historical interest, this document is still well worth reading.

Before work can begin there are many positions that must be manned continuously: at the pit-head, the vertical and horizontal haulage system, the underground management and supervision, and the various safety functions. The more output produced in a given working day, the smaller the share of these 'starting-up' costs borne by each unit of output. It follows that, if production is to be undertaken, fairly large outputs are required to make operation worthwhile.

The cost structure of an individual mine may therefore look something like the curves shown in *Figure 4.1*.

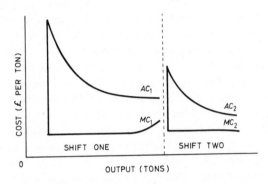

*Figure 4.1. Simplified cost curves of an individual
coal mine*

It will be noted that the *AC* curve is 'scalloped'. Multi-shift working is assumed: two out of the three possible shifts are employed for the cutting of coal. The third is organisational in the sense that preparation is made for the coal cutting (and should, therefore, be regarded as an overhead cost[4]). The upward sloping portion of MC_1 represents 'optional' overtime. The two sets of *AC* and *MC* curves do not overlap but 'add on' to each other. MC_2 relates to the marginal costs of production of the second shift alone. AC_2, however, represents average costs of production *as a whole* to that amount of output. Average costs for the second shift start at a higher level than those obtaining at the end of the first, because of 'unproductive' labour time: particularly travelling and preparation.

In traditional mining practice, the actual winning of coal was

4. A good description of the traditional system is given in DENNIS, N., HENRIQUES, F., and SLAUGHTER, C., *Coal is our Life: An Analysis of a Yorkshire Mining Community*, Eyre & Spottiswoode, London, pp. 38–48 (1956). This book gives an accurate and sympathetic account of life and work in a mining village.

limited to one shift per day; two other shifts were required for preparation and 'tidying-up'. In this case, we would have one U-shaped AC curve, the labour costs incurred by the 'preparatory' and 'cleaning-up' shifts being regarded as overheads. It is the introduction of mechanised excavation, power-loading and conveyor systems that has made multi-shift production possible. Sometimes this can almost be carried out on a round-the-clock basis. At the time of writing, there still exist technical problems preventing full utilisation of such equipment. Nevertheless, this kind of practice will eventually predominate.

The diagram shows a steeply falling AC curve that gradually flattens out towards the end of each shift. (The shifts define spells of work for the labour force.) Once labour is committed, given the existence of a minimum guaranteed payment, MC consists simply of, for example, power costs. MC 'curls up' quite sharply on account of escapable overtime payments at enhanced rates. The second shift is represented by a downward sloping MC curve that would also eventually turn up rather sharply.

Overtime payments apart, what short-run constraints would lead to this sharp upturn? Transport may become a bottleneck, both underground and vertical haulage; production cannot go on too long before further coal face preparation is required. There is also 'tidying-up' to do after the coal cutting is finished, i.e. withdrawal of props, etc. MC for both shifts may be very small, once the miners are underground.

The smooth curves of *Figure 4.1* will rarely be encountered in practice. On account of the natural factors mentioned earlier, there is a strong element of technical uncertainty.

Figure 4.2 depicts the average cost curve for a specific mine in the form of rather broad bands. Costs will oscillate up and down according to the natural conditions encountered. It may be that inputs have to be increased in order to maintain output. In this case, a vertical oscillation will take place (V_o). Average cost per ton will lie somewhere within that band. The probability that costs will lie on a particular line within that band will not be the same for all possible locations. The double-hatched small band may represent, say, the area of 0·5 probability for a specific mine, i.e. there is a 50% chance that average costs will lie within it.

For similar reasons, output may vary (H_o). (Even when measured on an annual basis output may vary appreciably in an apparently random manner.) The phenomenon of a backward bending supply curve of labour is reflected in figures of labour absenteeism. This

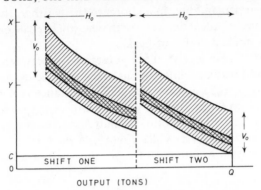

Figure 4.2. Effects of 'human' and technical uncertainty upon cost structure of individual coal mine

has obvious effects upon output. Indeed, in the short run, this kind of oscillation may be the more important in view of possible time lags in adjusting the amount of resources necessary to maintain output in the face of natural difficulties.

The 'shape' of such a cost function could be established statistically. Nevertheless, there would remain difficulties of output/cost forecasting and budgeting. One device might be to budget for total costs (which are not so variable) and set output *targets* so that a satisfactory financial surplus could be generated given the prevailing price level[4a].

In *Figure 4.2* output OQ can be obtained in suitable circumstances, at an average cost of OC. In real life, this would be an 'ideal' target, very difficult to achieve. Theoretically, average cost could be in the region of OX; certainly there would be nothing unreal about cost OY. It seems quite clear, however, that MC would be lower than AY in the region of output OQ.

So far, we have assumed that output consists of one homogeneous product. It must be remembered that, in the same seam, 'smalls' (mainly for power-station use), 'graded' (specialised industrial use) and 'large' (domestic) coals may be produced. The proportion of each will vary.

It should not be overlooked that there are risks and uncertainties also on the demand side. Coal can be stored, although there may be space problems and the risk of deterioration. There are seasonal

4a. *See*: OAKLAND, W. H., 'The Effect of Variation in Output on Colliery Profitability', *Statistical News*, No. 11, pp. 11.13–11.15, Central Statistical Office/H.M.S.O. (1970).

variations in demand but, in addition to the weather, the amount required to be supplied will vary with who stocks coal, and to what extent it is stocked in the off-peak.

Production cost levels* differ substantially between different coalfields and between different pits in the same fields. In 1967–68, for example, it cost £4·79 on an average to produce a ton of coal (at the pit-head) in Great Britain, with a profit of 13½p a ton before charging interest. In the South Midlands Areas, however, it cost on average £3·87; in West Wales £6·68[5]. In the former case, there was a profit (before interest) of 24½p: in the latter a loss of 17½p per ton.

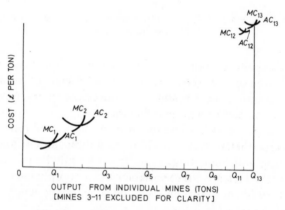

Figure 4.3. The cost structure of the coal mining industry

Figure 4.3 provides a highly simplified illustration of the cost structure of the industry. (The cost curves of *Figures 4.1* and *4.2* have, for example, been temporarily replaced by more conventional textbook ones.) The mines represented to the left of the diagram tend to be large and modern, regular beneficiaries of cost-reducing and output-expanding investment. The mines to the right of the diagram are older and relatively small. There is some positive correlation between size of colliery and depth of workings,

* These are accounting figures. Elements such as the historic costs of sinking the mine are included. As coal mines have very limited alternative uses, these 'costs' may be regarded as lost for ever. At least, a high proportion of them may be so regarded. This point is not as important as it once was, on account of the writing-down of the capital structure (in the financial sense) of the National Coal Board under the Coal Industry Act, 1965.

5. NATIONAL COAL BOARD, *Annual Report and Accounts*, H.M.S.O., London (1967–68).

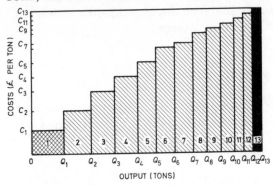

*Figure 4.4. Columnar representation of the cost
structure of the mining industry*

for many of the newer mines have been sunk through overlying
strata.

The families of cost curves may be transformed, for the sake of
simplicity, into a step function or columnar representation as in
Figure 4.4. Cost and price are measured along the vertical axis; output along the horizontal. Each individual mine is assumed to be in
short-run equilibrium.

Figure 4.5 illustrates the transformation process. The output of
Mine No. 1 is OQ_1 at which average cost (and marginal cost) is
OC_1. Similarly with Mine No. 2, whose cost curves are more
closely related to those discussed above.

The high cost margin (dark-shaded column in *Figure 4.4*) is constantly being cut back as older collieries are closed down; the low
cost margin (cross-hatched) on the other hand is extended as new

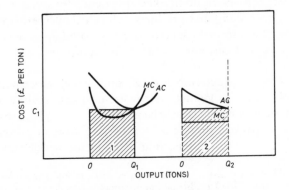

*Figure 4.5. Relationship of cost columns to cost
curves of individual mines*

collieries are sunk. The diagram, like the industry it reflects, is, therefore, constantly changing.

THE PRICE STRUCTURE

The *level* of coal prices is determined primarily by the financial objectives set for the industry by the government within the framework of institutional constraints. The prices★ of specific coal products are determined by a number of factors, such as:

1. The chemical composition, i.e. the heat-giving properties of the coal ('calorific value'). The importance of heat content is such that price is often expressed in terms of 'cost per therm'. Adjustments are made for the amount of water content, sulphur, ash, etc.
2. The size and preparation of the coal. Coal is sorted by a screening process into 'large' and 'small', with many intermediate gradings. With the advent of power cutting, large coal (coal that will not penetrate, say, a 5 cm diameter mesh) has tended to become relatively scarce. A further adjustment is made if the coal is washed.
3. 'Commercial' adjustments. These are demand premia reflecting such qualities as hardness and friability.
4. Coalfield adjustments. So far, the principles outlined relate to the demand side. These adjustments, broadly speaking, are a concession towards varying production cost levels as between different coalfields.
5. 'Special' bargains. In markets threatened by severe competition from alternative products such as fuel oil, there is a strong temptation to strike special bargains, based upon the costs of specific low-cost units. More is said about this later.

Price is therefore determined by a compromise between demand and supply factors, a 'points' system attempting to strike a balance between them. It would clearly be possible for the system to evolve further towards one more closely reflecting costs of production; equally, quality factors, reflecting value in use to the consumer,

---

★ It should be noted that we are dealing here with *pit-head* prices of industrial and carbonisation coals. The distribution of domestic coal is a separate field and much of it is in the hands of independent dealers having only commercial links with the National Coal Board.

could have even more emphasis placed upon them (i.e. 'charging what the market will bear').

It is not easy to translate this pricing system into simple diagrammatic terms. Consequently, the following attempt is bound to do some violence to the reality. It might, however, help to illustrate the principles involved.

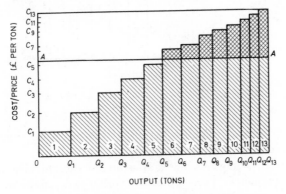

Figure 4.6. The price structure of the coal industry:
a first approximation

As already pointed out, different products make up the output of coal mines, and these products may continually change in proportionate importance in the individual colliery's product-mix due to natural factors. Let us assume that each mine depicted in *Figure 4.6* produces only one type of coal. The diagram also shows, as before, the cost structure of the given segments of the industry. Again, cost/price are measured on the vertical axis and output on the horizontal.

The price system in the coal industry is often spoken of as an average cost one, and we may accept this as a first approximation. The price level is set so as to attempt to recoup total accounting costs (although, of course, other pricing systems could perform the same task). Because of this averaging-out, however, a substantial number of mines operate at a financial loss, the deficits being offset by surpluses made at the low-cost mines. The line *A–A* represents the price charged. Mines 1–5 make a financial surplus; collieries 6–13 a loss.

But there is more to the pricing system than this simple averaging. One must take into account the coalfield adjustments. (We have abstracted away from chemistry and size by assuming that the diagram relates to only one type of coal.) The coalfield adjustments

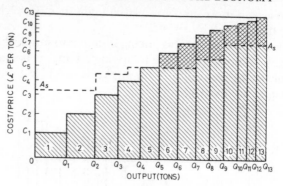

Figure 4.7. *The price structure of the coal industry:*
a second approximation

are taken into account by 'stepping' the price-line which now
becomes A_s–A_s in *Figure 4.7*.

Let us go a stage further and assume a substantial number of
'special bargains'. These consist of price concessions to specific
consumers based on the low costs of the mines to the left of the
diagram. Imagine that the necessary differentiation (or should it be
called discrimination?) is based upon the signing of long-term
supply contracts.

This system is still basically average cost pricing. The system is,
however, becoming gradually more sophisticated. The tendency is

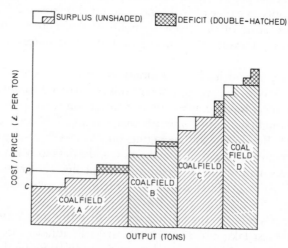

Figure 4.8. *The price structure of the coal industry:*
a third approximation

for the averaging-out to become more specific[6]. Relative prices as between coalfields are evolving so that the average costs of production of *each coalfield* are reflected in the prices charged by that coalfield. *Figure 4.8* illustrates this. The diagram is different in degree from *Figures 4.6* and *4.7*: the mines have been divided into four coalfields. The 'steps' are now located so that each field has surpluses and deficits. The transitional gulf between this situation and the one in which surpluses at least match deficits in each field is not unbridgeable.

Such is the existing system. History and custom apart, it developed against the background of the government-sponsored policy of maximising output discussed earlier. This policy involved maintenance and expansion of output at extra-marginal mines (i.e. mines that could not conceivably have covered their accounting or economic costs, given the conditions of demand, regardless of which kind of pricing policy was being pursued).

Purely financial calculation would certainly have led to the conclusion that much investment should have been diverted to new low-cost pits. With a time-constrained output maximisation policy, however, this was not feasible. Implicitly, the N.C.B., reflecting public policy, were employing a very high rate of social time preference. Immediate results were what counted in the post-nationalisation decade.

The policy of output maximisation is now a matter for historians. Would a policy of, say, *SRMC* pricing lead to allocative gains?

SHORT-RUN MARGINAL COST PRICING

What would short-run marginal cost pricing consist of? *Figure 4.9* illustrates the principle of average cost pricing (or rather a highly simplified version of it).

Employing the rule $AC = AR$, we derive price OP_a and output OQ_a.

Suppose that a policy of marginal cost pricing were introduced. We would have the situation as shown in *Figure 4.10*. The rule employed is now $MC = AR$, so price increases from OP_a to OP_m

6. *See*: SELECT COMMITTEE ON NATIONALISED INDUSTRIES, 'Future Pricing Policy', *National Coal Board*, Vol. II, H.M.S.O., London, Appendix 21 (part of Memorandum by National Coal Board), pp. 50–63 (1969). 'Pricing of Industrial Coals' in the same volume (Annex I reproduced a C.B.I. booklet *Coal: the Price Structure*) gives a detailed explanation of the pricing system.

80

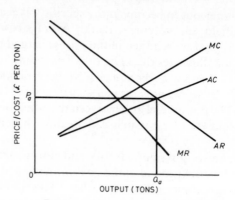

Figure 4.9. Average cost pricing in the coal industry

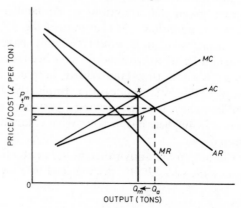

Figure 4.10. Marginal cost pricing in the coal industry

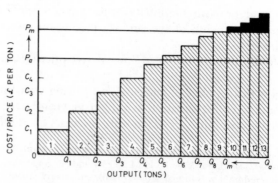

Figure 4.11. The effect of changing from AC to MC pricing upon the structure of the coal industry

and output decreases from OQ_a to OQ_m. A financial surplus is generated. This is represented by the rectangle $P_m xyz$.

Returning to our columnar exposition (*Figure 4.11*), the effect of deserting simple averaging for equally simple marginalism is to bring about the abandonment of productive capacity between OQ_m and OQ_a. The financial result is a surplus (the area below line P_m minus the cost columns). Remember we are not dealing with a long-run cost function for a single productive unit where the size of plant is being chosen from a wide range of possible sizes. We have an *existing* collection of pits each one of which has its own cost characteristics.

It will be noted that in this interpretation[7] an *SRMC* price is based upon the *average* costs of the marginal unit retained in production. The introduction of *SRMC* pricing, it may be held, would eliminate cross-subsidisation. Given the shape of the relevant *MC* curve it would also have beneficial effects upon the N.C.B.'s financial position.

It is, of course, possible to go much further than this and advocate complete decentralisation of pricing. Each colliery, or whatever would be the smallest possible unit capable of realising scale economies, could in effect act as a profit-maximising unit. Such decentralisation of price and output decisions would approximate to a marginal cost pricing solution. Investment could be evaluated by the profitability criterion. Profitable units would be expanded and unprofitable ones contracted.

Clearly, some financial cross-subsidisation exists, as we have seen. Would there really be substantial enough allocative gains to justify the adminstrative difficulty of cutting down the amount of this cross-subsidisation? Can costs and revenues be specifically enough attributed to productive units? Is it a fact that there are no joint costs sufficiently important to prevent meaningful attribution?

All these questions are highly relevant. Without answers to them, we can go no further.

It may be argued[8], however, that there are situations where apparent cross-subsidisation is wholly consistent with efficient

7. LONG, M., 'The Marginal Cost Price of Coal, 1956–7', *Economica*, New Series Vol. 29, No. 116, pp. 395–409 (1962).
8. This section is based upon Professor Shepherd's analysis. *See:* SHEPHERD, W. G., *Economic Performance Under Public Ownership*, Yale University Press, New Haven and London (1965), and SHEPHERD, W. G. (1964), 'Cross subsidisation in Coal', *Public Enterprise: Selected Readings*, Ed. R. Turvey, Penguin, Harmondsworth, pp. 316–349 (1968).

allocation. For example:

1. Stochastic (probabilistic) disequilibria. Year-to-year fluctuations in financial results take place at individual pits due to the 'natural' factors reflected in *Figure 4.2*.
2. Transitional disequilibria. Demand may shift inward or outward more rapidly than it is feasible to vary the size of productive capacity due to technical or human factors.
3. Demand fluctuations. Off-peak production levels may fall below the optimum scale of given plant and/or the opposite may apply to peak production levels.
4. Elements of rent (i.e. historic capital costs incurred for assets which have no value in alternative use) may appear in accounting costs.
5. Externalities and other divergences of market costs from social opportunity costs. Commercial decisions may directly violate marginal net social productivity conditions. Such divergencies may be common in industries like coal-mining.

The need for caution in applying pricing rules was emphasised in Chapter 1. Textbook logic can suggest means of securing efficient allocation from marginal cost pricing in the sense described or from attempting to simulate a decentralised private market.

One cannot guarantee that the private firm and marginal cost pricing approach will not yield different solutions. Indeed there is bound to be a difference unless the simulation of a private market can go so far as to attain a state of perfect competition. In particular, private market rules tend to break down where externalities, and divergences of private and social cost exist. And these factors characterise the most difficult allocation problems facing the National Coal Board.

Furthermore, it may be argued that a large number of individual mines is not sufficient in itself to ensure competitive conditions let alone approach perfect competition. The coal industry's mines and commodities find themselves in rather (perhaps highly) imperfect market conditions, on both the buying and selling sides.

On the whole, a fair conclusion would appear to be that coal pricing policy is evolving in a direction satisfying to economists. How far that evolution should go perhaps remains a matter of controversy.

LONG-RUN MARGINAL COST PRICING IN THE COAL INDUSTRY

If we look back to *Figure 4.4* we see that the long-run margin is to the left of the diagram. An *LRMC* price would be based upon the average production costs of the most efficient colliery (1). The financial effects would be as described in Chapter 1.

This is, of course, to discuss the matter in terms of our simple model of the industry. In practice, any other concept of *LRMC* would be extremely difficult to specify.

Consider the following interpretation of *LRMC* pricing:

The existing coal pricing system is a compromise between cost reflection and 'charging what the market will bear' (obtaining from the market for each grade of coal a premium reflecting the value in use of the coal). Theoretically, consumers can choose the pit-heads from which they obtain their coal. Price, remember, is 'at the pit-head', i.e. takes no account of transport costs. In some areas it may be cheaper for the consumer to take local coal at a high price rather than lower-cost fuel from distant pits at high transport costs. In any situation like this traditional supply patterns play an important role.

It may well be that some customers are not being supplied from lowest-cost (including transport) sources. Sales may, perhaps, be lost as a result.

It has been argued[9] that the price structure should be based upon coal from the cheapest source of supply wherever it may be located. Demand must first be met by the lowest-cost coal available plus whatever locally produced coal can match that cost because of low freight costs. If demand remains unsatisfied, more coal should be brought from the next cheapest source (including the transport costs). The price of *all* coal sold in the area would be based on this level until demand at resulting price levels was met. Within this basic policy, differentiation on account of quality differences could continue.

What we have done in the last few paragraphs is to view the coal industry and its distribution mechanism as an inter-connected system instead of as isolated productive units. (In the next chapter an analogy with electricity pricing will be noted.)

When looked at in this way, the calculation of marginal costs needs to be performed rather differently. What is now relevant is

9. SELECT COMMITTEE ON NATIONALISED INDUSTRIES (1969), op. cit.

the change in total costs to the entire system (production and distribution) brought about by given changes in demand[10].

COST STRUCTURE AND COMMERCIAL PRACTICE

With a cost structure of the type described there is scope for 'playing the market'. The pricing system may be substantially modified by offering to carefully selected consumers a price based upon the production costs of low-cost units. There is, however, the problem of 'undue preference'. Furthermore, such price differentiation★ obviously depends to a crucial extent upon whether such special arrangements can be concealed from, or justified to, other consumers of the product. An appropriate device here is a long-term contract. Clearly, the financial consequences of a price based upon the costs of the more efficient unit being generalised across the industry would have unfortunate effects upon the producer's profit and loss account. We would end up with the simple form of LRMC pricing discussed above.

The coal industry offers interesting case studies of this sort. A few years ago before the advent of natural gas, the Gas Council experimented with total gasification from low-grade coal (i.e. without the stage of producing coke) using Lurgi plant. The experiment was not developed into an investment programme. Although there were technical difficulties, it may be that N.C.B. pricing policy had some influence upon this decision.

Coal for electric power generation purposes was rising less rapidly in price than coal for carbonisation. Although one can never document such issues for obvious reasons of commercial secrecy, it seems likely that the N.C.B. considered gas to be a 'safe' market. The electric power market, on the other hand, was under pressure from fuel oil. In such circumstances, it would be very tempting to offer lower prices to the more competitive market. It would equally be difficult to explain away such practices to the consumer being discriminated against. (The N.C.B.'s position was that coal for gasification generally came from high-cost pits.)

10. For an analysis of this *see*: TURVEY, R., 'The Marginal Costs of Coal', *Economic Analysis and Public Enterprise*, Allen & Unwin, London, Ch. 12, pp. 133–139 (1971).

★ 'Differentiation' because the special price is based upon a cost difference, it would be 'discrimination' if there were no cost differences; only separate markets with different price (or quality) elasticities of demand.

Similar issues have arisen with the supply of coal to certain projected electric generating stations which have a nuclear option. The N.C.B. strategy has been to offer long-term contracts to the C.E.G.B. regarding supplies to individual stations. A specially low charge, based upon the production costs of a very efficient group of mines, has been offered by the N.C.B. The offer has been declined.

Why cannot that same low price be quoted in respect of other coal supplied *already* to power stations? This is the prospective customer's reaction. From the electric power generating industry's point of view there is no advantage in arranging contracts that make *particular* stations cheap to run: in their view already existing power stations should have first call upon such cheaper coal. (It should be noted that the C.E.G.B. are unable to convert certain of their high-cost power stations to alternative power sources on account of government policy to protect coal markets.)

THE INVESTMENT DECISION

Some of the obstacles to the use of rational investment criteria may now be seen. Questions have been raised about output policy and pricing structure. That apart, there is substantial protection against competitive products such as the fuel oil duty. There are certain 'guaranteed' markets provided when government 'persuades' the electric power generation industry to take so many tons of coal and re-phase conversion to other fuels. And one must not overlook the crucially important social costs of mine closure, some of which are reflected in current prices.

Nevertheless, some interesting issues arise from a study of colliery investment problems. In particular, there are difficulties of estimating exactly what returns consist of in a situation where one is often 'adding to' already existing capacity.

Firstly, one can estimate the financial return on *total* capital invested. This would be the estimated profit as a percentage of total investment, including the book value of the colliery, the *new* capital expenditure and the additional working capital required (Basis A, in the N.C.B.'s terminology).

Secondly, one can work out the return on *new* capital alone, i.e. the estimated improvement in financial results as compared with current results. Problems arise here when current results cannot be sustained without fresh investment (Basis B).

Substantial variations may arise from application of the two different methods, as shown by the following examples[11]:

COLLIERY X

Basis A: 6·6%

Basis B: 43·7%

New capital invested: £215 000

Total capital invested

(New plus Old): £350 000

How does this divergence arise? On Basis A, the colliery has gone from an existing loss of £71 000 to an overall profit of £23 000 annually. £23 000 on £350 000 gives us (crudely) 6·6%. On Basis B, £94 000 (£23 000 overall profit plus £71 000 deficit removed = profit on new investment) on £215 000 gives 43·7%.

Colliery X is not new and has some 35 years' deposits left in thin seams. The policy alternatives, as the N.C.B. saw them, were:

1. Close down, write off existing capital book values, thus losing the output and reserves; or
2. Continue without additional investment, at an accounting loss; or
3. Invest.

Let us suppose that the total return on capital invested is unacceptably low. Should the mine be closed? This is the crucial question. Before it can be answered, however, one would need to break down capital costs into those that are escapable and those that are not; the accountant's book figures are insufficient in themselves. If this process did not then reveal an acceptable rate of return, the policy issue arises: close or not?

The second example concerns

COLLIERY Y

Basis A: 19·7%

Basis B: 4·5%

New capital invested: £1 919 000

Total investment: £2 876 000

This is a large and profitable colliery with reserves of some 80

11. SELECT COMMITTEE ON NATIONALISED INDUSTRIES (1958), op. cit., Appendix 16, pp. 153–154.

years. With Basis A, an existing profit of £481 000 becomes one of £568 000 (plus £87 000). On Basis B, £87 000 (£568 000 minus £481 000) on £1 919 000 gives 4·5%.

The N.C.B.'s conclusion here is that production should obviously be maintained at a high rate. The rate of return on additional capital looks small but, in this case, surface equipment had to be replaced and substantial investment underground was also required. Thus Basis B understates the yield on new capital. The fact is that the existing substantial profits could not continue without this additional investment.

If all factors are taken into account, Basis B is the relevant method. The use of marginal resources must be compared with the marginal returns of employing those resources. In practice, however, some investment is needed to maintain existing output. So the marginal yield is generally greater than the estimates show.

One might argue here that the returns from undertaking such 'essential' investment (essential from the point of view of maintaining output) must be included in the Basis B figure. What would the rate of return on *total* capital become in the absence of that marginal investment? This should be quantified, however roughly.

Indeed, there is a danger in many firms and industries that such 'essential' investment will not be properly evaluated just because it is so essential. If the investment really is absolutely necessary, it should be quite easy to justify it in terms of rate of return. Such occasions may also be used to ask one of the economists' classic questions: have all possible alternatives been considered?

Readers should construct some arithmetical examples for themselves. One particularly interesting case is where one might obtain substantial returns by Basis B yet merely have reduced the loss in terms of Basis A. This may be legitimate if there is some policy constraint forbidding closure of the original facilities. Otherwise, it might simply be unsound economics.

So far we have merely mentioned the existence of externalities and social costs. These have immense importance in coal-mining.

There are two main types of social effect that require analysis: the human effects of colliery closure, and foreign exchange effects.

THE SOCIAL COSTS OF PIT CLOSURE

For obvious reasons of geology, the coal-mining industry is concentrated into certain areas. It is often the sole important source of employment. Moreover, the skills of the labour force are highly specific to that industry. Miners displaced are often at an age where it is difficult for them to obtain retraining in other marketable skills. In any event, they would frequently have to uproot themselves from their native environment and move considerable distances to areas of alternative employment.

Such transitional problems may be tackled as follows:

1. Taxes or prohibitions may be placed upon fuels competing with domestically produced coal.
2. Protected markets may be provided by, say, the electricity and gas industries under government persuasion (who will thus, themselves, be penalised in relation to their competitors).
3. Social elements in the policy of an industry (i.e. those that would not be taken account of by a profit-maximising entrepreneur in a competitive market) may be specifically financed. For example, the cost penalties inflicted on the gas and electricity industries could be reimbursed.
4. Government financial support can be given for redundancy schemes, redeployment and retraining.
5. Special inducements may be offered to industrialists to locate new plants in areas suffering from unemployment due to colliery closure.

Of these measures (1) and (2), it might be argued, are likely to have misallocative effects. To secure optimal allocation of resources, users of alternative fuels should have an uninhibited choice on the basis of prices that accurately *reflect costs* including social costs. Those users may then weigh up the technical advantages and operating costs associated with coal against the alternatives in relation to price differences. With such a policy, there would be no need for (3). Measure (4), it could be continued, has no such misallocative effects. The precise effect (5) is a matter for calculation.

On the other hand, optimal resource allocation is a means to an end. One important 'end' is the achievement and maintenance of full employment. In a second-best world where prices do not accurately reflect costs and where productive factors are immobile, the least-cost method of achieving full employment might well be the 'artificial' stimulation of coal demand. What is really the least-cost method is a question for the facts.

COSTS AND BENEFITS OF COLLIERY CLOSURE

Can the costs and benefits to society of colliery closure be quantified so as to come to a rational policy decision?

The costs of (4) can be specified. To this may be added redundancy payments by the industry and benefit payable to unemployed miners. Against such costs may be set the reduction in financial losses from the colliery closures.

It should be noted that accounting and resource costs may diverge significantly. (Resource costs are those involving the consumption of real resources as opposed to transfer payments, elements of rent, etc.) It would be useful for the reader to consider for himself how different a resource cost calculation[12] would look from this. Escapable costs, excluding specific assets without value in alternative use and elements of rent, could be matched with revenues. Redundancy payments (the coal industry's and the government's contributions combined) plus unemployment benefit for those miners unable to find alternative work could be substituted for the wages bill. Another important cost would arise from investment to bring alternative employment to areas affected to the extent that investment did not produce an equivalent rate of return to that available elsewhere.

The closure decision should clearly be taken on resource cost/benefit grounds. If the results of such calculation clash with the financial calculation, mines should be kept in existence. Prices should be set at a level that 'clears the market'. There is an economic case for subsidisation of such mines.

Suppose, however, that the result of resource cost/benefit calculation suggests closure. Social costs will still result. Should these social costs be reflected in coal prices? Disbenefits arise not because of the production of a given unit of coal output; they would arise in the *absence* of that production. Accordingly, the correct question is: at what point are financial losses on marginal output of coal *more than* counterbalanced by the human costs of closure?

The conclusion of this analysis appears to be that until the closure decision is justified there is a case for a specific public subsidy. After that point has been passed, there is a case for government meeting the resulting social costs instead. What is not clear is that there is a case for using administrative devices such as (1) and (2). From the

12. For a discussion of this *see*: SELECT COMMITTEE ON NATIONALISED INDUSTRIES (1969), op. cit., Ch. XIV and Appendix 4.

point of view, again, of resource allocation, the most acceptable policy might be specific assistance from the government to cover those social costs as soon as they appear. Coal prices would include no element in respect of this.

FOREIGN EXCHANGE EFFECTS

The ' . . . fact that coal is indigenous has . . . advantages for the nation: it is secure—the recent events in the Middle East have demonstrated the importance of that—and it costs nothing in foreign exchange; every ton of coal that is used in this country instead of oil materially assists the balance of payments'[13]. This may be a slightly oversimplified view of the structure of production: resources used in coal-mining could presumably be used in alternative occupations where they can contribute directly or indirectly to saving and earning foreign exchange.

In recent years achievement of a balance of payments surplus has been a major aim of government policy. Given a fixed exchange rate, such an aim may conflict with a policy of attempting to bring about optimal domestic resource allocation. One possibility of reconciling the two policies is by the use of 'shadow' rates of foreign exchange.

The opportunity cost of foreign exchange will exceed the nominal cost of such exchange where there is a substantial deficit. In a deficit situation, imports are, in real terms, more expensive than they appear to be by the difference between the actual (controlled) rate of exchange and the level that would apply if exchange rates were allowed to find their true equilibrium. The latter would obviously (in a deficit situation) be one that 'devalued' the pound in terms of other currencies. A 'notional' mark-up may be added to the price of foreign currency so as to reflect this 'true' exchange value.

Shadow prices could be employed in several different ways. Perhaps the most relevant one here would be to rework investment project calculations, revaluing the price of imported inputs. Referring back to the tables in Chapter 2, for example, the import element in initial capital outlay (col. 2) may be grossed up by, say, 15% to take account of this. So may raw material and other inputs, in which case the column of net returns (col. 3) would have to be

13. ROBENS, LORD, 'Consider the Record . . .', Address to the Annual Conference of the National Union of Mineworkers, 6 July 1967.

adjusted. In principle, it would be possible to make similar adjustments to the output side where exports were concerned.

A rate of return could be worked out on this basis. That rate of return would then serve as the basis for the allocation of investible funds. (It would be technically possible to transform this approach into a lower test rate of discount, but the reworking suggested is perhaps the simplest.)

The size of the appropriate shadow rate of exchange is an empirical question. It would be important to try to bring about the uniform adoption of a single rate to be used by *all* enterprises, public and private. The temptation might arise to use a bigger mark-up in respect of public enterprises than that indicated by the actual foreign exchange position to make up for the difficulty of imposing such a course on the private sector. The possible defects of such a policy hardly need to be emphasised. Adjustments for domestic or foreign subsidies or elements of protection would have to be made.

This would appear to be a situation where sensitivity testing should be employed before plumping for any one shadow price, i.e. the effects upon investment calculations of using different shadow prices should be ascertained. If a small change in the shadow price makes a big difference to the result, this is a reason for great caution.

(Alternative approaches to this problem might be undertaken from the direction of macro-economics. Balance of payments 'pressure' might, for example, lead to a policy-induced deflation of domestic demand. If one accepts this proposition, it might then be possible to estimate the improvements in G.N.P. (in terms of 'deflation avoided') resulting from reduced imports.)

There are severe practical problems associated with the use of shadow prices. For one thing, many public projects are slow to mature, and by the time such investments come to fruition the balance of payments position may have changed radically. Furthermore, current earnings of foreign exchange may be more valuable than future ones (i.e. should be discounted at a high rate). This assumes that policy measures are effective in moving the balance of payments towards equilibrium at the chosen rate of exchange. Clearly, the public sector decision-maker is faced by yet another forecasting problem.

Further questions are: at what point does the use of shadow prices turn into long-term protection of a 'senile' industry? How does one distinguish this kind of protection from assistance during a painful period of transition to a new equilibrium position? There is much scope for discussion here.

There are potentially a large number of decisions in the public sector with balance of payments implications. Implicitly a government may often take decisions on this kind of basis. The shadow price concept is very much a 'second' or 'third' best approach to solving balance of payments/exchange rates problems. The fact that one is literally dealing only with shadows does not allow a price/cost chain reaction to be communicated throughout all the relevant markets. Nevertheless, it is a technique for injecting some economic objectivity into an area that might be sensitive to political pressures.

THE ECONOMICS OF NATURAL GAS

As is well known, coal now faces competition from several other sources of primary fuel. An alternative source facing quite different problems from coal is natural gas.

There has been controversy about the principles governing the way in which such gas should be priced. Issues have arisen about the economic and technical conditions of exploitation of North Sea gas, the meaning of the objective of resource saving over time, and the general policy problem as to whether public enterprises should base prices on long-run marginal costs or instead meet all costs incurred, producing also a target financial rate of return.

It has been argued that a 'free market price system' will always lead to a better allocation of resources than government direction[14]. Misallocation would occur from the Gas Council's proposal to pay a relatively low price (say 1p per therm) based on the cost of making the gas available, plus a margin for 'adequate' profit for exploration and development.

It is held that a competitive solution is possible despite the monopolistic position of the Gas Council. This is because the suppliers have the power to lay pipelines and directly supply large customers.

A simple supply and demand model may be used to show how the 'free market' allocation of North Sea gas would operate. The demand curve for natural gas would depend on its price in relation

14. POLANYI, G., *What Price North Sea Gas?*, Hobart Paper No. 38, Institute of Economic Affairs, London (1967). This publication strongly puts the case for a 'competitive' solution.

to the price of substitute fuels. Thus at, say, 2p per therm, the gas would penetrate the market for high-grade fuels (where it commands a 'premium' over alternative fuels due to its cleanliness, reliability and absence of storage requirements). Lower-grade markets could progressively be invaded as supply increased and, as a consequence of this, the price of gas fell.

The supply curve is the long-run marginal cost curve of the industry (including 15% yield on capital including compensation for risk). Fixed capital costs make up a high proportion of total costs. The *LRMC* curve is constant and costs are relatively low over a wide range of outputs and successive market prices.

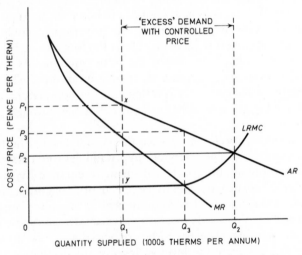

Figure 4.12.   The pricing of natural gas from the North Sea

The issues are illustrated with the help of *Figure 4.12* (after Polanyi, 1967). Suppose that OQ_1 therms per annum will be the amount of gas initially available (OQ_1 is the amount of gas from all sources currently available from the public system). A 'free market' price, given the *AR* curve of the diagram, would be OP_1. This would give rise to an excess profit of P_1xyC_1.

Now suppose that the price is controlled *from the beginning* at OP_2 per therm. This price may be chosen because it is the long-run equilibrium charge, i.e. the level at which an upturning *LRMC* curve intersects with the demand curve. Until amount supplied can be built up to the long-run equilibrium output, OQ_2, this price will lead to the existence of excess demand (OQ_2 to OQ_1). To complete the model, note that a monopolistic supplier would establish long-run output at OQ_3 ($MR = LRMC$).

The use of the price mechanism, it may be argued, will ensure that priority is given to those applications of the gas which yield the highest return to the national economy. To say that a low price will induce an abundance of fuel is to confuse cause and effect. To achieve cheap and abundant fuel one should operate on the supply and not the demand side.

Proponents of this view may concede the existence of a divergence between economic efficiency and social justice. For instance, given the assumed amount of gas initially available, a market price of OP_1 per therm would produce a rent or excess profit as shown in the diagram. This could be syphoned off, however, by applying an appropriate rate of tax. Similarly the government could bring pressure on suppliers to increase output and lower price below the monopolists' OP_3. (The use of the term 'monopolists' assumes collusion, of course, between the major producers.) The policy conclusion of such an analysis is that effective competition among sellers *and* buyers should be brought about (i.e. through private pipelines).

On the other hand, there are a number of oversimplifications in such an analysis[15]. The textbook supply and demand curves of the diagram imply smooth continuous changes; but in reality there are rigidities. These produce lags to changes in price in both supply and demand. On the demand side, for instance, even a low price for gas (OP_2) will not necessarily produce the excess demand shown in the diagram. Existing plant has to be converted and new plant built before this low price produces an increase in effective demand. If the lags in supply and demand were of roughly the same length, a low initial price would not necessarily mean rationing.

Another fundamental point relates to the time aspect of resource exploitation. A choice must be made whether to use more gas now and less in the future, or whether to use only a small portion of the known reserves of gas each year and hence spread the use of the gas over a much longer period of time.

Figure 4.13 illustrates some alternative possible depletion patterns. Suppose that OP rate of depletion corresponds to the long-run equilibrium of *Figure 4.12* (price OP_2 and output OQ_2). A solid line illustrates a short production build-up period (Ox) with maximum depletion between years x and z. Beyond z there is great uncer-

---

15. LLOYD, B., *Energy Policy*, Fabian Society, London (1968), puts an alternative view.

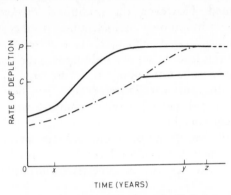

Figure 4.13. Natural gas alternative depletion rates

tainty. The dot/dash line shows an alternative slow build-up (Oy). At year y, there is the option of continuing to increase the rate of depletion. A more conservative rate of depletion (say OC) could, of course, be chosen in which case the period of exploitation would be lengthened.

Clearly, this is a social time preference discount rate problem. The government must consider the availability of future supplies. On the other hand, a longer depletion period would postpone any return from some proven reserves until far into the future. At a future date, technological and other developments might have made the gas less valuable than at present. Experience in other countries also suggests there is a good prospect of finding more gas. The best way to encourage further exploration is to bring the gas quickly into use. In this way, companies would obtain a quick return on their capital[16].

Whatever the depletion period chosen (i.e. the width of the plateau depicted in *Figure 4.13*) there are clear advantages in reaching this plateau as quickly as possible. Overhead capital (which as pointed out earlier comprises a large proportion of total costs) will thus be fully utilised and the need for investment in new town gas plant avoided.

Thus costs and therefore prices are also related to the 'load factor'. Gaswells, pipelines and other facilities have to be installed to meet the maximum demand catered for. The quicker and more fully this capacity can be utilised the lower the cost per therm of gas produced

---

16. *See*: SELECT COMMITTEE ON NATIONALISED INDUSTRIES, *The Exploitation of North Sea Gas*, H.M.S.O., London (1968). Observations by Minister of Power.

and distributed. However, the traditional market where gas commands a premium over equivalent heat from coal or oil is too small to produce a rapid build-up to the required level.

To ensure this level of supply and improve the load factor, gas prices will have to be low enough to ensure large enough sales to the bulk industrial market. Therefore price per therm is the main demand factor and gas will have to compete with the cheapest alternative fuel available. The resource saving will also be smaller in this market than in the premium and semi-premium markets (i.e. those in which *quality* of product is important). This result will not necessarily conflict with the objective of maximising resource saving.

Here we have a very interesting 'trade-off' exercise. Relatively small resource savings obtained now, or in the next few years, from the bulk use of some of the gas may be compared with the discounted present value of perhaps greater savings obtained from reserving supplies for long-term possible use in premium markets.

The resource costs of using the gas at alternative levels must be considered, including such effects as that upon the coal industry. With the manufacture of town gas, it is already much cheaper to make gas from oil than from coal. Thus, the true effect of introducing natural gas may be to displace oil and not coal. Hence, there are foreign exchange effects to be considered.

On balance, the choice of a rapid rate of depletion would appear to be appropriate.

Let us now consider the principles governing the establishment of charges to consumers by the Gas Council.

The Gas Council's policy is to sell gas (purchased from the various producers) to Area Boards according to a bulk supply tariff consisting of a standing charge related to peak demand plus standing charge for each take-off point plus commodity rate. (This is a form of multi-part tariff which was explained in Chapter 1.) All Boards will pay the same price subject to load factor.

An apparent inconsistency of policy exists here between a financial and a resource allocation approach to charging for gas consumption. On the one hand, it is established government policy that enough revenue should be generated to cover full accounting costs including overheads plus surplus in respect of financial objectives. On the other hand, there is a more recent emphasis that, while accounting costs should be covered if possible, prices should reflect costs. (This subject is discussed in Chapter 9.)

There is a conflict between an *LRMC* price of supplying

natural gas and a price which covers full accounting costs. This arises because of premature obsolescence of gas-making plant (approximately £300 million). The Gas Council accept that this is not part of the *LRMC* of supplying North Sea gas and did not intend to include an element in prices to pay for this. However, in the absence of a capital grant, the sum for premature obsolescence would have to be met out of general revenues (of which surpluses from sales of North Sea gas would be a part).

The government, however, insist that it is the industry's duty to cover its full accounting costs. A criticism made of this position is that there is a danger of market distortion, particularly as the original reasons for exploitation were based on arguments of resource saving.

A MODEL OF THE FUEL AND POWER SECTOR

There have been frequent references in this chapter to interaction between the various fuel and power industries. Such is the degree of interrelationship that it is hardly possible to take a decision of any consequence in one sector without affecting at least one of the others. How can this complex of interacting factors be analysed* so that the implications of different policies may be established?

An extremely interesting attempt to do this is being undertaken by construction of a model of the fuel and power sector of the economy[17]. The final form of the model may differ from that described here but the principles are clear enough.

The model is 'representational' in that it cannot at present be employed to arrive at an optimal solution (what is 'optimal' would depend of course, upon the choice of objectives). It is intended, initially, to provide policy-makers with answers to questions relating to the fuel sector *as a whole*. It will also provide information on demand for the various fuels, the resources required to satisfy physical demands and resulting prices. The model could, perhaps, be incorporated into one of the whole economy.

* Strictly speaking, some knowledge of the contents of Chapter 5 is required in order to appreciate fully this section. However, the material is included at this stage because it is perhaps most relevant to the problems of 'finding a role' for coal and natural gas.

17. FORSTER, C. I. K., and WHITTING, I. J., 'An integrated Mathematical Model of the Fuel Economy', *Statistical News*, No. 3, pp. 3.1–3.6 (1968). Readers should not rely on the brief summary in this book; it is important to read the original.

The supply side of the model is represented by four sub-models: coal, electricity, gas and oil. A distribution element is included, since this can be an important part of the total cost to the consumer. The demand sub-model deals with all fuels at the final consumer stage; intermediate demand by secondary fuels (e.g. coal for electricity generation) is dealt with in the supply sub-models.

DEMAND SUB-MODEL

This consists of three parts:

1. Information gained from outside the model about the growth of the economy is used to derive relevant activity indicators, such as consumers' expenditure, transport indices and output of individual industries. If no information is available, fairly simple assumed relationships may be substituted.
2. Energy consumption in each market corresponding to the various activity indicators is then derived. For example, the previous stage will have established the growth of steel output consequent upon the forecast rate of economic growth. If the energy input per unit of steel production is known, fuel requirements may then be calculated.
3. Market shares for individual fuels are derived, using relative price and other relevant information in two ways: (a) present market shares are projected forward. Techniques developed for use in 'modal split' (choice of mode of transport used for example in the journey to work) problems in urban transport studies have been adapted. Here a time lag needs to be built in, to represent cases where a change in fuel necessitates a change of appliance. Such models have been derived for some market sectors; (b) an alternative approach is to assume 'benchmark estimates' of market shares, corresponding to a specific set of price trends. These estimates are based on various alternative forecasting methods and 'informed judgement'.

SUPPLY SUB-MODELS

The coal sub-model is designed to show the effects of changes in such variables as labour supply, wage rates, degree of mechanisation and productivity. It can take into account the effects of colliery amalgamation, the closure of older, less efficient collieries and the results of specific investments at particular mines.

As with other sub-models, decisions about the amount of detail are based on data availability. Two attempts have therefore been made to build the sub-model. The first is based on readily available colliery data. It uses N.C.B. figures on variable costs per therm. Combining these with known capacity costs (and on the assumption that output is adjusted to the necessary level by cutting out production with the highest unit costs) figures for costs per ton are derived. The final figure is adjusted in the light of expected future changes in variables mentioned above. It can also be broken down into regions and type of coal.

The second attempt looks at individual collieries, and involves large data-collection problems. (Data availability and processing provide some of the most difficult problems in the field covered by this book. It is hardly an exaggeration to refer to them as the most important obstacles to progress.) Changes in cost and output as a whole are worked out from changes in scale and production techniques at individual collieries. Changes in relative costs of productive units may be allowed for. The exact changes at lower-cost collieries which will allow the desired output to be achieved may also be specified.

With gas, as might be anticipated from earlier pages, important problems are raised by the rate of conversion of consumers' appliances on the demand side and the expansion of the transmission system on the supply side. One approach is to use linear programming to select the least-cost alternative (an application of this technique is discussed in the next chapter). However, this model is directed to the production and bulk transmission of gas. Other costs have to be added in (distribution, services, overheads). Estimates of these are made in the light of expected future activity in the industry.

The electricity industry is viewed as having two separate functions, production and distribution. On the production side, selection and siting of large capital-intensive investments, choosing between alternative primary fuels and estimating the growth of peak demand, are the basic problems. As with the gas model, mathematical programming is used. This enables taxes and subsidies on the various primary fuels to be taken into account, and also any limitations placed on the installation of nuclear power stations.

The model incorporating distribution to the final consumer takes simple relationships between distribution costs and corresponding peak elements and units sold (i.e. as pointed out earlier, it is not an optimising model).

The situation with oil is unlike that of the other industries under consideration in that the U.K. is only a small part of a world market. As home demand has little effect on price, three model types are under consideration:

1. Assume that demand can always be met and that price is determined outside the model.
2. Again do not allow for factors outside the economy, but give more detailed consideration to factors within the U.K., such as quantities of crude oil to be imported from alternative centres, methods of refining, additional refining capacity required, which refined products should be imported or exported. Constraints can be built in.
3. Take *all* variables into account, and consider, in addition to the above, all international flows and interactions. This approach is unlikely to prove feasible simply as a means of deriving information about the U.K.

The two main requirements of a model of this type are realism and flexibility. The second of these is particularly important in a representational model of the fuel sector, since this is subject to continual change[18]. As additional data are obtained the more detailed aspects of the sub-models will become quantifiable. As this happens, the improved performance of the model will probably result in it replacing other forecasting methods.

One does not in any way detract from the work done by pointing out that methods such as these are still in the pioneering stage. Within the foreseeable future, however, there is the exciting prospect of being able to quantify fairly precisely the consequences of any desired policy. The sort of questions that might be answered, for example, are:

1. What price/output/investment policies in the various component parts of the fuel sector would minimise fuel costs to the economy (subject to demand constraints)? This to be done with or without 'social' benefits and costs.
2. If social costs are not explicitly included, what are the man-

18. *See*: MINISTRY OF POWER, *Fuel Policy* (Cmnd. 3438), H.M.S.O., London (1967).

power implications of particular policies? What other social implications would there be?

3. What tax structure is consistent with the policy objectives adopted, or would actively help to attain them?

4. Perhaps, most fundamental of all in the light of recent policy controversies, should the size of a particular industry be stabilised? Should, for example, the coal industry's 'size' be stabilised at 200 million tons output per year? (To be accurate, it has been recognised that such output had to be produced at competitive prices; nevertheless, such stabilisation is a leading principle.) What would be the benefits and costs of such a policy?

The reader will doubtless think of many more. From the academic point of view, such models might be developed to examine problems of welfare economics, e.g. marginal cost pricing and 'second best'. The results might well be surprising.

5

ELECTRICITY GENERATION ANI DISTRIBUTION

COST STRUCTURE AND PRICING

Demand for electricity fluctuates according to the season, the part of the week and the time of the day. Reasons for this are not too difficult to discover. More heating and lighting are required in winter than in summer; less power is required for industrial purposes at the week-end; the activities of domestic consumers in the early hours of the morning do not require as much current as in the early evening. As one might expect, the seasonal demand for electricity tends to be lowest in July; highest in January. The relationship to the state of the weather is perhaps obvious. Abnormal conditions may push the 'valley' or the 'peak' into another month, but on the whole, the seasonal pattern is remarkably stable.

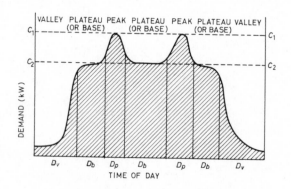

Figure 5.1. Peakiness of demand for electricity

The same can be said of the pattern of daily demand, as shown in *Figure 5.1*. Again, as one would expect, demand is at its lowest between about 11 o'clock in the evening and 6 o'clock in the morning. On either side of this valley there is a steep gradient and between 9 o'clock in the morning and 10 o'clock in the evening there is a high 'plateau' of demand. Two high peaks sprout through this plateau. In winter, the whole profile moves upward.

There are two basic sets of problems associated with such 'peakiness'. First of all, how much capacity[1] should be provided? Let us assume that *Figure 5.1* represents the day of maximum demand occurring in December.

Along the vertical axis is measured the demand in kilowatts (kW), i.e. the amount of generation capacity required. The horizontal line, C_1–C_1, represents capacity sufficient to provide *all* consumers with electricity even at the very tip of the highest peak. On the other hand, it would be possible to lower the level of provision to C_2–C_2. If this were done, some consumers would have to do without current at peak times; they would have to endure some power cuts.

The second set of problems is: how can demand[2] be 'evened out' so that peaks are 'shaved' and valleys filled in? (One would not want to level out demand to such an extent that the profile was completely flat; the engineers would almost certainly require time to undertake maintenance work.)

The first set of problems relates to investment decisions; the second to pricing policy. They are closely interrelated.

To begin with, however, let us abstract away from the peak complication and examine the cost structure of an electric power generating station.

THE COST STRUCTURE OF AN ELECTRIC POWER GENERATING STATION

Strictly speaking we ought to talk about a 'system' rather than a 'station'. It is simpler, however, to begin with an isolated station and to incorporate it into a network at a later stage.

1. *See*: MEEK, R. L., 'An Application of Marginal Cost Pricing: the Green Tariff in Theory and Practice, Part I', *Journal of Industrial Economics*, Vol. 11, No. 3, pp. 217–236 (1963).
2. MEEK, R. L., 'The New Bulk Supply Tariff for Electricity', *Economic Journal*, Vol. 78, No. 309, pp. 43–66 (1968).

The costs of such a hypothetical station may be divided into running costs (largely fuel) and capacity costs (capital costs, boilers, turbo-generators, fuel handling equipment, etc.). It may be convenient to include labour costs under the latter heading as these cannot be significantly varied with station output once operation is commenced.

Running costs per kilowatt hour (kWh) produced are constant in the short run, to the point that maximum capacity is taken up (kWh is the unit in which output is measured). Let us assume that it is physically impossible to squeeze out any further output beyond that point. This is reflected in the behaviour of the running costs

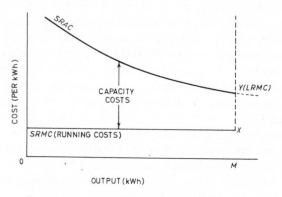

Figure 5.2. Short- and long-run marginal costs at an electric power generating station

profile of *Figure 5.2*, which turns vertically upwards once maximum capacity is reached. (On account of the 'notional' characteristics of this part of the profile, it is shown as a dotted line.)

Capacity costs are related only to the increment of capacity under consideration, i.e. that particular station. They are therefore constant by definition on a per kW basis but decrease with the production of additional kWh to the point of maximum output (for the usual arithmetical reasons when being spread over a larger quantity of output).

In *Figure 5.2*, therefore, capacity costs are shown as a line sloping gently downwards from left to right and intersecting the vertical part of the running costs profile (the dotted part). The portion of the line to the right of the running costs vertical line is also shown as a dotted line, as there would be no prospect of actually producing at such a level.

Running costs may be renamed short-run marginal costs, for

that is what they are. They are composed of fuel costs and have already been assumed to be constant per unit of output. Each increment of production in kWh costs the same until the point of maximum capacity is reached; so this particular cost curve is indeed identical with $SRMC$.

Capacity costs are 'added on' to 'running costs; and are represented by the vertical distance between the horizontal part of $SRMC$ and the $SRAC$ curve. The sum of the two categories may be taken to be the long-run marginal costs associated with that particular plant when it is optimally utilised, i.e. the point Y in the diagram may be taken to represent $LRMC$ of that plant. This relationship between $SRAC$ and $LRMC$ should be borne in mind throughout the analysis that follows. The $LRMC$ *curve* for the industry would link together all the points such as Y.

It has been assumed that $SRMC$ turns (notionally) upward and intersects $LRMC$ (or, rather, the 'added on' capacity costs line). This is plausible enough. Once the point of maximum capacity is reached, running costs may be regarded as 'shooting-up' vertically to infinity. There has been no similar development with capacity costs, which would merely be further shared out over any additional kWh were it possible to produce any.

OM shows the maximum possible output from the power station. XY, at maximum output, represents marginal capacity costs, when 'spread' over output OM.

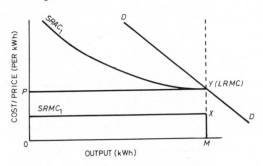

Figure 5.3. *Short- and long-run equilibrium of an electric power generating station*

The demand curve introduced in *Figure 5.3* intersects the vertical part of $SRMC$ and, by a happy coincidence, also the point where $SRMC$ meets $LRMC$. An $LRMC$ price has been established. This is equivalent to a combination of $SRMC$ with an optimal investment rule as we shall see in a moment. In the short run the consumer should cover at least the costs that would be escaped from if he did not require any output. Running costs (alias *SRMC*) are the relevant costs here. If demand moves to the right of *D–D* in the diagram there must be some rationing of supplies. Price will therefore exceed *SRMC* by whatever amount is necessary to do this. One can see from the position of the demand curve that, with price *OP* and output *OM*, price will exceed *SRMC* by *XY*. The reader will recognise that, with our assumption of output 'rigidity', *XY* represents a quasi-rent.

Consumers are prepared to pay for that output rather than do without it. This demonstrates that the utility obtained therefrom is greater than the cost of purchasing the current.

The principles of resource allocation also require that consumers should pay for incremental capacity costs, over and above marginal running costs. This they do in the situation depicted. The quasi-rent generated, *XY*, is equal to incremental capacity costs (as spread). *SRMC* equals *LRMC*.

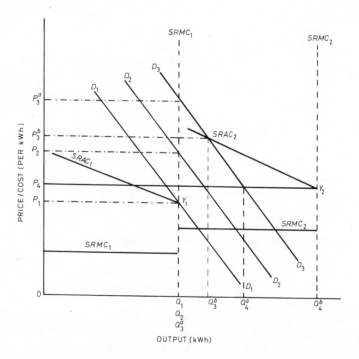

Figure 5.4. *Pricing and investment in electricity supply under conditions of shifting demand and full cost responsibility*

What should happen if capacity were to be expanded beyond this? Such expansion could go on providing short-run equilibrium price was higher than $LRMC$. Price would be used to 'ration' capacity in the short run. As *Figure 5.4* shows, the demand curve has swung to the right and, as a consequence, price has increased. Let us trace through the process to understand the stage at which capacity expansion becomes justified.

To start with, take as relevant data demand curve D_1–D_1 and cost curves $SRMC_1$ and $SRAC_1$. The plant is in equilibrium with price at OP_1 and with OQ_1 kWh of electricity being produced.

Then assume that demand grows, shifting to position D_2–D_2. Given existing plant and reliance on price as a rationing device, quantity sold stays the same (OQ_1, OQ_2) but price rises to OP_2. It can be seen from the diagram that if Plant No. 2 were to be installed ($SRMC_2$ and $SRAC_2$) only $SRMC_2$ would be covered with price OP_2; there is no case for an investment in an additional plant if the undertaking is required to recoup capacity costs and meet a financial target. This may be referred to as 'full cost responsibility'.

Demand, let us suppose, continues to grow until the demand curve reaches position D_3–D_3. If a policy of 'no power cuts' is adhered to there are two choices:

1. Keep plant size constant and price at OP_3^a. Quantity sold will thus also remain constant at (OQ_1, OQ_2, OQ_3^a).
2. Expand productive capacity by bringing in Plant No. 2.

In this second case $SRAC_2$ will be intersected by D_3–D_3. Price will now be OP_3^b and quantity sold OQ_3^b. Strictly speaking, (2) is the correct policy, but a cautious management may decide to wait until demand has increased further. This is an appropriate moment to point out that investment planning may not have been quite as accurate as desirable. Imagine that Plant No. 2 has been brought into operation when demand was still D_2–D_2. In that case, there would be an argument for basing price on $SRMC_2$ and keeping it there until it was possible to work the plant at full capacity.

Again, from the welfare point of view it could be argued that the capacity costs associated with Plant No. 2 are 'lost for ever' and therefore one should not attempt to recoup the marginal capacity costs until the outward growing demand curve eventually intersects the vertical part of $SRMC_2$. The practical difficulties of following such a course with full cost responsibility and a profits target would probably rule it out unless there were 'commercial' factors favouring a similar policy.

Managerial judgement will differ on the exact point at which to invest, given our assumption of commercial objectives. From one point of view it seems clear that Plant No. 2 should be installed as soon as it can cover its *SRAC*. In this case, where *SRAC*s are distributed over output of the marginal productive unit, this may be interpreted to mean any intersection of demand curve and *SRAC*$_2$.

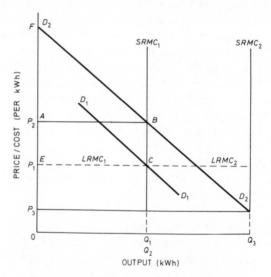

Figure 5.5. Marginal cost pricing, social surplus maximisation and the incremental plant investment decision in electricity supply

On the other hand, there are 'commercial' and administrative reasons which tend to make managements reluctant to change price levels frequently. It is conceivable that price OP_4 might be charged as soon as Plant No. 2 has been installed. Quantity demanded would thus be OQ_4^a. In other words, the forthcoming equilibrium situation (price OP_4, output OQ_4^b) could be anticipated.

Matters will be eased when we assume the existence of stand-by capacity that is only brought into operation during high peaks. This kind of transitional problem could be solved by working that capacity more intensively for a time.

What has been analysed so far is the range of possible decisions facing a manager who has commercial objectives. How is that analysis modified if marginal cost pricing is combined with social surplus maximisation[3] in the taking of the output decision?

Take the situation shown in *Figure 5.5*. Plant No. 1 is already installed; $SRMC_1$ and $LRMC_1$ (the latter suitably simplified by making the profile horizontal) have similar significance to the types of curve discussed earlier. D_1–D_1 is so located that the plant is in equilibrium: price = $SRMC_1$ = $LRMC_1$.

Now assume that demand rises to D_2–D_2. At what point should Plant No. 2 be installed according to this criterion?

First suppose that Plant No. 1 only is used to cater for the increased demand which is accordingly rationed by a higher price OP_2. Thus a producers' surplus $ABCE$ is generated. Additionally, we may note that a consumers' surplus FBA exists.

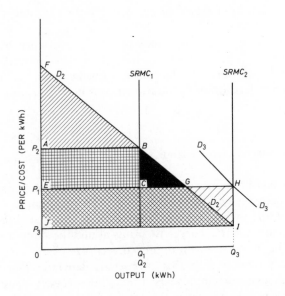

Figure 5.6. The social surplus investment criterion in electricity supply: gains and transfers of benefit

3. This analysis is based upon that of WILLIAMSON, O. E. (1966), 'Peak Load Pricing', *American Economic Review*, reprinted in *Public Enterprise*, Ed. R. Turvey, Penguin, Harmondsworth, pp. 65–71 (1968). *See also*: TURVEY, R., *Optimal Pricing and Investment in Electricity Supply*, Allen & Unwin, London, pp. 91–93 (1968). A good case-study that reflects also the marketing and engineering point of view is CREW, M., *Pennine Electricity Board: a Study in Tariff Pricing*, Bradford Exercises in Management No. 8, Nelson, London (1966).

What would be the change in consumers' and producers' surpluses brought about by investing in Plant No. 2? *Figure 5.6* illustrates the situation. Quantity produced would be OQ_3 and price OP_3.

The area of consumers' surplus *FBA* would be enjoyed as before. There is no change in welfare here.

The rectangle *ABCE* was hitherto producers' surplus. It now becomes consumers' surplus. Again, there is no welfare change; merely a transfer from producers to consumers.

Producers with price OP_3 and output OQ_3 now make a financial loss defined by *EHIJ*. But a considerable proportion of this producers' loss becomes consumers' surplus, i.e. *EGIJ*.

This leaves *GHI* as the amount of producers' deficit not thus offset.

But we have not yet taken into account the consumers' surplus *BGC*.

On this basis Plant No. 2 may be invested in when *BGC* is at least equal to *GHI*. Until demand has shifted so that position D_3–D_3 is reached operation will take place at a financial loss, but until then the loss is at least offset by additional consumers' surplus.

THE IMPORTANCE OF FORECASTING

The crucial importance of reaching equilibrium by matching plant size to demand will have been noted. To represent the process schematically, what is being attempted is the manipulation of *SRMC* and *LRMC* curves to bring about the desired equilibrium. The moral is: invest in the 'correct' size plant.

When it is pointed out that the relevant demand is one that will apply in seven or eight years' time (the necessary construction period of an electric power station) the importance of forecasting becomes apparent.

Any kind of economic forecast necessarily involves the making of a number of somewhat arbitrary assumptions and the use of incomplete data. This is not so serious a handicap providing these limitations are frankly recognised. An important part of this recognition is the need to weigh carefully the alternative risks posed by any specific investment project scheduled to come into operation at some future date.

The most relevant forecasts are those for six to eight winters ahead. Three sets of estimates are produced by the industry[4].

1. Area Boards make forecasts for their own area based upon local knowledge of building programmes, major changes in power consumption by users and so on.
2. The C.E.G.B. prepare a trend estimate by extrapolating past growth. This is done by 'fitting' an exponential curve to a ten-year moving series of winter peaks, the latter corrected for temperature, i.e. unusually severe or mild weather is adjusted for. The curve minimises the sum of squares of the percentage deviation from the trend.
3. The Electricity Council's staff integrates all the available data including that from government and important groups of users. Clearly, the existence of a national objective of economic growth has implications for growth in electricity consumption. The Council itself settles the actual forecast to be adopted.

The high degree of economic sophistication achieved should be noted. In the statistical analysis of industrial consumption, for example, demand is taken as a function of industrial production, electricity prices and a seasonal factor. But changes of consumption may not respond immediately to changes in those independent variables. There may be a delayed response (a 'lag') to such changes.

Regression equations may therefore be reformulated to reflect consumer behaviour in a given time period in a way that it depends upon changes in, say, production and changes in the *preceding* period. Hence we may end up with an estimate the independent variables of which are:

Lagged Index of Industrial Production
Lagged Price Index of Electricity Relative to Coal, and
Seasonal Factors.

THE PEAKING COMPLICATION

Now it is time to bring the peak complication into the analysis.

4. *See*: EDWARDS, SIR R., *Economic Planning and Electricity Forecasting*, Electricity Council, London (1966). A number of technical appendices are included by R. E. Baxter, J. G. Boggis, Mrs J. Hoque, P. T. McIntosh and A. R. Nobay and these are well worth careful examination by the reader possessing a little statistical equipment.

It has been implicitly assumed so far that 'demand' has been a summation of all the demands experienced at different times, or at least those contributing to the need to install capacity. Demand, for the purposes of the analysis that follows, is divided into:

1. Demand for consumption in the 'peaks'.
2. Demand for consumption in the 'base period' or plateau.
3. Demand for consumption in the 'off-peak' or valleys.

These concepts are broadly defined in *Figure 5.1*.

For the sake of simplicity, it is assumed that each of these periods of demand lasts for eight hours; together they comprise a full day's operation. (We are dealing with the problem of variation of the rate of demand, i.e. the amount of peaking, *within* this 24-hour period. The principles involved would, however, be the same if we were dealing with a larger time-horizon. Perhaps it is simplest to imagine that we are dealing with the daily peak within the winter seasonal peak.)

Two principles are involved. First of all, each demand must *at least* cover *SRMC* for familiar reasons. Secondly, marginal capacity costs (*MCC*) have to be recovered. How much, over and above *SRMC*, should each demand contribute towards them?

Take as an example the situation depicted in *Figure 5.7*. Here the cost/demand functions for the same power station are illustrated for each of the three periods. It could be argued that running costs (*SRMC*) might be different at the different times, but this is unimportant for the analysis. Also note that marginal capacity costs are really a 'lump' of cost. As the vertical scale is measured in per unit terms this cost is represented for convenience as a charge per kWh assuming that during one of these periods full capacity working is attained. But this is just a diagrammatic device. Remember that *MCC* should be regarded as a lump.

MCC is shown on the diagrams by *WZ*, which represents the same amount on each diagram, i.e. it would be double—or treble—counting to assume that *each* period *must* cover marginal capacity costs. Somehow they must do this *together*. *WZ* represents the charge per kWh for one period that would recoup total capacity costs.

Let us take the easiest case first. D_v–D_v intersects *SRMC* along its horizontal portion and it is obvious that no contribution to

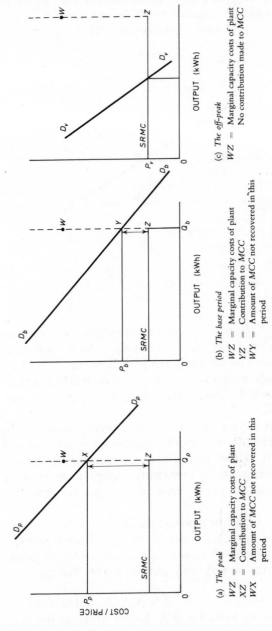

(a) The peak

WZ = Marginal capacity costs of plant
XZ = Contribution to MCC
WX = Amount of MCC not recovered in this period

(b) The base period

WZ = Marginal capacity costs of plant
YZ = Contribution to MCC
WY = Amount of MCC not recovered in this period

(c) The off-peak

WZ = Marginal capacity costs of plant
No contribution made to MCC

Figure 5.7. Peak and off-peak demand and pricing for electricity

marginal capacity costs will be forthcoming. 'Obvious', that is, if we stick to the principle of marginal cost pricing. A practical manager might be tempted to ration output in the off-peak in order to generate a contribution towards MCC. Take the example shown in *Figure 5.8*.

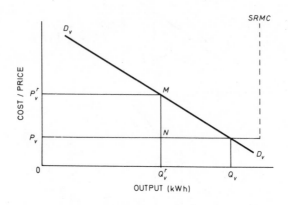

Figure 5.8. Alternative pricing policies for off-peak electricity

From the diagram it is apparent that marginal cost pricing would bring about price OP_v and output OQ_v. The management of the particular concern we are looking at, however, have braved the wrath of academic economists and set price at OP_v^r and are producing output OQ_v^r. This is generating a surplus over and above $SRMC$ of $P_v^r MNP_v$.

The exact degree to which such a policy would or could be followed depends upon market conditions (the relevant demand elasticity); it might attract new competition. In practice, the pronounced time lag in converting energy-using equipment and the specificity of many appliances might combine to tempt managers.

Now we turn to the base and the peak periods. *Figure 5.7* shows the relationship of demand to costs for all three periods. In the peak, D_p–D_p intersects the vertical part of $SRMC$ at point X. The resulting price is OP_p and output is the maximum possible, OQ_p.

The contribution to MCC is XZ. This falls short of covering full capacity costs by WX. In this situation the base period makes up the shortfall. In that period D_b–D_b intersects $SRMC$ at point Y. Output is again at full* capacity, OQ_b, and price is OP_b.

WY is exactly equal here to XZ, and so the two periods between them cover MCC. The plant is in equilibrium and, as it is the marginal plant, so is the entire system.

The examples discussed above relate to an equilibrium position. All we have done is to analyse the total demand curve for a 24-hour period by breaking it down into three sub-periods. Now the questions arise:

1. What if the demands in the three periods do not *together* cover MCC?
2. What if the sum of the three demands together *more than* covers MCC?
3. What if the periodic demands are shifting in relation to each other without necessarily together making a different total contribution to MCC?

(1) and (2) can be integrated into the earlier model, which is set out in *Figure 5.4*. The best way for the reader to understand the analysis is to work it out for himself.

Point (3) should not give much trouble either. Each period will be priced differently from hitherto. Capacity provided and current produced in the peak and the plateau will remain the same.

CHARGING IN PRACTICE

How does the theory of electricity charging compare with what the industry actually does when setting its prices? Let us look at the system employed in England and Wales[5].

First of all, some basic features of the industry's organisation should be noted. It is set up on a decentralised basis with the generation and distribution sides of the industry forming separate units. Generation and transmission are the responsibility of the Central Electricity Generating Board and distribution is that of a dozen Area Boards set up on a geographical basis. The C.E.G.B. *sells* electricity

---

* An alert reader might object here that *Figure 5.1* most definitely shows that full capacity working, if it is only attained during the peak, cannot from the information summarised on the diagram take place also in the base period. The answer lies in the fact that we really need an infinitely large number of diagrams in place of the three of *Figure 5.7* to record the minute by minute changes in load factor. It is simply that in the base period maximum capacity is called into use for a shorter time than in the peak.

5. MEEK (1968), op. cit., pp. 43–53.

to the Area Boards who, in turn, deal with individual consumers. (The only exception to this is that the C.E.G.B. has direct relations with certain large consumers such as the British Railways Board. This is not a factor of great importance and will not be referred to again.)

The C.E.G.B. is set a financial target by the government. The surplus must be recouped from the charges it makes to the Area Boards. In turn, each Area Board has its own accounts and a financial target to meet. The necessary surplus is obtained out of revenue from the final consumers of electricity. The Area Boards have a large degree of freedom in determining their retail charges: they have simply to aim at achieving their financial target.

This emphasises the importance of the wholesale price structure employed by the C.E.G.B.: the Bulk Supply Tariff. The form that this mechanism takes has great importance in that it is capable of transmitting economic forces to the whole of the industry and ultimately to the ordinary consumer. For this reason we may confine our analysis to the C.E.G.B.; the charging methods of the Area Boards simply reflect these principles in differing degrees.

With this form of organisation problems affecting the entire industry are likely to arise. They require for their resolution some form of machinery organised on that same scale.

This is an important function of the Electricity Council which, in addition to a small number of full-time members, has the Area Board Chairmen and members of the C.E.G.B. represented upon it. The council does not have formal supervisory functions, its main role being a consultative one.

The Electricity Council has two main responsibilities. The first is to advise the government. The second is to 'assist' the individual boards and to 'hold the balance' between them. In practice, this means the existence of a strong intermediary between the basic operating units of the industry and the relevant political authority. Although it would be theoretically possible for either operators or government to disregard the views of the Council, in practice, this would be most unlikely.

The C.E.G.B. and the Area Boards, for example, submit their investment proposals *directly* to the relevant Minister. Such submission would not take place without full prior consultation with the Council. Similarly, with technical questions of pricing and forecasting the Council's views carry great weight, although they have no powers to impose these views. (*Figure 5.9* illustrates the more important relations.)

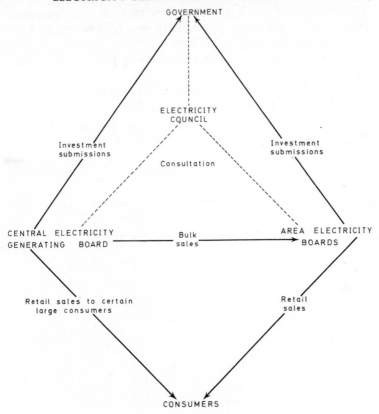

Figure 5.9. The organisation of the electricity supply and distribution industry in England and Wales

The appropriate point to begin the discussion of charging practice is with the Bulk Supply Tariff.

THE BULK SUPPLY TARIFF

This is composed of two parts: (i) a fixed charge and (ii) a running charge. This type of pricing has been discussed earlier and there is not much difficulty in reconciling it with the theoretical model outlined which was assumed to have a unitary charging system. It is convenient to begin with the running charge.

The C.E.G.B.'s generating stations are linked together by a grid.

The function of this grid is to allow current to be exchanged between consuming areas (particularly valuable when peaks do not coincide, and when station breakdowns occur), and to concentrate operation so far as is possible upon those stations with the lowest running costs.

Power stations are run in 'merit' order. From the point of view of daily—indeed hourly or minutely—dispatch of electricity throughout the network from generating stations to points of demand, capacity costs are not relevant. The task of dispatch engineers is to ensure the minimum cost operation of a *given* complex of plant and distribution network.

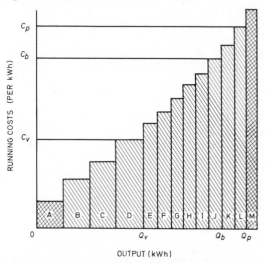

Figure 5.10. Short-run minimum cost operation of electric power generating plant

Thus we have the situation depicted in *Figure 5.10*.

Generating stations are ranked from left to right in terms of their running cost levels. Station A is a modern installation, perhaps nuclear, whereas Station M is an old, small unit nearing the end of its physical life. It is only brought into operation during unusually high surges of peak demand or emergencies.

Now let us examine the effects upon the use of this capacity of three different levels of demand: D_p, D_b and D_v of *Figure 5.7*.

1. In the peak period marginal running cost (i.e. the running cost of the marginal unit of generating capacity employed) is OC_p when quantity produced is OQ_p. (Note that there exists

an extra-marginal unit, Station M, which provides possible stand-by capacity.)

2. In the base period, marginal running costs is OC_b. Stations K and L are now out of operation.
3. In the valley period only modern, low-cost stations A, B, C and D are employed. *MRC* is OC_v and quantity sent out OQ_v.

To reflect such different cost levels the running charge part of the Bulk Supply Tariff employed by the C.E.G.B. varies by time of day. Each 24-hour period is split into three ('Peak', 'Day' and 'Night') and charged accordingly. The 'Peak' period (lasting about 250 hours or just over) applies only during December and January, with a few exceptions such as Christmas Day. The other rates apply for the whole year, the 'Day' rate taking over during the 'Peak' hours outside the December and January period.

OTHER FORMS OF DIFFERENTIATION IN RUNNING CHARGE

These are largely geographical in basis. Some Area Boards have to be supplied by long-distance high-voltage transmission systems, others have low-cost primary fuel supplies within their areas.

Different administrations in various countries do not tackle the problem in exactly the same way. The C.E.G.B. have, in the past, dealt with it through 'fuel clause' adjustments to the running charge. Over time, running costs are adjusted as the price of primary fuel inputs (e.g. coal) changes. Each Area Board pays more or less according to how the cost of fuel in that particular area varies from a national 'standard'. Some areas contain coalfields that are heavy net 'exporters' to other parts of the country. The principle is therefore modified to take account of this and Area Boards pay whichever of the two possible charges listed below is the *lower*:

1. The adjustment for 'local' fuel costs; or
2. The adjustment calculated from the national average price of fuel *surplus to local requirements* plus a transmission charge.

There are clear implications for investment here. New stations will be 'steered' to low fuel cost areas providing that 'wholesale' transmission costs do not outweigh those cost advantages plus the saving in transporting raw fuel such as coal.

THE CAPACITY CHARGES

The principle here is again to charge users according to the demands they make upon the use of generating capacity *at peak times*. It would be possible (and once was done) to share out capacity costs over the estimated demand (in kW) at peak times. One simply measured how much each Area Board consumed on certain high peak days and attributed capacity costs accordingly.

This sort of calculation, however, averages out the costs of two different kinds of capacity. One is capacity installed to deal with the 'winter plateau' of *Figure 5.11*. The other is that required to supply

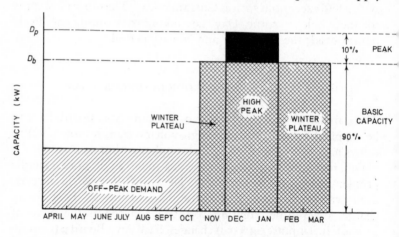

Figure 5.11. Attribution of capacity costs in electricity supply

the high peak, again shown in *Figure 5.11*, experienced in the months of December and January. The latter can be most economically supplied by 'old' plant that may be very lightly employed, or not employed at all, for much of the year. (An alternative might be investment in new gas turbine equipment.)

Why is it important to differentiate between the two types of capacity? The gains from lopping the peak requirement are clear in terms of scrapping of old plant, with its high running costs, and of saving investment in gas turbine capacity. But the savings from doing this are exaggerated by the 'sharing-out' method. Suppose that this leads to a charge of £10 per kW. This charge reflects, to a considerable extent, the large amount of modern equipment forming part of the system and *which will not be dispensed with by such 'peak lopping'*.

A realistic figure for such 'old, marginal' capacity saving might be of the order of £4 per kW per annum. Additional capacity can be installed for a similar sum. The incentive to shave-off the peaks is therefore unrealistically high under the simple share-out system.

The current method provides for two capacity charges. One is related to the provision of capacity to meet winter plateau demand D_b; the other to that required to cater for incremental demand in the high peak, D_p. Before the appropriate charges can be established, it is necessary to define D_p in terms of the marginal generating equipment involved.

The capacity/running cost characteristics of 'new base-load' and 'old, marginal' plant are different. In particular, the lower capacity costs of 'old' equipment are offset by high running costs, and which plant offers the lowest cost performance depends upon the degree of utilisation. Broadly speaking, the marginal plants are more economic if called upon to meet loads of 250 hours per year or less. Above that kind of use the wider spreading-out of capacity costs, allied to lower running costs, allows modern conventional plant to perform better.

Let us say, from operating data, that the plant brought into use when system maximum demand soars above 90% use of installed capacity is not employed for more than 250 hours per year. That residual 10% of installed capacity used for less than 250 hours per year is shown on *Figure 5.11* by $D_p - D_b$ (solidly shaded).

Now for the two peak capacity charges. The total Peak Capacity Charge is based upon the £4 per kW figure multiplied by 10% of the forecast maximum demand placed upon the system (the solidly drawn quadrilateral of *Figure 5.9*). (Note that all we have done is to establish the total amount to be recouped from the Area Boards. No attempt has yet been made to formulate a peak charge for individual Area Boards.)

The total Basic Capacity Charge is established by:

1. Taking the total estimated costs of the C.E.G.B. plus the financial surplus the Board is expected to achieve;
2. Deducting from this total, estimated income from the running charges, taking into account the fuel cost adjustment; and
3. Deducting also the Peak Capacity revenues.

The Basic Capacity Charge (in per kW terms) can thus be worked out by dividing this residual lump of costs by the 90% of system maximum demand in kW. In illustrative figures, the total Basic Capacity Charge may yield a rate of about £11 per kW of basic capacity as compared with the above-quoted £4 per kW of peak capacity.

It now remains to attribute these two kinds of capacity costs to the different Area Boards. This may be done by:

1. Measuring the demand of each Area Board when *total system demand* (D_b) is about 90% of the possible maximum (D_p) as shown in the cross-hatched winter plateau portion of *Figure 5.11*. (Note that the peaks and troughs depicted there refer to time of year, by month, rather than time of day as in *Figure 5.1*. Imagine the whole profile of daily consumption shifting up and down according to season.)
2. Summing each Area Board's contribution to demand at these times and expressing them as a proportion of the total. The total Basic Capacity Charge may then be attributed in these proportions.
3. Each Area Board's contribution to maximum system demand is based upon the average of their measured demands during periods when maximum output (D_p) has been sent out.
4. The contribution to system maximum demands having been thus determined, the use of peaking capacity is measured by the difference between this contribution and the use of basic capacity as in (1); i.e. the contribution to D_b is subtracted from the contribution to D_p.
5. Such a difference exists for each Board. The differences are added together. Each Board's difference is expressed as a proportion of that sum of differences. The total Peaking Charge is then attributed in those proportions.

Let us summarise with the help of *Figure 5.11* (based upon that of Meek, 1968). When total demand placed upon the system rises to D_b kW (cross-hatched area), a Board's use of peaking capacity is measured by the average of its contribution to that level of total system demand. It would be charged at a figure of, say, £11 per kW of this average.

So far as the solidly shaded high peak is concerned, a Board's use of such capacity would be measured by the *difference* between the average of its demands when total system demand was D_b kW, and the average of its demands when total system demand was D_p kW, in relation to such differences for other Boards. The rate of charge would be say, £4 per kW.

The period of off-peak demand (diagonally shaded) has no significance for capacity charging.

The development described here has rightly been hailed as a major advance towards economic principles of charging. The best way for the reader to master the analysis is to experiment for himself with the diagrams illustrating the theory in the light of what is practised.

THE NUCLEAR OPTION

The main difference between the 'conventional' coal or oil-fired power station and a nuclear installation is the substitution of the atomic reactor for the conventional steam-raising boiler. For a long time there has been no doubt about the *technical* feasibility of raising steam to power turbo-generators in this way. Indeed, at the time of writing claims are frequently being made that this form of power generation is economic. These claims have caused controversy.

Some fundamental economic issues arise:

1. Are there circumstances in which nuclear stations are economic?
2. If so, how important a role should such stations play in programmes of investment in new generating capacity?
3. If there is no *immediate* economic case, is there an argument for 'protecting' nuclear power until it does become economic?
4. What is the form of design organisation most likely to bring about rapid innovation and improved economic performance?

COST CHARACTERISTICS OF NUCLEAR POWER GENERATION

Capacity costs are a high proportion of the total. The reasons are not far to seek. A very complex nuclear installation is required to replace orthodox steam-raising equipment. A coolant system must be installed to transfer heat from the reactor to the turbo-generator.

Special construction materials are needed. A certain minimum amount of fuel must be inserted into the pile before reaction can take place. This initial fuel input cost may be regarded as a capacity cost. (For this, and other reasons, the early reactors were physically large.)

Elaborate control equipment is essential. The charging-up and handling of radio-active materials demand great care. Again, this means heavy capital expenditure and elaborate safety measures, e.g. shielding.

The capacity costs of a nuclear station are therefore proportionately high in relation to those of a conventional installation, although there may be a tendency for them to come down. On the other hand, once the reactor and its associated equipment are raising steam, running costs are relatively low. The high current expenditures on coal or oil, and the costs of transporting and handling it do not exist. All that is required, in effect, is supervision and maintenance.

As capacity costs are such a large proportion of the total the life of plant that is assumed plays an important role when calculating returns on investment. These are primarily technical questions: how long can the reactor core withstand the effects of irradiation? What is the life of the reactor container?

There are also questions of obsolescence. With the scale of the research and development effort being carried on (particularly into advanced concepts such as the Breeder Reactor which produces more fissile material than it initially burns) and the gradually accumulating operating experience of existing stations, technological progress is likely to be rapid. In addition, there is the rapidly improving technical performance, and hence reducing costs, of conventional plant. Certainly, the forecaster has a very difficult job in making technical projections here.

The load factor at which the stations are, or will be, operated is also of great importance. This follows from the differing proportions of capacity and running costs in the two main techniques between which the choice is being made.

Let us assume to begin with that we are choosing between an investment in *one* nuclear and *one* conventional station. These are isolated stations in the sense that they are not part of a system. In this case, the comparison is relatively straightforward.

We may construct a diagram like that of *Figure 5.12*. Taking demand to be given, and the size of the appropriate station (with each technique) to be thus determined, the comparison boils down

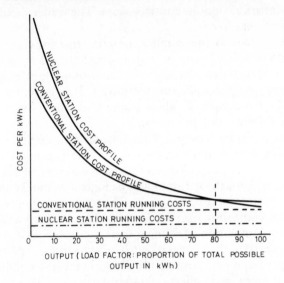

*Figure 5.12. Cost profiles of comparable nuclear and
conventional power stations*

to a question of the anticipated load factor. Two rather different
cost profiles would emerge: the nuclear station's curve would
demonstrate the existence of high per kWh costs at low output, but
relatively low costs at high output. The opposite would apply to the
cost curve of the conventional station. Running costs for the two
types of station are separately plotted; capacity costs are represented
by the vertical distance between running cost and total cost profiles.

In the diagram, it will be observed that the two cost curves intersect at a fairly high load factor (let us say at approximately 80%,
both stations having the same capacity) given the underlying cost
assumptions.

Let us assume that capacity costs include rate of return on capital,
i.e. a return at least equivalent to the current public sector discount
rate. The nuclear station is more capital-intensive than its rival. As,
therefore, a greater investment in capacity is required to provide a
given amount of electricity by nuclear technique than by conventional, the nuclear station is more sensitive to changes in the
required test rate of discount (or, historically, in the rate of interest
on capital paid to the Treasury).

The 'break-even' load factor will be affected by changes in this
price of capital. An increase in the discount rate will penalise the

capital-intensive option; and vice versa. The reader should satisfy himself that this is true.

Let us now relax the simple assumption that the choice lies between two isolated stations and examine the effect of fitting a newly constructed station into a system of inter-connected stations. These may employ different techniques. Rarely will an undertaking be faced with an 'all or nothing' decision with one kind of station dominating the system.

Let us begin by recalling that, in order to minimise short-run generating costs, stations are operated in 'merit order'. Those with lowest *running* costs are employed, as far as is practicable, as much as possible, whereas the stations with the highest running costs might only be operated during the peaks. The total costs of operation are irrelevant in the short-run decision-making process. The objective must be minimisation of running costs.

The effects on the system of introducing a given type of station will depend upon the position it will take in the order of merit (this 'order of merit' is, in effect, a kind of League Table, and we will henceforth refer to it as such). A station with high capacity costs and low running costs will occupy a high position in the table; another, even though its total costs per kWh produced are lower, might have an inferior position. These effects must be taken into account.

The total cost streams over the lifetime of a nuclear station may be expressed as follows[6]:

$$C_n = I_N + \sum_{t=1}^{T} \frac{R_n - S_n}{(1+r)^t}$$

where C_n is the present value of the total costs stream incurred by the nuclear station; I_N is the initial investment 'lump' of cost; r is the rate of discount; R_n are the estimated annual running costs of the station; and S_n are the *fuel* cost savings due to base-load requirements being met by a station with lower running costs than hitherto—an effect which extends throughout the system; T is the estimated life of the station and t the specific year of station life.

Similarly, for a coal-fired station, we may write:

$$C_c = I_C + \sum_{t=1}^{T} \frac{R_c - S_c}{(1+r)^t}$$

6. *See*: WEBB, M. G., 'Some Principles Involved in the Economic Comparison of Power Stations', *Manchester School*, Vol. 35, pp. 1–18 (1967).

The notation is the same as that used above, with the exception of the subscripts which refer to the different type of station.

Abstracting away, for the moment, from possible differences in the life of the two stations being compared, decision-makers will select the station with the lowest discounted total costs. This looks straightforward enough. What has been done is to place initial capital costs and running costs (after discounting) side by side and see how a given amount of power can be provided at lowest cost.

Note that for the sake of simplicity the initial sum invested has been shown as taking place in one year. Usually construction periods are fairly lengthy and expenditure spread accordingly. They should thus be discounted over the construction period. If the base year is taken as the first year of operation, this will take the form of grossing up expenditures to reflect lost investment opportunity. Perhaps it is simplest to think in terms of compound interest payments upon assets not yet brought into operation.

S_n and S_c are more difficult to handle. The introduction of Plant N with its very low running costs will cause some existing stations to operate at a lower load factor. Apart from the additional demand, to cater for which the new capacity has been provided, there is some existing demand which will now be met by the *new* station rather than by an *existing* station. It is necessary to assess that cost reduction and to take it into account.

Let us examine the situation depicted in *Figure 5.10*. Stations A to M are ranked in merit order as discussed earlier. Then, the prospect of installing a new nuclear power plant (N) is examined and the effect portrayed in *Figure 5.13*.

Station N takes first place in the league table. The output Ox of electricity, hitherto produced by Station A at a running cost of OR_A is now generated by Station N at a running cost of OR_N. In turn, the position of Station B is taken by Station A: a similar economy in running costs is experienced with outputs Oy to Oz. And so it goes on with stations possessing relatively high running costs losing places in the league table to newcomers with relatively low running costs. The 'relegated' stations are not necessarily retired. Indeed, that will not happen until they reach the margin. They will, however, experience lower load factors as they will progressively bear the brunt of the peak instead of being worked 'round the clock' as in their youth.

To summarise, then, the running cost economies resulting from the introduction of Station N throughout the system are added up.

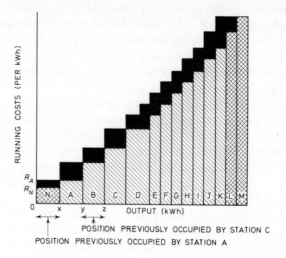

Figure 5.13. Changes in merit order and system running costs after introduction of Station N

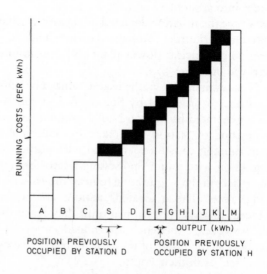

Figure 5.14. Changes in merit order and system running costs after introduction of Station S

These economies are discovered by subtracting the new running cost profile from the old as shown in *Figure 5.13*. (This diagrammatic exposition is necessarily somewhat schematic. As stations displaced will in general experience lower load factors, many of the columns to the right of the diagram should be narrowed to reflect the lower output.)

So far, the analysis has referred only to the case where a new plant is introduced at the very top of the league table. If a new conventional plant is installed, this will not be the case. However, in principle, the calculations of system running cost economies is the same. *Figure 5.14* shows the consequences of introducing a new conventional station (S). Once again, the 'old' profile for *Figure 5.10* is taken and the 'new' one 'subtracted'. The system effects may then be traced out. These system effects will be relatively smaller for the variant of technique with proportionately high running costs.

NUCLEAR POWER AND SOCIAL TIME PREFERENCE

Some fundamental policy issues arise about nuclear power programmes. One is the degree to which nuclear power should be 'protected' in the interests of *future* supplies of low-cost power (a variant of the infant industry argument). Another is the question of which organisational arrangement will best achieve the earliest possible arrival at a state of, at least, economic parity with other power sources.

Implicitly, or explicitly, the first question involves taking a position about a social time preference discount rate (although there may be numerous arguments about national prestige, export prospects, etc., many of which lie outside the economist's sphere). It is difficult to find systematic application of an S.T.P. discount rate in the case of any developed country's atomic energy investment programme.

A strong case might be made for such protection if it can be demonstrated on the technical level that operational experience is essential to achieve some future state of economic parity or superiority for the new technique. Such evidence will no doubt be supplemented by data about primary fuel availability and long-term price trends.

A related point here is that of the difficulties, already discussed, of making technical projections. This applies to existing techniques as well as to the new. Forecasts of 'break-even' dates (i.e. the time at which nuclear power will become economic) have gone astray partly because conventional power techniques have shown unexpectedly good cost-reducing performances.

There is no substitute for broad judgement here. That judgement will weigh up the technical and economic uncertainties involved.

Uncertainty is not the same thing at all as the weighting of the respective interests of present and future generations which is reflected in the discount rate. The economist will almost certainly conclude that it is better to make the weighting explicit rather than leave it buried beneath political verbiage. He will also insist that competing techniques are evaluated on the same basis: if a nuclear power programme is justified on an S.T.P. basis, it may make little sense to apply 'commercial' criteria to the alternative techniques.

The principle involved in the development of the technology would appear to be the minimisation of resource consumption in reaching the specified goal. The latter one would take to be the achievement of a certain rate of technical progress calculated to bring about the 'break-even' point by a certain date. The consequences of achieving such break-even by different dates should naturally be tested.

There has been some interesting controversy here. There is a choice, for example, between allocating the task of developing reactor systems to a central group or to various groups located within the manufacturers of the system[7]. To what extent should alternative lines of approach be encouraged? A further decision relates to the number of manufacturing units to be kept in existence by means of orders for plant (i.e. how should programmes be shared out after their total size and timing have been determined?) and, perhaps, subsidies in various forms.

It may be a long time before economists—or should one say economic historians?—will arrive at a concensus on these matters. That is certainly not to say, however, that the economic point of view should not be heard. To undertake economic analysis in the sense of outlining the different consequences of alternative choices is to provide the basis for more rational political decisions.

7. On this subject *see*: BURN, D., *The Political Economy of Nuclear Energy*, Institute of Economic Affairs, London (1967), and SELECT COMMITTEE ON SCIENCE & TECHNOLOGY, *United Kingdom Nuclear Reactor Programme*, H.M.S.O., London (1967).

CHOICE BETWEEN ALTERNATIVE TECHNIQUES: THE USE OF LINEAR PROGRAMMING

It is possible to approach the problem of planning investment in alternative techniques by the use of mathematical methods. In this example we shall look at one of the simplest of these: linear programming. This is a set of tools for analysing, and arriving at optimal decisions where the functions involved are linear (straight line). It is possible, in undertaking such calculations, to take account of large numbers of constraints[8].

All that linear programming really consists of is a set of simultaneous equations representing all possible states of the system under study. Here we shall undertake a simple graphical exposition involving choice between only two techniques. This will illustrate the principles involved; the addition of further alternative techniques would merely require more graphical dimensions. In practice, multi-dimensional geometry would give place to algebra. Thus could be obtained the combinations of various types of power stations required to meet, for example, projected increases in the annual and peak demands for electricity. As we have seen, nuclear plant typically has high initial capital cost and low running costs. It is a low-cost method of catering for a steady base-load demand for electricity, but an expensive means of meeting peak demands. Conversely, gas turbine or coal plant has lower capital costs and higher operating costs per kWh, making it more suitable to meet peak demands and less suitable to meet the base-load demand.

In this simple example the planning exercise consists of weighing up the relative importance of the peak demand against the estimated annual increased demand for electricity, and deciding what combination of plants will meet both these demands at least cost.

In the following example an estimated annual increased demand for electricity of 12 000 GWh has been assumed. The need to provide a guaranteed hourly capacity of 1 500 MW is taken with a peak January demand of 2000 MW.

Suppose that each power station has the following technical and cost characteristics per unit of guaranteed capacity. For example, coal-fired stations are more flexible in increasing capacity for a short period to meet peak demand, while nuclear stations are slightly superior in meeting the annual demand because they are out of commission for a shorter period of time in the year.

8. *See*: LANGE, O., *Introduction to Econometrics*, Pergamon, London (1959).

Table 5.1

	Nuclear (X_1)	Coal (X_2)
Guaranteed capacity (MW)	1	1
Peak capacity (MW)	1·25	1·4
Annual output (GWh)*	8·0	7·5
Construction cost (£000s)	160	55
Annual operating cost (£000s)	64	67

* Note: GWh = Gigawatt hours, where 1 gigawatt = 1 000 megawatts.

We can now formally state the problem as the satisfaction of the following inequalities or boundary conditions:

$$X_1 + X_2 \geqslant 1\,500 \text{ (Guaranteed capacity) } K_1$$
$$1·25\,X_1 + 1·4\,X_2 \geqslant 2\,000 \text{ (Peak capacity)} \qquad K_2$$
$$8·0\;X_1 + 7·5\,X_2 \geqslant 12\,000 \text{ (Annual output)} \quad K_3$$
$$X_1 \geqslant 0 \qquad X_2 \geqslant 0$$

The projected peak demand for electricity can be met by installing 1600 MW capacity of nuclear plant or approximately 1400 MW of coal-fired plant or any combination of coal and nuclear along the straight line joining these two extreme points (K_2). Similarly, the increased annual demand of 12 000 GWh can be met by installing coal plant of 1600 MW, or a combination of coal and nuclear as shown by any point along the straight line joining these points (K_3).

It can be seen that for all non-negative values of X_1 and X_2* the area of feasible solutions is given by the area farther from the origin than the lines K_2 and K_3. Capacity *at least* equal to the combinations shown along the boundary must be installed. It can also be seen that if peak demand and annual output are satisfied, then the technological conditions are such that the condition relating to guaranteed capacity is automatically satisfied. Line K_1, indicating the minimum total guaranteed capacity, is therefore redundant in this particular example.

The problem can be made more difficult by imposing a maximum constraint on the system. Suppose that both coal and uranium fuel must be imported and that a balance of payments deficit exists. Only foreign exchange sufficient to provide fuel for a coal-fired power station of a maximum capacity of 1100 MW or a nuclear

* We have to state $X_1 \geqslant 0$ and $X_2 \geqslant 0$ because if we reach a point where costs are minimised by having, say, all X_2, mathematical reasoning may tell us that costs will be further reduced by making X_1 negative!

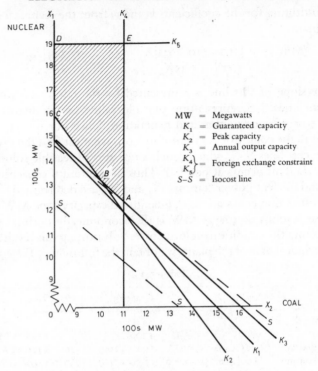

Figure 5.15. The linear programming approach to choice between alternative techniques

station of 1900 MW is available. According to these constraints, the area of feasible solution lies under the lines K_4, K_5.

Combining the determining constraints of peak and annual demand satisfying capacity with the foreign exchange constraint, gives us an area of feasible solutions equal to the area $ABCDE$. It now remains to select a point in this space which provides the economically optimal solution. An optimality criterion is therefore introduced. This is defined as the solution which minimises the joint discounted construction and operating costs. Formally we must find the minimum of the following linear form:

$$\text{Min. } S = \sum_{i=1}^{2} k_i \, x_i + \frac{1}{r} \sum_{i=1}^{2} g_i \, x_i \text{ (discounting to infinity)}$$

where k = construction costs, g = running costs, x_i, etc., = the 'ith' plant (Plants X_1 and X_2) and r = rate of discount (10%).

Substituting for the coefficients k_i and g_i from the technical data we obtain:

$$\text{Min. } S = [160+(10\times64)]X_1+[55+(10\times67)]X_2$$
$$= 800X_1+725X_2$$

The slope of this line is represented by the family of broken straight lines $S–S$ representing possible values of the discounted joint cost of construction and generation. Since our object is to satisfy all the conditions at minimum cost, we must find the lowest of the cost lines $S–S$, which touches our area of feasible solutions $ABCDE$. This occurs at point A. Thus the optimum capacities of coal and nuclear power stations, X_1 and X_2, are determined.

Constructing coal stations of guaranteed capacity 1100 MW and nuclear stations of 468·75 MW is the economically optimal way of meeting the conditions at least cost*. Substituting this result into our technical data of the plants we obtain the following (*Table 5.2*):

Table 5.2

	Nuclear (X_1)	Coal (X_2)	Total
Guaranteed capacity	468·75	1 100	1 568·75 MW
Peak capacity	$(1\cdot25\times468\cdot75)=586$	$(1\cdot4\times1\,100)=1\,540$	2 126 MW
Annual output	$(8\cdot0\times468\cdot75)=3\,750$	$(7\cdot5\times1\,100)=8\,250$	12 000 GWh

* It is not necessary to find the capacities exactly by trying to read these values off on a graph. It is easier and more precise simply to determine which constraints are operating at the point of least cost (in our case K_3 and K_4) and to make these inequalities into equalities and solve the simultaneous equations:

(1) $8\cdot0X_1+7\cdot5X_2 = 12\,000\ (K_3)$

(2) $1\cdot0X_2 = 1\,100\ (K_4)$

Multiply (2) by 7·5 and subtract to give $8\cdot0X_1 = 3\,750$, i.e.
$X_1 = 468\cdot75 \qquad X_2 = 1\,100.$

6

RAILWAYS

Upon casual observation it might be thought that railways produce
just one or two commodities: passenger-miles and ton-miles. In
fact, railway output consists of hundreds or even thousands of
different products. These are transits between different points on
the route network which make use of common facilities (stations,
marshalling yards, track, signalling, selling effort, etc.) to various
extents at different times of day, week and year. The 'quality' of the
service to the consignor or passenger, measured in such terms as
speed, reliability, convenience, safety, will show much variation.
Often these variations will exist only in the minds of the users[1] in
the sense that individuals will value the same quality of service
differently.

THE PATTERN OF RAILWAY OPERATION

The problems facing railway costing personnel may be illustrated
with the help of a diagram such as *Figure 6.1*, which shows the
traditional pattern of railway freight operation, based upon the
movement of individual wagons.

The process begins and ends with road collection and delivery
apart from the important exception of traffic to and from private
sidings located upon the premises of traders. The individual wagons
are 'picked up' and taken to a local marshalling yard and preliminary
sorting is carried out. In all probability, the wagons will then find

---

1. For some indication of the relative importance of service quality factors
   see: BAYLISS, B. T., and EDWARDS, S. L., *Transport for Industry*, H.M.S.O.,
   London (1968), and BAYLISS, B. T., and EDWARDS, S. L., *Industrial Demand for
   Transport* (1970), H.M.S.O., London.

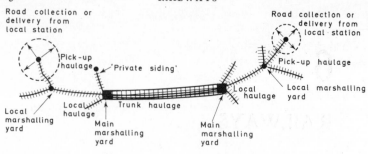

Figure 6.1. Schematic representation of railway freight wagon-load operation

their way to a main marshalling yard and be resorted. Trunk freight trains operate between the main yards. Upon arrival at the destination yard, a similar process is undertaken, but in reverse.

One can imagine the cumbersome nature of this kind of operation. The progress of a given wagon is slow and the amount of work obtained from it very small. Men and locomotives are used wastefully in 'local' work. The existence of myriads of rail/road transhipment points (dating from the era when each goods depot had to be located within horse-and-cart distance of traffic generating points) creates difficulties when the logic of modern operation demands rationalisation of difficulties.

Such a picture of traditional railway operation is schematic and highly simplified. The complexity becomes greater when each wagon is occupied by more than one consignment and when the route network resembles that in Great Britain twenty years ago★.

Take the example of a package sent from one small town to another. The package may be collected by a road vehicle engaged full-time upon such work and dealing, perhaps, with several hundred such consignments in a week. The package may be handled at the local station by personnel who also spend some of their time on dealing with passenger traffic. Let us suppose it is then consigned to a large urban terminal in the guard's compartment of a passenger train. Upon arrival there, it is carried by road vehicle to another terminal in the same city. Arriving thus at the appropriate trunk terminal, the package may be carried a long distance by a specialist parcels train. Upon arrival at a parcels terminal the

★ In Great Britain, the route 'system' developed as a result of the unco-ordinated efforts of many different companies. As a result, much unnecessary technical duplication and incompatibility occurred, e.g. the absence of a uniform loading gauge.

package may be transferred to the brake van of a local freight train. Eventually, the package arrives at its final destination by road van.

During its trip the package has been handled or carried by a variety of different means. At each stage, it will have shared the use of those facilities with a large number of packages or other traffics of various kinds.

This is an extreme case, but it illustrates an important railway problem: how should costs of using the system be attributed to individual traffics? Some proportion of the costs are simply incurred in common but can nevertheless be attributed to the traffics giving rise to them. A significant proportion may, however, be strictly 'joint'.

Such problems arise to some degree in practically every kind of productive enterprise. Railways are unusual in that there is such a large proportion of costs which are said to be insensitive to variations in output. They are therefore joint in the sense that they are not 'escaped from' unless the whole, or a considerable proportion, of that output is discounted.

Not only did such a system lead to high operating costs and difficulties of attribution; there were effects upon the demand side in terms of low quality of service. Both these supply and demand factors were (and to some extent still are) severe handicaps in meeting competition from road transport.

Charges are but one factor in determining consignors' choice of mode of transport. Consider the 'quality' of service offered by wagon-load operation. Speed? Road haulage competitors might, in certain circumstances, be able to deliver a consignment by the time a rail wagon had reached the first local yard. Freedom from damage? Each shunting added to the risk of breakage. Reliability? Wagons could easily be mis-sorted or even be completely 'lost'.

To a considerable extent, matters could be improved by modernising and streamlining such a system. The number of depots could be reduced and marshalling yards concentrated. Thus, much more road vehicle milage could be substituted for costly local rail milage. Bigger and faster trains could be run between the concentrated yards. Much investment has taken place in railways to bring about this kind of operating change. Modern practice is increasingly tending to emphasise *train*-load operation. Examine the simplicity of the operating system illustrated in *Figure 6.2*.

Transhipment operations are concentrated upon a relatively small number of strategically located terminals. Between them run trains of semi-permanently coupled flat wagons carrying containers.

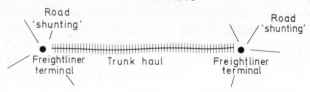

Figure 6.2. Schematic representation of railway freight train-load operation

The containers are 'shunted' by road vehicles. (Not all, or even most, train-load operation takes exactly this form but the principle of not breaking the train down into individual wagons is now common. Many such trains operate between specialist terminals, e.g. oil refineries and distribution depots. They may involve no road operation.)

The effect upon service quality will be apparent: greater speed and reliability are but two benefits. Equipment of all kinds may be used far more intensively. The costing problems are simplified, although not removed. It may now be useful to look at the way the railways tackle them.

THE COST STRUCTURE OF RAILWAYS

The basic cost categories used are those of Direct and Indirect Costs. It should be emphasised that these categories are *not* equivalent to the variable and fixed costs of the economist. Direct Costs are those considered to be directly attributable to specific traffics, services or operations on 'reasonably firm foundations of fact'. They are specifically related to the actual performance of particular operations such as the stabling and servicing of locomotives; or can be directly related to the provision of a particular train service; or the conveyance of an identifiable traffic flow.

Broadly speaking, Direct Costs (henceforth D.C.) are items which, in the long run, are expected to vary in relation to substantial changes in traffic volume. They are said to reflect the resources *directly* absorbed in providing the service. The area of Direct Costs, it has been argued, corresponds broadly to that of the long-run marginal cost of the system or service as a whole[2].

2. *See*: BRITISH TRANSPORT COMMISSION, 'Some Notes on Traffic Costing', *Report for 1951*, H.M.S.O., London, Appendix to Ch. 2 (1951), and SELECT COMMITTEE ON NATIONALISED INDUSTRIES, *Traffic Costing*, H.M.S.O., London, Appendix 39 (1960). Although now somewhat dated this Report is still a valuable source of information.

In effect, this may be taken to mean that Indirect Costs (dealt with below) were variable in relation to traffic volume only over a period that was too long for practical investment purposes. In other words, it was not practicable to 'tailor' the capacity reflected by such costs to traffic volume.

To a certain point, therefore, D.C. may be established for individual traffics. The costs of providing a train, for example, may be worked out with reasonable precision; 'allocating' the costs of that train to individual consignments or passengers carried on it then becomes necessary. This is how the railway traffic costing officer sets about his job. To ascertain the D.C. of a given transit, he looks up tables of what are, in effect, specific average costs for each component of the operation.

Returning to our original example of the package, he will extract the average costs per parcel for road collection and delivery, the average costs of handling, and those for every other link in the total operation. These costs will be added up to give total D.C. In this case, D.C. would appear to be somewhat arbitrarily established but in others, such as the movement of the train load of *Figure 6.2*, costs can apparently be calculated with great precision.

Account may be taken of varying levels of asset utilisation and

Table 6.1   BASIC RAILWAY COSTING CATEGORIES

---

1. Direct Costs (passenger and freight)
      Haulage★
            Provision and maintenance of locomotive
            Wages of crew
            Wages of guard
            Fuel and lubricants
            Stabling and servicing of locomotive
      Provision and maintenance of carrying units
      Marshalling
      Terminal shunting
      Handling (freight)
      Documentation/booking passengers
      Loss and damage (freight)
      Collection and delivery by road (freight)

2. Indirect Costs
      Track
      Signalling
      General administration

★ In freight working the cost involves: trunk haulage; pick-up haulage; feeder haulage; haulage between main yards.

Table 6.2 REVENUE AND ASSESSED COSTS BY MAIN TRAFFIC GROUPS FOR BRITISH RAILWAYS, 1961

Type of traffic	Receipts	Direct Costs	Margin— surplus or shortfall of receipts over Direct Costs	Allocated Indirect Costs	Total Indirect Costs	Net revenue or deficit over total costs	I.C. as % of D.C.
	(£m.)	(£m.)	(£m.)	(£m.)	(%)	(£m.)	
Passenger							
Fast and semi-fast	91·2	72·7	+ 18·5	40·3	24·0	− 21·8	55·4
Stopping	30·8	56·9	− 26·1	29·8	17·7	− 55·9	52·4
Suburban	39·8	40·3	− 0·5	24·5	14·6	− 25·0	60·8
Total	161·8	169·9	− 8·1	94·6	56·3	− 102·7	55·7
Freight by coaching train, mainly parcels and mails	57·3	40·2	+ 17·1	10·3	6·1	+ 6·8	25·6
Freight							
Coal	108·3	83·5	+ 24·8	22·0	13·1	+ 2·8	26·3
Minerals	44·5	36·9	+ 7·6	11·3	6·8	− 3·7	30·6
General merchandise							
Wagon load	64·8	96·6	− 31·8	22·0	13·1	− 53·8	22·8
Sundries	38·0	51·5	− 13·5	7·8	4·6	− 21·3	15·1
Total	255·6	268·5	− 12·9	63·1	37·6	− 76·0	23·5
Grand total	474·7	478·6	− 3·9	168·0	100·0	− 171·9	35·1

changes in the disposition of staff. Sample studies can be undertaken to ascertain costs in 'representative' circumstances and to test them for sensitivity to changes in such circumstances.

On the other hand, it is far more difficult to attribute the costs of track and signalling to particular traffics or services. The same applies to such items of expenditure as central administrative costs. Where costs of this kind can only be allocated on a 'reasonable but arbitrary' basis, they are referred to as *Indirect Costs*. *Table 6.1* illustrates the basic costing categories employed.

To establish in *broad* terms the profitability or otherwise of main groups of traffic, annual expenditure may be broken down into those categories shown in *Table 6.2*. In the table a broad division is first made into Passenger and Freight traffics with Freight by coaching train as a separate category. Direct Costs are then further sub-divided as shown.

The table is based upon that published in the *Reshaping Report*[3]. The estimated costs in this table include interest and the provision for depreciation is calculated in terms of 1961 money values. (The percentage of total Indirect Costs allocated to each type of traffic is not published in the table; this has been derived.)

Some types of service demand a higher standard of track maintenance and more elaborate signalling than others. Express passenger trains, for example, make necessary far higher standards than do slow freight services. The *additional* expenditure incurred by the requirements of the express passenger trains could be escaped from if they did not run. It is therefore attributable *wholly* to those trains.

A residual amount of track and signalling costs, perhaps a large one, is left over. These may be considered to be true joint costs. The course adopted here is to spread the balance of track costs *pro rata* according to gross ton-miles run over the track and signalling costs according to train miles. It is held that the weight of the traffic passing over the system is responsible for track wear and tear (the effects of high speeds, provision of smooth riding qualities, etc., having already been isolated and debited to the trains making such demands on the track). The amount of signalling depends on the number of trains and the different speeds at which they run.

This kind of exercise provides a broad summary of the profitability of the system as a whole and its main component parts.

Two interesting sets of questions arise out of this process. The

3. BRITISH RAILWAYS BOARD, *The Reshaping of British Railways*, H.M.S.O., London, Part 1, Table No. 1, p. 8 (1963).

first is the extent to which standards of, for example, track mainten-ance are economically justified. Are they based upon traditional engineering and operating notions or are they established by analysis of the relationships between the costs of providing track and the costs of operating trains? There may be scope for 'trading off' higher expenditure on track against lower costs of operation, or vice versa. It may well be that there is an important demand aspect, e.g. the smoother riding.

The second question is the extent to which cost attribution can take place. Statistical methods may be employed to discover the true behaviour of costs in complex situations[4].

THE STATISTICAL APPROACH TO COSTING

This approach may be adopted with railway infrastructure* costs once the traditional assumption that there are a limited number of 'plant' size possibilities to choose from is discarded. It may offer a chance to go beyond the formula approach to Indirect Cost attribu-tion described above. If track-milage is taken as the main long-run size variable, the size of the productive unit may be varied almost continuously in the long run.

In a period which is too short to adapt plant size completely, some costs will be incurred even with near-zero output. For example, maintenance must be at a certain minimum to operate any railway system. And, even in the long run, there will be a certain, unavoidable, level of expenditure to be incurred before relatively economic operations can be carried out.

The costs of handling a given traffic volume may thus be obtained from a linear function of the following type:

Cost = fixed or 'threshold' costs plus output variable costs (given by a coefficient representing the relationship of these costs to out-put multiplied by the relevant traffic volume).

In the long run it is assumed that producers have had sufficient

4. See: JOHNSTON, J., Statistical Cost Analysis, McGraw-Hill, New York, Toronto, London (1960), and MEYER, J. R., PECK, M. J., STENASON, J., and ZWICK, C., The Economics of Competition in the Transportation Industries, Harvard University Press, Cambridge, Mass. (1960). The latter contains much material relating to railways.

* 'Infrastructure' is frequently used to refer to the whole complex of track, signalling, bridges, earthworks, etc.

time to adjust operating methods and costs to the prevailing volume of traffic, i.e. they will be as efficient as current practice permits. Plant capacity will thus be as ideally adapted to output needs as possible.

It cannot be assumed, however, that plant size will vary exactly with output. Different transport situations often require different amounts of capital to produce the same output efficiently. So measures of plant size can be included as explicit, separate variables in the cost function wherever needed:

Cost = threshold costs plus output costs plus size costs, as given by the product of the size variable (e.g. track-milage) multiplied by the coefficient representing these costs in relation to plant size.

The basic technique of statistical costing is multiple regression analysis. It is used to derive the coefficients with which to multiply the output and size variables in ascertaining total costs. This is done by analysing a cross-section of situations in which there are (relevant to this example) many different relationships of plant size and output. An equation is obtained:

$$C = T + r_0 O + r_s S$$

where C = total costs, T = constant, representing threshold costs, r_0 = output regression coefficient, r_s = size regression coefficient, O = output and S = size.

The statistical analysis provides the values of T, r_0 and r_s. It then remains to insert O and S and to multiply them with their respective coefficient to arrive at total costs.

THE SETTING OF CHARGES

The difficult task of pricing[5] railway products, few of which have any clearly defined cost, has to be attempted. What kind of rules may be laid down?

Assuming the existence of a commercial target pricing rules as follows may be laid down:

5. *See*: HALL, R. L., and HITCH, C. J., 'Price Theory and Business Behaviour', *Oxford Economic Papers*, Vol. 11, pp. 12–45 (1939), on the subject of full cost pricing. For a practical railwayman's view of the problem *see*: STEWART, J. C., 'The Marketing and Pricing of Railway Freight Transport', *Institute of Transport Journal*, Vol. 31, No. 10, pp. 377–382 (1966).

1. Identifiable costs, including return on that portion of capital assets giving rise to those costs, must be *at least* covered, i.e. Direct Costs.
2. The whole range of different prices charged to different users must *in total* cover the costs incurred jointly, including return on the portion of capital assets giving rise to these joint costs, i.e. Indirect Costs.

To these rules a further one needs to be added:

3. Within rules (1) and (2) the misallocation of resources between railways and competing products should be minimised as far as possible. For instance, the price of urban rail commuter transport could be raised to such a high level that, even granted the low demand elasticity for this particular product, significant amounts of traffic would be diverted to the urban road network. The social costs of traffic congestion imposed on road users might outweigh any financial gain to the railways from the pricing policy adopted above. Clearly, commercial railway management would be reluctant to take such factors into account. This is really a matter for government intervention, and, perhaps, a specific compensating subsidy.

How does this kind of policy work out in practice? The operation of rule (1) is relatively straightforward. Rule (2) can, however, be implemented in various ways. Rule (3) we shall leave for the moment.

One approach is to employ some variant of 'full cost' pricing, i.e. D.C. plus an 'allocated' contribution to I.C. The allocation could be carried out on the gross-ton-mile and train-mile basis described earlier.

An alternative is to take D.C. as an irreducible minimum plus some minimal contribution to I.C. The view can then be taken that, above such a charging 'floor', any contribution to I.C. is better than nothing. Traffic might be accepted if this minimum level could be obtained in the knowledge or hope that elsewhere sufficient revenue is being gathered in to ensure that I.C. would be fully covered.

Theoretically, there is nothing wrong with this. Joint costs cannot be precisely attributed; they must be recovered from the demand side by charging each traffic the contribution to I.C. that it 'will bear', i.e. contributions will be taken from each consignor according to his respective demand elasticity. To put it another way, prices will be set by market forces where there is a high degree of competition. Where the railways are in a strong competitive position, they will extract a proportionately large contribution to I.C.

One method of institutionalising the latter approach might be to require different parts of the railway undertaking (passenger and freight would be the simplest division, although the principle could be carried much further) to put in competitive bids for the use of common facilities. Track and signalling would then be 'sold' to the freight and passenger operators. This would ensure that impulses from the demand side would be transmitted to the basic railway plant and its use shaped accordingly. If freight traffic was the most profitable its use of, and payment for, track and signalling would be proportionately the most important; and vice versa. If both categories of traffic between them could not manage to cover the costs of the jointly used facilities, this would indicate the need for contraction.

The operational and administrative complexity of a modern railway system would make this solution difficult to achieve. The system would have to embrace all parts of the network that were being 'bid for'. A long, complex transit would take in a very large number of track sections and junctions, even if it were a train-load operation with the minimum of terminal processing and a complete absence of marshalling *en route*. At each point of the transit, the volume and intensity of demand—and the composition of the bidders—would probably be very different. A sophisticated computing system would probably be required. Even then, a highly simplified version of the principle would be necessary if it were to prove at all workable.

If one accepts that railway charges are determined by long-run competitive forces, and that the management has little power to influence such forces, the basic decision is: shall we accept traffic at such market prices? If decisions to accept traffic on the 'D.C. plus' basis lead to failure to cover I.C. in total, the appropriate policy is to contract the system until the financial target is attained.

Failure to cover total costs may be facilitated by the traditional kind of railway organisational structure which lacks a method of matching originating receipts with costs imposed on the railway network as a whole by particular traffics. To do this, special costing exercises are necessary. What is really essential is that this matching should take place as a matter of routine in order to measure profitability of particular traffics. Otherwise there may be the temptation, difficult to withstand, to accept traffic in order to present a favourable 'originating receipts' picture.

We have noted the view that 'D.C. = L.R.M.C. of the system as a whole'. This implies that, even in the long run, the mass of track and signalling costs cannot be varied: '. . . the total cost of providing the route system . . . is a fixed cost, in the full sense of the term, all the while the route system remains unchanged.'[6]

If this argument is accepted, a policy flows from it of channelling on to the route system as much traffic as possible because it may be carried at zero, or very low, marginal track and signalling cost. The specialised track required may, it is true, give rise to high fixed costs, but high-capacity trains may be operated. These have very low movement costs per unit carried. Moreover, dense flows of traffic are possible and, if realised, will bring fixed costs per unit down to a very low level.

If this reasoning be accepted it follows that railway management is faced by an 'all or nothing' decision in regard to an uneconomic route. The decision must be: keep the route as it is or close it down entirely. Recent research has tended to challenge this view. Route capacity may be varied by changing the quantity and quality of the physical plant much more than hitherto thought possible*. The number of tracks may be altered. The standard of maintaining them can be set at a number of different possible levels, allowing different maximum speeds and riding qualities. There is a great deal of possible flexibility in the number and sophistication of signals that may be installed. This gain will determine the capacity of the route and influence the speeds at which trains may be run[7].

The prospects of tailoring capacity, including track and signalling, are therefore much more favourable than traditionally thought. Statistical analysis of the kind mentioned earlier has helped to provide evidence to shake the traditional view.

So far the discussion of pricing has taken place on the assumption that total accounting costs must be covered. This requires that prices should cover not only short-run costs but also the costs of

6. BRITISH RAILWAYS BOARD, op. cit., p. 9.
7. JOY, S. C., 'British Railways' Track Costs', *Journal of Industrial Economics*, Vol. 13, No. 1, pp. 74–89 (1964).

* One probable reason for the persistence of the older view was the pursuance by engineers of their own traditional professional objectives (i.e. the maintenance of 'high' standards) without much regard being paid to the objectives of the organisation as a whole. Indeed, such overall objectives may not have been explicitly formulated.

replacing assets plus a return on the latter. (The costs of these assets are reflected in both D.C. and I.C.)

There are certain assets, such as cuttings and embankments, that will never have to be replaced*. Such assets, let us suppose, have no value in any alternative occupation; once excavated, there is little or nothing else that a cutting can be used for. The capital sunk into its construction is 'lost for ever'. But it should, with a bit of luck, last 'for ever' if called upon to do so.

From the economic point of view such assets (maintenance apart) are costless. Any earnings in respect of them constitute a rent. If that rent cannot be earned, it might be rather unfortunate for the original investors but they cannot recoup their funds. Neither is there any principle of resource allocation that justifies an attempt to recoup the original capital sum or a rate of return on those assets if the market will not allow this.

This is, of course, a somewhat extreme case. If such an asset could obtain a return in alternative use, it would be put to that alternative use as soon as it failed to obtain at least that return in its present occupation. In real life, however, there may be many reasons why it is difficult to switch assets about in this way.

So far as retention of the assets goes, it is the *future* costs of using them that are important. Prices should reflect the resources employed in using these assets from the *present moment onward*. They should include the replacement cost of assets (and exclude the 'cost' of assets that will never need to be replaced). Thus will replacement be assured[8].

Let us suppose, however, that consumers do not wish to continue purchasing that product, at least to the extent originally forecast at the time the investment was made. Two sets of questions arise:

1. Which assets reaching the end of their economic life, if any, should be replaced?
2. Suppose that, before the end of their economic life, it has become obvious that the business is not generating sufficient revenue to justify their replacement. What contribution (if

---

* Theoretically, anyway. In practice, embankments crumble and tunnels begin to fall in after about a century of use. A special accounting provision is made for this kind of eventuality.

8. SELECT COMMITTEE ON NATIONALISED INDUSTRIES, op. cit., and MUNBY, D. L., 'Investment in Road and Rail Transport', *Institute of Transport Journal*, Vol. 29, No. 9, pp. 271–279 (1962).

any) should then be made towards the historical costs of those investments?

The answer to (1) is: replace if enough revenue can be obtained (i.e. a high enough price charged) to cover costs on a replacement basis.

The answer to (2) is not so clear cut. Imagine an undertaking whose costs can be divided into simple short- and long-run categories. (Short-run costs are variable costs and long-run costs are variable costs plus fixed costs.) In the short run, before the fixed equipment reaches the end of its economic life, production will be maintained if *at least* variable costs are covered. When the equipment needs to be replaced, the undertaking will retire from that

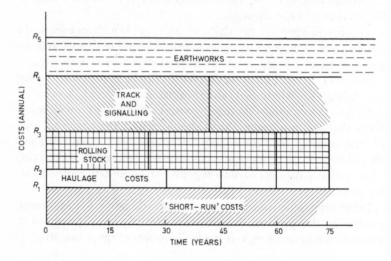

Figure 6.3. Time horizons and the renewal decision on a railway system

line of business if long-run costs have not been covered. Renewal will probably take place if long-run costs have been covered, although such costs will have been defined as above.

This straightforward rule cannot be applied to a railway system without modification. For there is not simply one long-run but a whole series of time horizons[9]. *Figure 6.3* summarises the position schematically.

9. Highly relevant here is LEWIS, W. A., 'Fixed Costs', *Overhead Costs*, Allen & Unwin, London (1949).

In the diagram four categories of 'fixed' cost are taken. These are haulage, rolling stock, track and signalling, and earthworks. Along the horizontal axis is measured time in years, and the lives of the assets are marked off. Along the vertical axis is indicated the level of earnings needed to remunerate those assets, i.e. to cover replacement costs plus the 'normal' rate of return on capital. It will be noted that costs almost *immediately* escapable in the short run are also included. These are largely wages, fuel, materials and similar costs that must be covered if operation is to take place at all.

Each rectangle represents an amount of revenue over a given time period. For example, locomotives are assumed to have a life of 15 years during which they must cover their capital costs (on an annual basis) each year. The vertical line denotes the end of the locomotive's life; the decision whether or not to replace can then be taken.

The cost range up to OR_3 broadly represents Direct Costs; OR_3 to OR_5 broadly Indirect Costs. The reconciliation of the two sets of categories to the right of the diagram should be noted.

For the system to operate at all, annual revenue OR_1 must be forthcoming. In the simplified scheme represented in the diagram, the first equipment renewal opportunities do not arise for 15 years★. If revenue level OR_2 is not being achieved, operations will continue until year 15 on the (now, let us hope, familiar) principle that 'bygones being bygones', any contribution to that category of 'fixed' costs is better than nothing within the relevant time horizon, i.e. 15 years.

Suppose revenue OR_2 is, at least, being gathered in but the level falls short of OR_3. In that case, locomotives would be replaced but not the rolling stock. The system would close down in year 25. Similarly with track and signalling: revenue OR_4 is required to ensure replacement there.

Earthworks are in a rather different category, as pointed out earlier. The system will remain in operation if receipts OR_4 are taken. Anything above that is in the nature of a rent, and although OR_5 would doubtless be very welcome to investors it is not essential.

What conclusions for policy emerge from such an analysis? Take the case of an electrification scheme which does not live up to its original promise: demand does not attain the forecast level and no

---

★ The assumption is made that the locomotives have no alternative use value so that there is no point in not continuing to use them until they reach the end of their economic life. The same point applies to the other categories of fixed equipment.

amount of fares adjustment can secure enough revenue to meet the replacement cost of the assets. 'Short-run' pricing (say a price based upon revenue level OR_2 or OR_3 in *Figure 6.3*) is relevant if resources are to be allocated as well as possible in this situation. There is no economic case for attempting to recoup the full replacement cost of the assets by charging, say, at a level reflecting OR_4 or even OR_5.

Perhaps the greatest danger in such a policy is that if management is following some such objective as maximising system size, it may (consciously or unconsciously) invest in assets which have no hope of ever earning their replacement costs. Once installed, they may calculate, a satisfactory 'return' may be earned by the use of 'short-run' pricing.

This is another practical difficulty of laying down a broad rule such as 'undertake marginal cost pricing', to add to the interpretative one about what is the relevant margin.

INVESTMENT IN NEW RAILWAY ASSETS

Difficulties of the kind discussed above are compounded when one attempts to calculate the rate of return on investment in new railway projects. Suppose that it is desired to introduce a new kind of freight service using special terminals and rolling stock. The costs of investing in these assets are not too difficult to establish (i.e. the Direct Costs part of the exercise). What is more difficult is to deal with the infrastructure (track and signalling) and network effects.

With infrastructure, there are two possibilities: either no additional infrastructure costs are incurred by the new service or such extra costs *are* incurred.

If no additional track and signalling costs are incurred, should returns be related solely to the expenditure on the facilities specific to the service, and those alone? Should the investment make a given contribution to Indirect Costs? In other words, to what extent should that investment be regarded as 'marginal' to the existing system?

These kinds of issue have been raised in public discussion about the London to Liverpool and Manchester electrification scheme[10].

Three questions are relevant. The first two have already been touched upon:

10. SELECT COMMITTEE ON NATIONALISED INDUSTRIES, op. cit., pp. c–ciii.

1. Should replacement take place at all?
2. If so, when?

A third question relates to choice of technique.

3. Should replacement of steam traction take place on the basis of diesel or electric power.

The principles involved with (1) have been discussed earlier. As for (2), replacement should take place when the discounted stream of gross returns from existing assets (i.e. receipts minus short-run escapable costs, with depreciation and interest ignored) falls below that of the discounted stream of net returns from the new assets under contemplation (i.e. receipts minus short-run escapable costs and minus depreciation and interest).

This assumes that the discounted revenue stream will at least cover either of the two cost streams. If, for example, receipts will not even cover short-run escapable costs, and there is no prospect of salvation from new technique or operating practice, the system (or relevant part of it) should be closed down. Once again this follows from the analysis of *Figure 6.3*.

The principles involved with (3) are not, perhaps, so clear. One possible method might be to compare the forecast cost/revenue situation *after* the electrified system was fully operational with the estimated position if the existing assets had been replaced 'like-with-like', i.e. assuming continuance of steam traction.

Next, increases in revenue and reductions in operating costs due to electrification could be worked out. This improvement might then be related to *incremental* outlay on electrification. In other words, this would assume that a considerable renewal and replacement programme would take place *anyway*, regardless of electrification. That expenditure should not, therefore, be counted in; only the investment in electrification and any associated improvements over and above what 'like-for-like' replacement would have necessitated.

Figure 6.4 illustrates this method, together with an alternative. In Version One, annual returns (£8 m.) are related to 'non-unavoidable' expenditure (£110 m.)

In Version Two it may be argued that the discounted revenue stream had to provide an acceptable return on the *whole* of the investment. If not, neither the 'avoidable' nor the 'unavoidable' investment is justified.

It is quite conceivable, however, that within the framework of

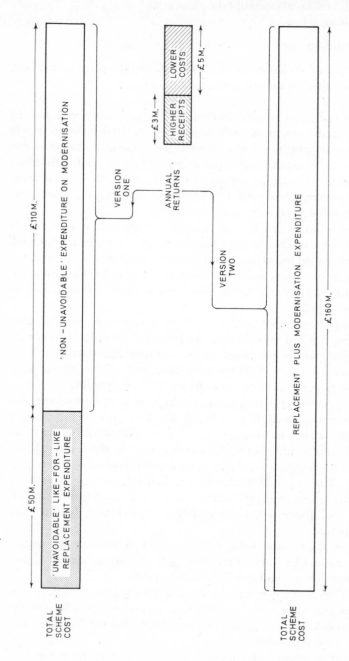

Figure 6.4. *Alternative methods of calculating returns from railway electrification scheme*

the analysis of *Figure 6.3*, incremental investment in, say, engines and rolling stock should proceed. This could go on until longer-lived assets came up for renewal, only to find that renewal could not be justified.

This does not deal with the fundamental problem of whether Version One or Two is relevant. There are two sets of circumstances in which Version One is acceptable. In the first place if the system is already profitable enough to justify like-with-like replacement, the approach is legitimate.

Secondly, however, if a loss is being made, this does not automatically disqualify the investment if it cannot bring about an overall profit. If, for any reason, a policy decision is taken that the basic system will continue to operate willy-nilly, the incremental approach is legitimate.

This brings us back to our original problem: to what extent should the returns from, say, freightliners be required to contribute to Indirect Costs? If the basic system is not in doubt, and if it has spare capacity, it is not illegitimate to use the incremental approach.

Nearly all railway investments form part of a very complex, interlocking system. There are often individual links in the network that 'require renewal' on the grounds that, without such renewal, it will be difficult for the system as a whole to continue functioning.

Let us think of a bridge, over which runs an important trunk line, that has seriously weakened with time. It obviously cannot be allowed to collapse, for a large part of the system will then simply have to be discontinued. Consequently, the railway management may see little point in doing other than prescribe automatic renewal. All over the system, similar decisions may be taken piecemeal. At no time may the aggregate amount thus invested be related to the total returns forthcoming. Indeed, there are great dangers of counting benefits from such 'automatic' renewals over and over again.

It may be argued that the decision to renew individual assets forming part of a network may sometimes *worsen* the current financial position, but that the position may become even worse if the investment is not made. The answer to this is that the decision to renew or not must be extremely carefully examined.

Given the difficulties of costing specific services and calculating returns on investment, is there any economically acceptable method of establishing the 'correct' size of a railway network? (We shall leave aside for the moment the complication of non-paying services.)

THE CONSTRUCTION AND USE OF POLICY MODELS

One interesting approach to this problem is to attempt the construction of long-run cost functions. This may be done for both rail and road operation, including infrastructure. (Infrastructure may be defined as the complex of track, signalling, bridges, tunnels and earthworks.) A study is required of how total costs for each transport mode vary as traffic volume changes. The further question may then be asked: what happens to total road *plus* rail costs as the proportion carried by each mode changes, and as the types of traffic carried alter? There is therefore no 'allocation' of joint or indirect costs. Such allocation is irrelevant, for it is the global costs of operation that are being examined in relation to total traffic volume.

A model may be built to look 30 years ahead[11]. The case for such a period is that, at the end of it, most existing capital will have been renewed out of existence. It is therefore unnecessary to calculate any costs in terms of depreciation reserves. Actual renewals in contemplation over the period may be used. Additional capital expenditure plus maintenance occurring within the 30-year span are the relevant quantities. Current costs of operation are added on.

The exercise thus begins with a clean sheet. 'Bygones are bygones' and, after the initial year of the exercise, only incremental costs are counted in. These will vary with the traffic volume assumed. The point of doing this is to escape completely from conventional accounting problems to build a model reflecting economic factors.

What results could be expected to flow from such an exercise? It may be that both rail and road have potential long-run economies of scale. The appropriate division of traffic between them (together with associated problems of charging) is a complex matter to evaluate. It would be possible, in principle, to test whether the market machinery was bringing about an optimal division of traffic between competing modes, i.e. that which minimised private and social costs (embracing quality of service to users).

Minimum operating cost situations could be sought in the first place. These would not have much, if any, economic meaning in

11. *See*: MINISTRY OF TRANSPORT, *Road Track Costs*, H.M.S.O., London, Ch. 10, pp. 38–39 (1968).

themselves. Cost and demand functions need to be integrated. If social costs were included, light could be thrown on investment shares between road and rail, the possible implications of changing taxes and subsidies and the effects of constraining road traffic by various policy measures. Questions about the general nature of pricing on road and rail consistent with achieving low total costs for both modes and feasible in terms of road/rail competition could perhaps be answered. Some light might also be thrown upon the problem of 'track costs' discussed in its traditional form in the next chapter.

A model of the entire national rail and road network would be the appropriate tool. To be more realistic, from the point of view of resource expenditure the specific form such research may take is that of an inter-urban trunk route model. Such a model together with companion studies of the demand for transport, without actually producing conclusions or decision, can provide an informed basis for discussion.

This kind of work demands the handling of data on an immense scale and would simply not be feasible without the help of computers. With the prototype model, two trunk corridors of different characteristics were selected for study because good traffic data were readily available, and because they were important main routes which might require further capital expenditure. At a later stage it may be possible to construct a more elaborate model taking in many more trunk routes.

Such work may be divided into four broad phases:

1. Data preparation,
2. Forecasting,
3. Costing, and
4. An investigation of demand.

The following paragraphs describe the approach under each of these headings. They may be useful in bringing out some of the practical problems that research workers in this kind of field encounter.

It was first necessary to reconcile the commodity classification employed in the Road Goods Surveys[12] with that used by the

12. MINISTRY OF TRANSPORT, *Survey of Road Goods Transport, 1962*, H.M.S.O., London, published in various instalments from March 1963. By the time this appears the Department of the Environment may have published the results of the 1967–68 Survey.

railways. This compromise classification involves 13 commodity groups on the freight side and, on the passenger side, there are three journey purpose groups (viz. journeys to and from work, business trips, and other journeys).

The country is divided up into terminal zones, a very detailed division being made in the case of 'on route' terminals and a rather more general scheme adopted in respect of 'off route' terminals. It should be noted that any traffic touching either of the two routes in the study, for however small a proportion of its journey length, is included in the exercise.

A series of commodity matrices, each cell of which corresponds to a flow between two terminal zones, was completed manually, and later converted into a form suitable for computerisation. Computer programmes were then developed which convert this data into any form required by the various costing processes.

It is not possible to obtain passenger traffic information in such a detailed form. But work to prepare flow data in respect of private cars, long-distance coaches and short-distance buses was carried out. Similar work was undertaken in respect of railway traffic.

Having established the facts about traffic volume and composition, freight and passenger, along each selected corridor, it is then necessary to forecast how the pattern will change and develop. A period of 30 years (1968 to 1997) was selected for reasons already outlined. Traffic forecasts, for each of the commodity and passenger groups, were made for each year of the exercise. Two different overall economic growth rate assumptions were employed, an upper and a lower limit.

The second stage is to share out the total traffic (freight and passenger) for each year of the 30-year period between road and rail in different ways. Three allocations were analysed: 'road pessimistic'/'rail optimistic', which presents the split that might be achieved if a very high proportion of those kinds of traffic best suited to rail did in fact go by rail; a 'road optimistic'/'rail pessimistic' allocation which assumes that road haulage carries a correspondingly high proportion of traffics best suited to it; and a 'central' assumption lying between the two.

The third stage is to cost the flows of traffic determined above, thus providing estimates of both favourable cost situations for each means of transport. This also provides a first estimate of how the total costs of road and rail transport might vary according to the traffic allocation assumed.

It is also necessary to make forecasts of future cost trends, i.e. those brought about by real rather than monetary developments. This involves the making of assumptions about technical and operational developments on both road and rail.

The costing is carried out by a number of sub-models. The road haulage model, for example, takes as inputs flows of traffic (broken down into commodity groups, bulk/weight ratios, etc.). First of all, operating criteria are applied, e.g. to divide into trunk or tramp categories. Further processes deal with such problems as what to do about 'unbalanced' traffic. The traffic having been analysed into different categories, costing programmes take over. Depending upon vehicle fleet and crew requirements, miles run, operating speeds, etc., various cost results emerge from the model. If any of the operating or cost assumptions are changed, the total costs vary accordingly.

Throughout the 30-year time-span of the model, it should be noted, maximum capacities of new vehicles, maximum permitted driving hours, pay and conditions, and so on, are assumed to be changing. The alternative sets of assumptions can be tested.

It then remains to bring into account studies on the demand side of the money value placed by transport users (freight and passenger) on the various qualities of the different transport media.

This necessity brings out an important problem of cost treatment. From the point of view of national resource allocation, it is real *resource* costs that are important (i.e. costs stripped of transfer elements such as indirect taxation). If one wishes to predict the behaviour of consignors or travellers, however, quite clearly such elements should be kept in.

There is little doubt that, as with models of the fuel and power sectors, such models will be an important aid to policy making in the future.

Another type of problem upon which economic analysis can throw some light is represented by the 'stand-by' controversy[13].

THE CONCEPT OF 'STAND-BY' CAPACITY

Should a public enterprise railway have enough capacity to provide stand-by transport for the users of private transport when it suits

13. *See:* JOY, S., 'The "Standby" Concept on Railways', *Journal of Transport Economics and Policy*, Vol. I, No. 3, pp. 243–248 (1967).

the convenience of those users? There has been little doubt historically about the existence of such surplus capacity. This transport 'service of last resort' has in the past been financed by cross-subsidisation; more recently by subsidy.

How may the issue be approached? A railway is a system that integrates the outputs of terminals, trains and tracks so that certain objectives are attained.

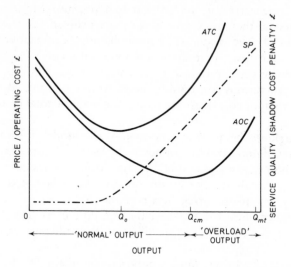

Figure 6.5. 'Normal' and 'overload' ranges of output
on a railway system

Each of these sub-systems can produce output in two separate ranges as shown in *Figure 6.5*. The first is from zero to where average operating cost *AOC* is minimised ('normal' output OQ_{cm}). The second is the range of output where factors such as traffic congestion and operating problems cause average operating cost to rise with increased output until the maximum possible amount of traffic is carried ('overload' output OQ_{cm} to OQ_{mt}).

This relates only to the private cost to the railway. Beyond a certain level of output, quality of service will go down. This is depicted as a 'shadow cost' penalty, *SP*, it being assumed that lowered service quality can be measured as a cash disbenefit. Curve *ATC* represents the summation of generalised cost: operating costs plus shadow cost penalties, i.e. average total costs. If the decrease in quality is experienced regularly there will be traffic losses, given no compensating reduction in prices. The optimal output, i.e. that where the price/quality combination is optimal for most users, OQ_o, will probably be significantly lower than the cost-minimising output.

Assuming a price over which they have little or no control, the railway management will be under pressure to minimise their costs. They will therefore risk operating at an output level where service quality, at a constant price, is unacceptable to some users, i.e. up to OQ_{cm}. Stand-by capacity is therefore available at the cost of diminished quality of service.

Given constant traffic levels, the railways could attempt to match cost-minimising output to that at which the price/quality combination is optimal. (In terms of *Figure 6.5* this would involve organisational and/or investment measures so that OQ_o and OQ_{cm} coincide.) Where demand is peaked, though, the management must decide whether to install enough capacity to handle the peaks without imposing a cost penalty. An important factor is the commercial judgement about the reduction in service quality acceptable to users during peaks.

At terminals, queuing can be temporarily allowed, but this cannot continue beyond a certain point. The alternative is not difficult to imagine. Trains and rolling stock are largely interchangeable between traffics and thus can often be supplied at close to cost-minimising output. Peak requirements for one traffic or area may be catered for by facilities surplus elsewhere. With track, however, a disparity between actual output and average cost-minimising output is likely. The output of infrastructure may be varied over a very wide range indeed and the commercial judgement about the amount of capacity provision is accordingly complex.

In what situation is apparent surplus capacity likely to develop on a route?

Firstly, it may be that a large number of trains must be dispatched on a route in a short period for commercial reasons. The track capacity to handle such a quantity of output is then available for the rest of the day. A railway in this situation will recover the cost of the peak capacity from the peak users.

Secondly, capacity in excess of that currently required may have been installed in the past. Rather than scrap such surplus it may be less costly to retain it in operation until replacement is due. A combination of retirements and renewal may be used to reduce capacity to the appropriate level, in accordance with the philosophy of *Figure 6.3*.

Thirdly, the installation of, say, high-quality track with normal capacity greater than existing traffic requirements might provide cost savings. In this case it would be appropriate for the cost of the superior facility to be covered by revenue from existing traffic.

Finally, a railway may maintain a route to a particular standard primarily to provide alternative routes for trains when their normal routes are unavailable because of engineering work or emergency. Here again there is no compelling economic reason why users should not be charged the cost of such provision.

Should a publicly owned railway go beyond these rules of capacity provision? One likely cause of temporary demand for capacity is because of weather conditions. One choice is to accept such 'casual' traffic which would impose reduced quality of service upon existing users. Another choice would be to ration capacity in such circumstances, the casual users being turned away.

None of this analysis adds up to a strong case for possible subsidy of stand-by capacity by the general tax-payer. This does not mean to say that there is no case for rail subsidisation in any circumstances. Circumstances where such subsidisation does take place are discussed later.

NOTE ON OTHER COST CATEGORIES SOMETIMES EMPLOYED

In other contexts the British Railways Board have sometimes employed slightly different cost categories. For example, in *A Study of the Relative True Costs* . . .[14] the categories of *Operating* and *System* Costs were employed. In this case Operating Costs may be regarded as being roughly equivalent to Direct Costs with an addition to cover general administration. They comprise train operating costs and terminal costs, including collection and delivery. System Costs are composed entirely of Indirect Costs with the exclusion of central administration charges.

A slight variant of this classification was used in the *Reshaping Report* when dealing with passenger service costs: *Movement* and *System* Costs. (Most of the *Reshaping Report* uses the Direct/ Indirect Costs terminology). In this case, with Movement Costs (mainly locomotive provision, haulage, shunting, ancillary movement, etc.) some Direct Costs are excluded (i.e. terminal costs

14. BRITISH RAILWAYS BOARD, *A Study of the Relative True Costs of Rail and Road Freight Transport over Trunk Routes*, London (1964).

which are included under the heading 'Cost of Stations'). The System Costs here are those attributable to the passenger service alone.

The Direct/Indirect Costs classification is the basic working tool of the Traffic Costing Officer. The other categories mentioned were evolved for different purposes: to attempt a road/rail trunk route cost comparison on an exactly similar basis and to establish the costs of passenger services.

7

ROADS

If rational allocation decisions are to be taken, the economics of roads must be analysed and principles of costing and charging employed that are consistent to the greatest degree practicable with those used on the railways★. The great difficulty here is the lack of a specific enough charging mechanism. We are therefore presented with a 'second best' problem.

THE COST STRUCTURE OF ROAD PROVISION AND USE

The costs of the road system[1] can be broken down into three broad categories:

1. User costs are costs which are incurred directly by road users. Examples are fuel, oil and tyres, and the time involved in travelling.

★ Assuming the railways to be a significant competitive provider of services. On the continent, the argument would have to be broadened to take in inland waterways.

1. Important reading here is MINISTRY OF TRANSPORT, *Road Track Costs*, H.M.S.O., London (1968). This section follows quite closely that of *Road Track Costs*. *See also*: the interesting controversy in MUNBY, D. L., 'Mrs Castle's Transport Policy; Section 4, Road Track Costs', *Journal of Transport Economics and Policy*, Vol. 2, No. 2, pp. 162–179 (1968), and FOSTER, C. D., and HARRISON, A. J., 'Mrs Castle's Transport Policy', *Journal of Transport Economics and Policy*, Vol. 2, No. 3, pp. 389–392 (1968), with rejoinder by Munby. A different approach to the problem is represented by BRITISH RAILWAYS BOARD, *A Study of the Relative True Costs of Rail and Road Freight Transport over Trunk Routes*, London (1964).

2. Public costs consist mainly of road construction and maintenance expenditures, and are borne by central and local government.
3. Social costs are those imposed by road users upon other members of the community.

User costs are broadly analogous to railway direct costs. Road users cover the resource costs of the assets they use, and pay something additional in the form of taxation.

Taxation is a cost to the road user, but unlike the other user cost items does not represent the consumption of resources. It is a transfer of incomes from one group, road users, to the state. Subsequently there is a further transfer to other social groups through services such as health and education. Such payments are not, therefore, costs from the standpoint of the economy as a whole. From another point of view, however, such taxation is at least partly the way in which road users pay for their use of the roads. To include these payments *and* public road expenditure in the same expenditure account would involve double-counting.

By definition user costs are met directly by users. Taxation paid by road users which does not represent the consumption of resources may be set against non-user road costs. Thus one may compare total road user payments with the total costs incurred in road provision and use.

Public costs present more difficulty. It is not obvious exactly which public costs should be attributed to road users either individually or as a group. A further question is how capital expenditure should be attributed to vehicle users in any given year. It may be argued that police costs, accident costs not covered by insurance, and all administration costs should be attributed to road users and not regarded as community overheads. Other items, such as capital, maintenance and cleansing, are all clearly road costs.

For capital costs, two approaches are possible. The first is to charge capital to the users in the year it is spent. The second is to estimate a capital charge on the basis of an analogy with another nationalised industry, electricity supply. This example was taken because it was held that its economic circumstances most closely resembled those of roads: it is rapidly expanding, prosperous and a major investor of capital.

Social costs present severe problems of evaluation. This subject is taken up later in the chapter.

Table 7.1 PUBLIC ROAD COSTS 1965–66

	Current expenditure basis (£m.)	Public enterprise basis (£m.)
Capital: new roads and major improvements	179	390
Minor improvements	36	
Maintenance	96	96
Cleansing	23	23
Lighting	9	9
Policing	52	52
Administration	40	40
Accidents	15	15
Totals	450	625

Source: *Road Track Costs*, Tables 3.1 and 3.2, p. 10.

Table 7.1 shows public road costs 1965–66 and *Table 7.2* revenue raised from road users 1965–66.

Road users contribute to government revenues in three principal ways: through payments of purchase tax, fuel tax and vehicle excise duties.

Table 7.2 REVENUE RAISED FROM ROAD USERS 1965–66

Source	(£m.)	(£m.)
Fuel tax	679	
Vehicle excise duty	247	
Total excluding purchase tax		926
Purchase tax		144
Total including purchase tax		1 070
Road haulage charge (notional) (later superseded)		30
Grand total		1 100

Source: *Road Track Costs*, Table 4.1, p. 13.

PRINCIPLES OF ROAD CHARGING: ROAD USERS IN GENERAL

Four possible charging principles may be employed. They are: the public income and expenditure account basis; the public and

social income and expenditure account basis; short-run marginal
cost pricing; and long-run marginal cost pricing.

THE PUBLIC INCOME AND EXPENDITURE ACCOUNT BASIS

This requires that revenue paid should cover the public costs
incurred in any given year. The only complication relates to the
appropriate treatment of capital. How should capital costs be
'spread out' over different years? Whether the current expenditure
or the public enterprise basis are used a surplus of revenues over
costs emerges under present circumstances.

THE PUBLIC AND SOCIAL INCOME AND EXPENDITURE
ACCOUNT BASIS

There are strong grounds against taking the former as a basis
for comparison. It may be argued that account should be taken of
social costs: loss of amenity due to vehicle noise, fumes, etc., and
accident costs. These are likely to be very important.

At the present time, it is only possible to make a broad comparison of total social costs with total revenue. If it were possible to
charge these costs to road users (particularly individual users) there
would be a reduction in the demand for use of road space. Reduced
demand would lower total social costs, i.e. given the relevant
demand elasticities the traffic remaining would consist of those
users prepared to cover the full social costs they imposed.

If costs were lower than revenues to start with, low charges
would stimulate extra journeys. The additional journeys would
generate additional social costs which would be reflected in higher
charges. Again, equilibrium would be reached when road users
were individually covering the social costs they generated.

In principle, a combined public and social account is the correct
economic basis of comparison between road user costs and revenues. It is so difficult to construct such an account, however, that
society will have to be content with the public account alone for
some time.

So far the problem has been discussed largely in terms of public
finance. Marginal charging principles are concerned with the use of
prices to allocate resources efficiently. There are, in principle, considerable advantages to be gained from applying such a rule to

roads. The principal difficulty is the lack of a practicable charging mechanism.

Once the decision to provide a certain amount of capacity has been made and the necessary capital invested, the only resources used by the decision to produce an additional vehicle mile are those which vary directly with the level of output. Other resources are either 'lost for ever' in the form of fixed capital without any alternative use or cannot be released quickly for other uses.

S.R.M.C. charging appears particularly suitable for roads for two reasons.

Firstly, the gap between total and marginal costs is very large for most roads. Costs of running the road system which may be taken as a reasonable approximation to S.R.M.C. may amount to only 5–7% of the annual capital charges of, say, a motorway. Once such a road is built one additional user imposes very little public cost. Expenditure on carriageways, embankments, drainage works, etc., once committed, produces resources that cannot be switched to other uses even in the long run. The proportion of capital and other long-run costs being high, the difference between prices based on total and short-run marginal costs will be considerable. Consequently, the potential for greater efficiency by introducing an S.R.M.C. pricing policy is, in principle, correspondingly great.

Secondly, the time gap between initial investment and replacement or expansion is usually very long by ordinary industrial standards. Thus only infrequently does the long-run capital investment decision arise. As total costs are so large relative to short-run costs and incurred infrequently, there are long periods when the chief resource allocation problem is one of obtaining the best use of *existing* resources.

There is a wide range of variation in the public costs of providing roads of different types. If costs vary significantly between one part of the road network and another, there is a strong case for a system of road charging which reflects the variation. This would encourage users to travel where marginal public costs were low and vice versa.

The benefits of such a system may not be large. Although the proportionate variation in marginal costs from one road to another is large, the absolute figures are not great. Hence it is possible that the proportion of users diverted to roads with a low S.R.M.C. of additional use would be low. At the same time there is an important disadvantage: if marginal public costs are below average public costs, as will usually be the case on the road system, total costs will not be covered. On the other hand, if this were to be judged the correct pricing rule, the current surplus revenue over short-run marginal public costs is very large. That surplus, however, has no importance in the context of the rule. S.R.M.C. can be justified only in terms of its effects upon the pattern of road use, i.e. the allocation of resources. If the charges are small or non existent, the case for the rule is greatly weakened.

There would be more important consequences if variation in congestion costs were also included[2]. The economic benefits of making charges reflect congestion costs might be very high. This would particularly be true in urban areas where congestion costs are much greater than public costs.

The inclusion of congestion costs represents an approach quite different from those so far considered. Until this stage in the argument the revenue/cost relationships have been those between road users and non-road users. The latter have been either public authorities or the community as a whole. But congestion costs are already borne by road users as a group. Reflecting congestion as well as other costs in charges will, it may be argued, bring about the correct revenue/cost relationship between each user and other users, as well as between users and non-users.

How revenues would compare with total public costs if congestion costs were included in charges is clearly an empirical question. Because of congestion in urban areas, receipts might cover or even exceed existing revenue levels. Can it therefore be said that road users would be worse off? The answer is negative because they would simultaneously be gaining through the consequent reduction in congestion costs. Road use on congested roads would be discouraged; vice versa where there was no sign of congestion. Journeys would be quicker and cheaper in terms of operating costs. These benefits would provide the justification for S.R.M.C. pricing, not the level of revenue it produced.

---

2. *See*: SMEED REPORT, *Road Pricing: the Economic and Technical Possibilities*, H.M.S.O., London (1964), and ROTH, G. J., *Paying for Roads: The Economics of Traffic Congestion*, Penguin, Harmondsworth (1967).

LONG–RUN MARGINAL COST PRICING

Long-run marginal cost, as defined in Chapter 1, includes all costs associated with the production of an extra unit of output, capital as well as running costs. Existing users must cover the costs that will actually be incurred by replacing the facilities they are using; additional users will pay what it costs to provide facilities for them.

Thus charges calculated on this basis do not relate to costs incurred in the past. They relate to the costs that *would have to be incurred* to produce an additional unit of output on an entirely new facility. Thus, if total costs of provision are generally falling, charges will fail to cover past costs. If they are rising, the opposite will apply (*see Figure 1.12* in Chapter 1).

With roads, there are difficulties in determining what long-run marginal costs are. Demand in one place cannot be met by facilities located in another. Furthermore, capital invested in roads has a virtually infinite physical life so that in practice it is not necessary to replace capital, only to add to it or modify it to meet additional demands. For these two reasons, it has been argued that the concept of L.R.M.C. cannot, in terms of its strict definition, be applied to roads.

A possible solution is to charge for capital expenditure as though it were a current item, i.e. in the year it is spent. Thus the spirit of the principle is retained in that past expenditures are ignored and only the actual commitment of resources considered. In practice, the argument continues, L.R.M.C. pricing is equivalent to the current expenditure version of the public income and expenditure account basis discussed above. L.R.M.C. may be defined to include community costs as well, but the practical difficulties of estimating future levels of community costs are much greater than those of gauging existing levels.

There are two further weaknesses of L.R.M.C. as a charging principle for roads. Firstly, as with S.R.M.C. pricing the necessary charging mechanisms are not available. The rule can only be applied to roads as a whole. Consequently, L.R.M.C. charging could only represent the costs of providing for particular users or groups of users. It would have to be assumed that such users did not confine themselves either to roads needing improvement or to roads with spare capacity.

Secondly, assuming that a suitable charging mechanism were available it could not distinguish between small parts of the network for charging purposes. Although it might be possible to differentiate between L.R.M.C. in urban and in rural areas, the rural network would have to be treated as a whole. If charges were set higher on one part because of the expenditure being incurred there, road users would divert where possible to other parts. Such diversion would often not be welcome. Improved roads are usually uncongested and are less expensive to maintain per vehicle mile run on them. It would therefore be preferable for them to be used rather than old and unimproved facilities.

L.R.M.C. pricing nevertheless retains significant economic advantages. On these grounds the Ministry of Transport employed the current expenditure basis when making cost allocations in *Road Track Costs*, arguing that L.R.M.C. for roads as a whole is adequately approximated by charging all expenditure to users as it occurs.

It should be remembered—how could it be forgotten?—that fiscal policy requirements will not allow the unrestricted application of any of these principles.

PRINCIPLES OF ROAD CHARGING: PARTICULAR CLASSES OF VEHICLE

So far, the relationship between costs and revenues for roads as a whole has been discussed. The problem next arises of determining the appropriate revenue/cost relationship for each category of road user. There are two possible approaches: the relationship of benefits to costs and the cost responsibility approach.

THE BENEFIT/COST APPROACH

If the L.R.M.C. rule is valid for road users as a whole, it can be argued that it should apply to individual road users, i.e. that *each* road user should be charged the cost incurred for him.

The relationship between benefit and L.R.M.C. is not straightforward. Road revenues at present cannot be related to particular expenditures. If benefits for a particular vehicle class exceeded costs, then more specific investment should take place on behalf of that class until the disparity were removed. Consequently it would pay more. In this way three elements, costs, benefits, and revenues paid, should tend to equality.

This approach is difficult to apply. Firstly, community costs

cannot yet be estimated in total. They certainly cannot be related
to individual vehicle classes. Secondly, fiscal and other policy
requirements apply just as much to individual vehicle classes.

It therefore appears that the benefit/cost approach cannot help to
indicate what proportion of the total costs of road provision each
vehicle class should bear. Because many road costs are joint, there is
bound to be some indeterminacy.

There are practical difficulties too. Estimates of some relevant
benefits are not available. These are the check on the justification of
expenditures, the suggestion, in certain circumstances, of modifica-
tions to the expenditure pattern. Thus pricing and investment
policies both for roads as a whole and for individual vehicle classes
are related as clearly as possible.

THE COST RESPONSIBILITY APPROACH

This approach *assumes* that expenditure incurred because of the
special requirements of certain groups of road users is justified in
terms of benefits to them.

Each cost item may be examined in turn. Any component
incurred for a particular vehicle class is then isolated. Such costs are
then allocated to that class. This done, the remaining costs can be
shared between vehicles by their proportionate road usage. So far
as possible allocation of costs is directly related to the cost of road
provision.

The approach provides an equitable basis for charging. This is
important from the point of view of public acceptability.

The cost responsibility approach does have important deficiencies. It is not possible to charge for particular types of road or
particular journeys, so it is likely that the charge on some will be
too high and on others too low. The costs to road users are not the
public costs that would be saved if those users were to disappear
from the roads. Partly this is because the charges that result from
allocating the total roads cost over all vehicles must necessarily be
averages of cost conditions over all roads. It is also because of the
nature of road costs. In most circumstances a given change of traffic
does not bring about a proportionate change in cost, i.e. marginal
costs are unlikely to be the same as average costs. In some circumstances they may be more, in others less. This is likely to occur
wherever there are significant elements of joint cost.

How may cost attribution be made in practice? With capital

costs, the task may be commenced on the same principle as with railway infrastructure costs; what capital costs are, for example, incurred *solely* because of the need to provide for heavy commercial vehicles? Such costs will consist principally of additional carriageway and structural costs to cater for extra weight and height.

For the residual capital expenditure, it is not so easy to identify any part of it with a particular vehicle class. It is assumed that heavy vehicles should pay more per mile than light. Capital expenditure is required, it is argued, because roads are congested and speeds low. For rural roads, it has been estimated that on average a heavy vehicle causes three times as much congestion as a light. In *Road Track Costs* they are allocated only twice as much capital cost per mile as light vehicles.

Surface maintenance is another item where costs caused by heavy vehicles are very different from those caused by light. It is occasioned almost entirely by heavy vehicles.

In the case of the remaining costs, other than accidents, there is little evidence to suggest that any class of vehicle is more expensive than any other to provide for. Consequently these costs are shared out between each vehicle class according to the miles they run on the system. This allocation method is also applied to police costs. Accident costs are allocated according to the frequency of involvement of each vehicle class in accidents and the relevant medical costs.

Road Track Costs found that there was no exact correspondence between revenue shares and cost responsibility. Cars, for example, pay proportionately more in revenue than the costs allocated to them; for heavy goods vehicles the situation is reversed.

THE INVESTMENT DECISION

One of the great difficulties in deciding *how much*, *where* and *when* to invest in road construction and improvement is the lack of 'feedback' from the revenue side. (This statement is not quite true as it stands: revenue accruing to the Treasury from a new road scheme might easily *diminish*. This is because an important economy benefiting road users would be reduced fuel consumption, with consequential effects upon fuel tax revenue. Reduced vehicle requirements would have a similar effect.)

Clearly, it would be wrong to conclude from this that there was no case for investment. An appropriate criterion must, however, be found. Let us first recall the policy a profit-maximising entrepreneur would follow if he were providing toll roads. His first step would be to establish the shape of the demand curve for the use of the facility.

Leaving aside the complication of current costs (maintenance, administration, etc.), a profit-maximising toll road company would set a price at which total profits were as large as possible. The number of users would then be a function of the selected toll.

This would depend upon the position and shape of the demand curve. It may be that a relatively low price would maximise profits; or vice versa. Note that the demand curve reflects amongst other things the existence or otherwise of alternative facilities.

As argued in Chapter 1, it may be possible to measure the whole of the benefits accruing to users of the proposed road by measuring the area of the entire triangle of consumer surplus, i.e. the area under the demand curve for the use of the road. After all, that triangle represents the benefits prospective users will obtain from the use of a 'free' facility. The demand curve is 'there' and could be discovered by anyone who wishes to introduce some form of pricing system.

How may the shape and position of such a curve be established? In the absence of a charging mechanism an indirect approach must be resorted to. The information a demand curve conveys relates to the amount of consumption individual users, or users in total, will undertake at varying price levels. If we ask the question 'What benefits will users obtain from this road?' we can estimate what they might be prepared to pay to obtain those benefits. Clearly, they would not pay more for the use of the road than they would obtain in benefits. On the other hand, it might pay some users to give up a substantial portion of those benefits rather than do without the use of the facility.

The principle is therefore to assume that benefits are totalled up by asking what a perfectly discriminating monopolist could extract from such a market. The result is a consumers' surplus rate of return.

The pioneering work of this kind done in the U.K. was the study of the economic justification for the M.1 motorway[3]. *Table 7.3*

3. BEESLEY, M. E., COBURN, T. M., and REYNOLDS, D. J., *The London–Birmingham Motorway, Traffic and Economics*, Road Research Technical Paper No. 46, Department of Scientific and Industrial Research, London (1960). *See also*: DAWSON, R. F. F., *The Economic Assessment of Road Improvement Schemes*, Road Research Technical Paper No. 75, Ministry of Transport, London, p. 78 (1968). This publication is the nearest approach to a handbook of instruction that is available, despite the disclaimer in the foreword.

Table 7.3 ECONOMIC APPRAISAL OF THE M.I MOTORWAY

Estimates of savings (−) and increases (+) in costs resulting from the building of the motorway	*Changes in £ thousands per annum*		
	First assignment	*Second assignment*	*Third assignment*
Saving in working time by traffic transferring to motorway	−453	−624	−766
Reduction in vehicle fleets	− 80	−161	−227
Change in fuel consumption for vehicle milage transferred to motorway	−117	− 84	− 18
Change in other operating costs for vehicle milage transferred	−200	−200	−200
Costs of additional vehicle milage incurred in transferring to motorway	+229	+307	+375
Reductions in cost to vehicles remaining on old roads	−128	−128	−128
Total vehicle costs	−749	−890	−964
Reductions in accidents	−215	.−215	−215
Maintenance costs of motorway	+200	+200	+200
Net annual measured saving (1955)	−764	−905	−979

Source: *The London–Birmingham Motorway*, Table 32, p. 58.

Table 7.4 ESTIMATED RATES OF RETURN ON INVESTMENTS IN MOTORWAY (%)*

1955 basis	*Rates of return*		
	First assignment	*Second assignment*	*Third assignment*
1. Benefits enumerated in Table 7.3	3·3	3·9	4·2
2. *Plus* benefits to generated traffic	3·8	4·5	4·8
3. *Plus* the benefits of non-business time valued:			
(a) at 20p per hour	5·4	6·4	7·1
(b) at 30p per hour	6·2	7·4	8·3
(c) at 40p per hour	7·0	8·3	9·4

4. Allowing for the effect of growth in traffic over time at 6% per annum: predicted rate of return in:

1960	9·9–15·2	
1965	17·6–27·3	

* Estimated cost of motorway including interest charges at 5% during period of construction: £23 300 000.

Source: *The London–Birmingham Motorway*, Tables 33 and 34, pp. 61 and 62.

shows the most important benefits calculated to be made by users of the motorway.

The rate of return from the investment in the motorway is set out in *Table 7.4*. It will be noted that an important benefit was time savings. The time of all people travelling in working time was valued at their average hourly earnings. At the first stage (that represented by the first table) no value was given to non-business time. The second benefit to be estimated was savings in vehicle use. The quicker the journeys, the fewer vehicles would be required, it was argued. Then came savings in fuel costs and other kinds of operating costs.

Against this had to be set the costs of additional milage incurred by vehicles transferring to the motorway from the old route. On the other hand, traffic on that old route could now flow more smoothly and receive corresponding benefits. (*See Figure 1.5* for diagrammatic representation of this.)

The above categories may all be grouped together as vehicle costs. To complete the calculation it was necessary to add in the value of the expected decrease in accidents. This may be done by estimating the effect on output, medical and administrative effects and damage to property.

Subtracted from the total were the anticipated average annual maintenance costs.

Three sets of rates of return were worked out, as may be seen from *Table 7.4*. (The assignments represent different forecasts of how much traffic would divert to the motorway.) It can be seen that, on this basis alone, the rate of return is quite small.

But new traffic will be generated. There is a relationship between journey time and the volume of traffic between towns. If journey time falls traffic volume rises. Such benefits must be included. (They are valued at half the rate used for non-generated traffic.)

Non-business time was then brought in. Several different assumptions were made about this, as can be seen from *Table 7.4*.

Finally, allowance was made for growth in traffic due to growth in national income.

Full-scale exercises of this magnitude are expensive and decision-makers require simpler, less costly analytical tools for routine use. Clearly the results thus obtained will be more rough and ready. There will be situations where a cost/benefit analysis of the alternative techniques of cost/benefit analysis is required. Much will depend upon the accuracy of the results required.

Let us draw attention, for example, to the Ministry of Transport's technique for quantifying the deficiencies of roads in monetary terms known as Travel and Accident Loss (T.A.L.)[3a]. The 'loss' is the difference between operating and accident costs as they *are* on the roads currently existing compared to what they *would be* if the roads were built to the appropriate standards of design for the traffic volume in question. (It will be observed that a somewhat arbitrary element is introduced here: how does one decide the 'appropriate' standard of design?) T.A.L. is calculated for a stretch of road from measurements of traffic speeds and flows, and accident data.

T.A.L. thus takes account of factors (e.g. gradient, alignment, lane-width, and the effect of junctions and frontage development) that influence traffic flows. Even so, there are some omissions such as the losses of amenity or environmental quality from the noise and traffic fumes and the pain and bereavement from road accidents.

The T.A.L. for each stretch of road is calculated and expressed as a 'first year' of operation rate of return. This provides a knowledge of where the trunk road system is currently most deficient. By making assumptions of traffic growth, T.A.L. measurements may be projected several years ahead and improvements and new construction already programmed taken into account. The results focus attention on those stretches of road where costs, thus defined, are highest and where the need for improvement is greatest. Thus T.A.L. is an important planning tool, and is a very interesting example of how a sophisticated form of analysis may be adapted for practical regular use.

The theoretical notion of social surplus maximisation (Chapter 1, *Figure 1.7*) has also been clothed in numerical flesh and blood in studies such as that of the London Transport underground railway link, the Victoria Line[4]. The purpose of this approach was to be able to make a relatively accurate economic comparison with a competitive road project evaluated according to the consumers' surplus criterion.

The Victoria Line project, on a commercial basis, would have lost some £3 m. per annum. *Table 7.5* shows what happened when consumers' surplus was brought into account.

3a. MINISTRY OF TRANSPORT, *Roads in England and Wales*, H.M.S.O., London, pp. 21–23 (1964).

4. FOSTER, C. D., and BEESLEY, M. E., 'Estimating the Social Benefit of Constructing an Underground Railway in London', *Journal of the Royal Statistical Society*, Series A, Vol. 126, Part I, pp. 46–92 (1963).

Table 7.5 ECONOMIC APPRAISAL OF THE VICTORIA LINE

	Presented discounted value at 6% (£m.)
Costs (annual working expenses)	16·16
Benefits	
Traffic diverted to Victoria Line	
Public transport users: Time savings	13·83
Comfort and convenience	3·96
Motorists: Time savings	3·25
Savings in vehicle operating costs	8·02
Pedestrians: Time savings	0·28
	29·34
Traffic not diverted to Victoria Line	
Public transport: Comfort and convenience	5·22
Cost savings	9·10
Road users: Time savings	21·54
Savings in vehicle operating costs	8·93
	44·79
Generated traffic	11·74
Terminal scrap value	0·29
Total benefits	86·16
Net annual benefits	70·00

Value of capital expenditure	38·81	
Net benefit (net present value)	31·19	
Social surplus rate of return	11·3%	

Source: Foster and Beesley (1963), Table 2, p. 49.

It will be observed that no figure for the financial loss mentioned earlier appears in the table. This is because the fares charged by London Transport gather in a part of the benefits listed. To count in fares revenue as well would be double-counting.

Such items as time savings and road vehicle operating cost reductions are worked out in the same way as for road projects.

It will be observed that the value placed on 'comfort and convenience' is very important in helping to determine the final outcome. This was calculated largely as a function of the value of time by surveying the habits of people who had the choice of travelling in a fast, though crowded, train as against a slower but emptier one.

THE ECONOMIC ANALYSIS OF ROAD NETWORKS

The analysis so far deals, in effect, with single, isolated links of road. It must be generalised to take account of network effects, for in real life there is no such thing as an isolated link: any investment decision, or indeed any 'failure to invest' decision, upon one part of a road network will have important effects elsewhere. The elimination of a traffic bottleneck, for example, will attract traffic from other routes. This point has already been made in earlier discussion.

Once a network exercise is undertaken, a very elaborate programme of work is involved[5]. A first stage will probably be to divide up the area served by the network into traffic zones. Statistical analysis may then be undertaken to obtain 'trip generation' forecasts. A very simple example of this would be to construct a statistical model relating household income and population density (say) to trip-making. As income went up, probably car ownership and use would do likewise; public transport trip-making might decline. (The making of trips might be treated quite separately in such models from the process of 'modal split' which is the technical term for the division of trips made between the different modes of transport.)

Having made forecasts of traffic to be 'generated', the traffic needs to be 'distributed'. One procedure here might be to construct a 'gravity model' that, as the term implies, distributes flows between the zones of the model in direct proportion to the size, in terms of population and employment of originating and terminating traffic, and in inverse proportion to the distance between such zones. Gravity models exist in many different forms.

The next stage is to 'assign' traffic to a detailed path through

5. See: GREATER LONDON COUNCIL, *Movement in London: Transport Research Studies and Their Context*, London (1969), particularly Appendix F, 'Economic Evaluation'. Other examples of recent complex cost/benefit analyses are: MINISTRY OF TRANSPORT, *Report of a Study of Rail Links with Heathrow Airport*, Parts I and II, H.M.S.O., London (1970), and COMMISSION ON THE THIRD LONDON AIRPORT, Report, H.M.S.O., London (1971). For a commentary on the latter *see*: MISHAN, E. J., 'What is wrong with Roskill?', *Journal of Transport Economics and Policy*, Vol. 4, No. 3, pp. 221–234 (1970).

the network. This might be done on the basis of simple time minimisation (i.e. traffic is held to take the minimum time route between two zones, taking into account both distance and road congestion). A more sophisticated method is to assign on the basis of minimisation of 'generalised costs'. These costs are an aggregate of operating costs and time required to undertake a given journey. The purpose here is to forecast the behaviour of road users and such costs are consequently sometimes called 'behavioural' costs.

Finally, it is necessary to undertake an economic evaluation of the proposed new link, road improvement or perhaps a complete 'package' involving the reconstruction of the whole of an urban transport network.

With the help of computers, alternative schemes may be tested. Traffic forecasts may be undertaken on the assumption that no investment is going to take place. In this 'do nothing' situation, the additional traffic of future years has been distributed and assigned. A picture has been drawn of what the situation will be *without* any investment.

It now remains to test the alternative networks. Let us suppose we are testing Supernetwork A. The schemes comprising this network are added on to the original network and the whole process of distribution, assignment and economic evaluation gone through again. The do-nothing situation offers a bench mark; the benefits of the new network are the *improvements* in operating costs, travel times, accident savings, etc., *compared with what would have happened* if nothing had been done.

The technique of evaluation is no different in principle from what has been described earlier. We are simply taking a wider view of the effects of a given investment.

It is not enough simply to test alternative networks and then select that network giving the highest rate of return upon capital. Each component part of the package should have its economics separately assessed, or else there is a danger of cross-subsidisation. Similar exercises should be carried out in regard to the timing of individual parts of the scheme.

The generalised costs mentioned above are those which are held to govern the behaviour of travellers. It may well be that car users, in particular, will choose to disregard certain elements of cost; perhaps they will make their travel decisions on the simple basis of fuel costs and time taken. Certainly the costs of operating road vehicles of any kind to the user are a complex kind of multi-part tariff. It is not difficult to imagine the classic commercial effects of that tariff working upon the motorist: the attention of the consumer being focused strictly upon his very short-run marginal costs when making consumption decisions. (The fixed parts of the tariff are licence fees, depreciation, etc.)

This notion of cost is crucially important at the traffic assignment stage and can be checked upon by observing whether it does give good predictions of users' behaviour. When it comes to assessing the economic benefits of road schemes, however, different concepts of cost become relevant.

In the first place, the 'fixed' elements excluded hitherto may be brought in. Clearly, if this is not done, one can hardly count such items as vehicle fleet reductions as benefits. Secondly, the calculations, from the point of view of the national economy, should be undertaken on a resource basis, as when weighing up the true economics of coal-mine closure.

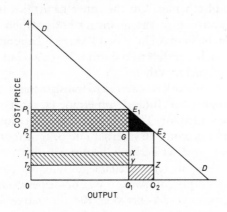

Figure 7.1. Change in consumers' surplus and non-resource costs due to road investment

We now have a basis for showing diagrammatically the technique of measuring benefits from road investments, as in *Figure 7.1*. Remember that such a diagram will exist for each flow of traffic between every pair of zones represented in the transportation model. Total benefits are arrived at by summing those on each individual diagram.

We begin with demand curve D–D. Existing 'price' of travel to the motorist is OP_1 and quantity of road space demanded OQ_1. Let us assume away the complication that behavioural costs do not take proper account of fixed costs. Every relevant cost and price relationship is shown on the diagram.

OT_1 represents the transfer payment element in the price to the road user: fuel tax, excise duty and so on. Total costs to the motorists are therefore $OP_1E_1Q_1$ of which OT_1XQ_1 does not represent the consumption of resources in the provision of the system. A consumers' surplus P_1AE_1 is enjoyed.

Suppose now that additional road capacity is provided and the price of travel sinks down to OP_2. The transfer element now decreases to OT_2. What are the total benefits flowing out of this investment?

There is a gain in consumers' surplus to existing traffic of $P_1E_1GP_2$; and of GE_1E_2 to 'generated' traffic. Tax revenue T_1XYT_2 is 'lost' from existing users, but YZQ_2Q_1 gained from the new users.

Two alternative treatments are possible with the 'transfer surplus' change. It can be ignored, as it commonly is in the economic appraisal of road schemes. On the other hand, this is a form of *public* surplus accruing to the financing body which might well wish to include the item. (The Road Research Laboratory's treatment excludes such transfers in economic appraisal but the Greater London Council includes them[3, 5]).

A vast amount of work is required to translate theoretical notions into practical application. Indeed, something far short of perfection may have to be settled for. The London Transportation Study, for example, did not produce an internal rate of return or a figure of net present value as described in Chapter 2.

Travel and other data were available for only one particular year in the future. A simple comparison was made between the annual benefit for that one year as between the alternative schemes and the do-nothing situation. In other words, a one-year rate of return was produced.

SOCIAL BENEFITS AND COSTS

So far the analysis has concentrated upon fairly tangible factors such as operating costs and travel time. Severe difficulties arise when it is desired to bring environmental and other social effects into the calculations.

Many large investment projects have important external effects. A topical example of this is the selection of a site for a new airport. It is possible to calculate the construction and operating costs of the airport and to total the travelling time of passengers, etc., with a fair degree of acceptability. When one comes to noise and visual intrusion, which are imposed upon residents in wide areas around the airport, the 'quantification' process becomes far more difficult.

Such phenomena have important subjective elements; there is no simple technical measure of their psychological effects. This is perhaps best explained by the example of accident costs.

The costs of road accidents may be established by finding out resource costs incurred by the health service, the police, actual damage to property, etc. To this may be added the net losses of national product due to death or injury of people involved in accidents. The future probable contribution of a casualty is assessed and his or her forecast consumption subtracted. If one wishes to be very sophisticated, no doubt all the various national income multiplier effects can also be included.

Let us suppose, however, that an old age pensioner is killed. On the basis described above it will probably be concluded that the economy will make a net *gain*—a conclusion that society is most unlikely to accept.

It follows that the 'cold blooded' or 'objective' costs of such accidents have to be supplemented by some subjective evaluation of the suffering, pain and distress imposed by accidents. This is now done. Somewhat arbitrary, but presumably socially acceptable, figures are included in accident cost calculations[6].

Similar problems arise with the evaluation of noise, fumes and environmental intrusion. It has been powerfully argued that difficulty of quantification is no excuse for ignoring these[7]. Yet the difficulties of such quantification, at least in economic terms, are extreme[8].

Before economic measurement can take place, there must be technical quantification in whatever units are appropriate. Noise levels, for example, may be measured in terms of 'A weighted decibels (dBA)' or a related scale. If this can be achieved, two basic treatments of the costs imposed can be attempted.

Firstly, the problem may be tackled by regulation. Standards may be laid down to the effect that certain levels of disbenefit must

6. DAWSON, R. F. F., *The Cost of Road Accidents in Great Britain*, Road Research Laboratory Report No. LR 79, H.M.S.O., London (1967).
7. MISHAN, E. J., *The Costs of Economic Growth*, Staples, London (1967).
8. A survey of the problems involved may be found in FOSTER, C. D., and MACKIE, P., 'Noise: Economic Aspects of Choice', *Urban Studies*, Vol. 7, No. 2, pp. 123–135 (1970).

not be imposed by individual agents upon non-users of the system (e.g. roads or airport noise and fumes regulations). In extreme cases or when poisonous chemicals are being inserted into an ecological system, the authorities may simply impose a complete ban on the practice.

The main difficulty here is in saying what the standard should be. Inevitably, there would be some arbitrariness. Once standards were set and enforced, however, the effects would become internal to those agents originally creating the social disbenefits. Cost penalties would be imposed upon those hitherto responsible and marginal adjustment of now unprofitable activities undertaken.

With roads, possible strategies might be (to deal with noise):

1. Require noise at source to be suppressed by the installation of mufflers or the redesign of engines to make them quieter;
2. The insulation of houses and buildings within a certain radius of the road, the cost thus imposed to be met by road users;
3. The erection of noise barriers around the road; or
4. A combination of these measures.

Secondly, a more strictly economic approach could be adopted by attributing the social disbenefits to those responsible for imposing them. The costs themselves could be evaluated by observing the behaviour of the relevant market when such costs were imposed upon it. To put it somewhat crudely: how much would individuals be prepared to pay to escape from noise?

One possible approach here would be to observe the depreciation of property values consequent upon the imposition of a noise or other nuisance (the revealed preference approach). This depreciation would give an indication of the social valuation of the nuisance; it would be charged to those responsible; they would adjust their operations until the compensation arising from their activities exactly balanced the nuisance imposed, as valued by the market.

There are several problems here. The first is the practical one of thus evaluating the costs. Technical data have to be transformed into money terms somehow so that it can be fitted into the conventional cost/benefit framework. Then there are the practical problems of identifying those responsible and charging them.

A serious objection to the property depreciation method is that it assumes that disbenefits are proportionate to value of property owned. As in the case of road accidents involving old age pensioners, society might find difficulty in accepting such a view. It is therefore necessary to supplement the revealed preference approach with one that takes into account the subjective costs in terms of nuisance and distress.

Such an approach might be based upon, say, household removal costs. One can assume that disbenefits will accumulate until a household finds the situation intolerable and then moves away in order to escape. Household turnover rates may be one guide here, and it could be argued that quite arbitrary social valuations are again preferable to nothing.

Most serious of all is that many important costs such as damage to health may not be perceived at all. They lie completely outside the market mechanism. An individual may become progressively accustomed to noise because his hearing deteriorates. A study of his market behaviour might indicate a growing acceptance of noise. Clearly one cannot leave such factors out of account.

Finally, there are some factors that are so intangible that the analyst cannot even begin to put a value on them: historic buildings, tranquil countryside, access to nature reserves and preservation of the wild life within them. All is not hopeless however. We may attempt to use the shadow price technique discussed in Chapter 2.

How could this work? Suppose a road was planned to cut straight through an area of beautiful parkland which it was desired to preserve in its natural state. An alternative would be to re-route the road so as to make a detour. By doing this, additional construction, maintenance, operating and time costs would be incurred. These would represent the 'price', a shadow price, of maintaining the parkland. Society could then make the judgement: should we pay this price for such preservation? Indeed, society may ask more fundamental questions such as: do we need this road at all?

Such are some of the main problems associated with what has come to be called cost/benefit analysis[9]. There can be no doubt that economists must be frank in declaring the limitations of their techniques here. However, to deny the need for such analysis is to declare in favour of complete arbitrariness in decision-making. Although it cannot perhaps do the whole job, economic analysis can provide an informed basis for policy discussion.

9. A survey of the whole field of cost/benefit analysis is provided by MISHAN, E. J., *Cost-Benefit Analysis*, Allen & Unwin, London (1971).

THE 'RATE OF EXCHANGE' PROBLEM

The reader may feel, by now, that there is a bewildering array of alternative possible rules for working out the returns on investments on projects. Leaving aside the complication of different pricing policies, we have:

1. Producers' surplus (the basis for orthodox financial calculation; Chapter 1, *Figure 1.1*).
2. Consumers' surplus which, for the sake of convenience, we will bracket together with social surplus (producers' and consumers' surplus combined; Chapter 1, *Figures 1.6, 1.7*).

These 'internal' calculations need to be supplemented by the inclusion and evaluation of 'external' effects, which may be divided into two main types:

3. Network effects (broadly speaking, the effects on similar or related facilities making up part of the system to which the project being invested in belongs; Chapter 1, *Figure 1.5*, and discussed in this chapter).
4. Environmental effects (phenomena of the kind just discussed: noise, fumes, etc.).

One of the basic problems facing public decision-makers when allocating relatively scarce investment funds is how to convert these different returns into one common 'currency'; we may speak of a 'rate of exchange' between projects.

It will be recalled that a profit-maximising entrepreneur would, if it were feasible, charge each user an amount *just short* of what would drive him off the facility. Theoretically, it would thus be possible to come close to gaining the *whole* of consumers' surplus. However, it is assumed here that such 'perfect' discrimination is not possible and that a single charge prevails, as illustrated in *Figure 7.2*.

Consumers' surplus is represented by D_1AP (diagonal shading). It is evident that, given the shape of the demand curve, consumers' surplus is about half the size of the receipts rectangle $PAQO$ (cross-hatched). Toll receipts are therefore approximately two-thirds of total benefits represented by D_1AQO, the total shaded area. As on a previous occasion, it is assumed that there are no

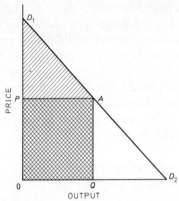

*Figure 7.2. The investment rate of
exchange: example one*

running costs associated with provision of the road. (Naturally,
different results would be forthcoming from different 'shapes' of
demand curves.)

If no charge was levied, usage would increase from OQ to OD_2
and the incremental benefits AD_2Q would be enjoyed by users. If
these extra benefits were to be added on to D_1AQO, total benefits
would increase to about double those of receipts $PAQO$, given the
assumption of the diagram.

We therefore have a choice of two ratios if a rate of return thus
calculated is to be compared with a commercial one: we can either
argue for 1·5:1 (i.e. that 1·5 units of consumers' surplus returns are
comparable to each unit of commercial returns) or for 2:1 (i.e.
halve the consumers' surplus return for comparative purposes).

Perhaps the most relevant comparison is that which assumes
adoption of a common pricing rule. This means that we are left
with a ratio of total benefits to financial surplus of 1·5:1, assuming
the toll of OP*[10]. On the other hand, it could be respectably argued
that the relevant price is zero and output thus OD_2. This would
imply a rate of exchange of 2:1.

* Note that this 'rate of exchange' adjustment is quite different from the discount rate. The latter, it will be recalled, reflects the weighting placed upon
current as opposed to future consumption. It has nothing to do with the definition
and calculation of costs and benefits.

10. There is little published material on this theme. For a pioneering contri-
    bution *see*: CARR, J. L., *Efficiency in Government Spending . . .*, Part IV,
    'Comparisons with other uses of resources', pp. 54–60 (1967), reprinted
    from Institut International de Finances Publiques, Congres de York, XXII
    Session, September 1966 (Proceedings).

Naturally, these particular results depend upon the assumptions built into the analysis. Change the shape and position of the demand curve, insert cost curves, and different ratios will emerge.

To carry the analysis further, we must depart from the special case considered so far: that of a completely new investment. Can it be assumed that any kind of *general* conclusion can be drawn? To answer that we must undertake some further comparisons. Let us recall the example of a railway electrification project from the previous chapter. This had two aspects:

1. A cost-reducing investment.
2. A demand-expansion project.

For the sake of simplicity let us take the cost-reduction aspect first, as illustrated in *Figure 7.3*.

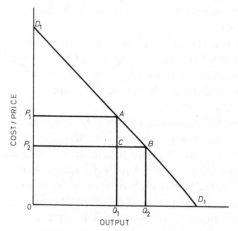

Figure 7.3. The investment rate of exchange:
a cost-reduction case

We begin with price OP_1, output OQ_1 and total receipts P_1AQ_1O. Then suppose that costs fall, as the result of investment, so that the costs no longer intersect demand curve D_1–D_1 at A, but instead at B. If, as a result, price is lowered to OP_2 and output increased to OQ_2, we may ask about the benefits gained by consumers.

In this case, there is a gain of utility measured by P_1ABP_2, all of which is reaped by consumers. If this area can be measured, at least approximately, the total benefits will be included. The returns will then be commensurable with the consumers' surplus benefits of the

new road investment. Both sets of return being directly comparable, the rate of exchange should be 1:1.

It is unlikely, however, that an undertaking required to secure a
specified rate of return would thus allow consumers to reap all the
benefits. Suppose that the undertaking did not pass on the benefits
of reduced costs to consumers. Would the conclusion be radically
altered? In this case price would remain at OP_1 and output at OQ_1,
but the undertaking would gain a surplus P_1ACP_2. The return on
investment would now be smaller by the amount of unrealised
consumers' surplus, ABC. But no benefits would be 'lost' in the
appraisal process. Again the conclusion points to a 1:1 exchange
rate.

Let us set aside the cost-reduction effect for a moment to consider
the situation in which investment improves service quality without
affecting production costs: electrification produces a faster, cleaner,
more reliable service. The consequences of this is an outward shift
of the demand curve as shown in *Figure 7.4*.

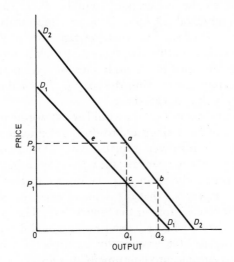

Figure 7.4. The investment rate of exchange:
a demand-expansion case

Original demand is represented by curve D_1–D_1 but, as a result of
electrification, demand increases to D_2–D_2. Price had formerly been
OP_1 and output OQ_1. The enterprise has two main alternative
policies:

1. Maintain output OQ_1, 'rationing' by the setting of price OP_2 (or, of course, tolerating a physical shortage by reservation control with price remaining at OP_1); or
2. Alternatively, price may be held steady at OP_1 and output expanded to OQ_2, presumably at the cost of investment funds, in, say, locomotives and rolling stock additional to those already expended.

A public enterprise with a financial target will wish to convert some of the consumers' surplus thus generated into producers' surplus. If output is held to OQ_1, but price raised to OP_2, total benefits will be D_2aQ_1O. An additional producers' surplus P_2acP_1 will thus be generated. Some of this will be a transfer of surplus from consumers to producers, but part of newly created consumers' surplus D_2acD_1, will not be captured in the returns. In other words, only the triangle *eac* will represent genuinely new benefits resulting from the investment and *included in the calculation of the benefits*.

If output is increased to OQ_2, total benefits will be D_2bQ_2O. Total revenue to the undertaking will be P_1bQ_2O, of which cbQ_2Q_1 is incremental. D_2bcD_1, however, represents additional benefit that is not reflected in whatever rate of return calculation has been undertaken. In this case, there may well be serious under-representation of benefits. A high rate of exchange with the consumers' surplus return from the road (i.e. something like the $1 \cdot 5 : 1$ ratio) may thus be called for.

The additional benefit D_2bcD_1 would be extraordinarily difficult to quantify in real life. Rough and ready approximations would be called for. There is, however, a further complication. In this situation, as perhaps in the former case, the railway management would probably attempt some form of price discrimination. It will be observed from *Figure 7.3* that the demand curve has shifted outward proportionately more at the 'upper' end. The management would almost certainly take advantage of this by differentiating the market, running de luxe services, for example, or especially fast trains, and thus cutting into consumers' surplus.

To this one may add some further difficulties of measurement and interpretation:

1. The measurement of consumers' surplus is necessarily indirect. For example, it is crucially important to make a correct valuation of time savings to road users. The problem was tackled by dividing users into journey-purpose categories,

e.g. business and non-business, but a single value assumed for each category. Similarly with operating costs: what is measured is the difference between the *costs* to users before and after the investment, not their preparedness to pay. We have already noted that there might be a wide divergence between behavioural and true costs.

2. One has to be very careful that one is comparing like-with-like. So far it has been assumed that road investments are new and represented by a fresh diagram. There are many cost-reduction situations with road investment too.

3. On the other hand, it may be slightly misleading to call the returns from a road scheme consumer surplus, as opposed to the returns from a railway investment. Much of the 'consumers' surplus' consists of operating cost reductions to users. These would be included in a railway appraisal, but would be internal to the agency installing the project.

4. With environmental externalities it would appear to be very difficult to lay down any principles at all governing the exchange rate. This will vary with actual circumstances. The most fruitful course may be to 'internalise externalities' by regulations.

It would appear from this discussion that the establishment of a common exchange rate is most unlikely. The safest conclusion would appear to be that it is dangerous to generalise and that specific investments should be individually investigated.

Policy making, however, can rarely wait for such analysis and the economist may be required to give a quick, though admittedly rough, judgement. It can be argued that, in some of the cases discussed, e.g. the cost-reducing projects, the rates of return are comparable *at the margin* with those from new roads. It is evident, though, that situations often arise in which the latter are relatively over-stated. The evidence may well point to this conclusion.

8

PUBLIC ENTERPRISE AND THE STATE: I

THE RAILWAYS

The state has involved itself in railway affairs right from the earliest days of the steam locomotive's dominance. After all, an Act of Parliament was required to start a railway and this Act bestowed both rights and privileges upon the new mode of transport.

There were privileges because it often made no economic sense to have more than one concern serving a given area or route; a degree of monopoly power was inevitable. Some would argue today that the physical system that emerged did not show *enough* signs of monopoly: there was far too much duplication of facilities, with high costs incurred when traffic was transferred between companies. There was also joint stock status before this was generally available to industry. Without it, the necessary mobilisation of capital would have been far more difficult.

There were also elements of public control or obligation. The first railway in the modern sense, the Liverpool and Manchester Railway of 1830, had written into its Act, for instance, a clause compelling it to reduce freight charges if dividends above a certain level were declared.

As market forces were denied full expression in the construction of facilities, commercial conflicts were reflected on the political and juridical planes.

There was far more to the relationship than the Acts setting up the various companies. The history of the railway system could be written largely in terms of general legislation (such as the famous 1844 Act), Royal Commissions, Departmental Committees, Tribunals, and so on. It often has been[1].

The process can be summarised like this. Most users of railways strongly supported 'freedom' of enterprise for the economy as a whole. But they did not feel that it was good for railways. Traders preferred to be part of a vast impersonal market process than to be controlled by guilds or magistrates; they were less enthusiastic about free market ideas being applied to the vast new transport undertakings upon which they were so dependent.

The economic confrontation being unequal, users were compelled to band together *politically*. This they did. And the result of their pressure remained with us until comparatively recently. Indeed, they have still not completely disappeared. The result was the control of charges and their basing upon what the 'traffic would bear' so that users should not be subjected to monopolistic exploitation or 'unfairly discriminated' against.

There had also to be 'equality' of treatment, and the right to 'reasonable facilities'. The formidable battery of legislation, added to a powerful common law tradition, in effect transformed the railway companies into a public service rather than a commercial enterprise.

Control of monopoly went further. The process of amalgamation or even the introduction of working agreements between companies was hampered for a long time. Policy did not change until the experience of the First World War (when the state operated the railways directly by means of a Railway Executive Committee) transformed opinion on that particular question. Indeed, amalgamation was sponsored *from above* by the 1921 Act which brought about the 'Big Four' grouping.

But the great network of public obligation and charging control was to remain until after the Second World War. Its removal does not seem to have been seriously contemplated even after the advent of motorised road competition, carrying no such burdens. Legislators found other techniques, more dubious from the economic point of view, such as the imposition of licensing control on road services.

The attitude of the state until comparatively recently was thus

1. A good account of the development of public obligation is provided by MILNE, A. M., and LAING, A., *The Obligation to Carry*, Institute of Transport, London (1956). *See*: CLAYTON, G., and REES, J. H., *Economic Problems of Rural Transport in Wales*, University of Wales Press, Cardiff (1967).

largely negative*. The railway system was something to be controlled from without. It was not the business of the state to *initiate* developments; merely to see that the railways behaved themselves. The criteria of good behaviour were somewhat vague and had more to do with what was 'fair' rather than what was economic. In return, the railways were given an element of protection.

It is curious that when the railways were taken into direct state ownership little was done about public obligation. In this regard, modernisation had to wait for the Acts of 1953 and 1962.

Although the existence of a highly developed road haulage industry made such obligation a historical curiosum so far as freight was concerned, it was politically very difficult to change the public attitude to passenger services; the concept of 'transport-as-a-service' was far too deeply rooted. There was strong public opposition to the closure of uneconomic railway services.

THE STATE AS 'BUYER' OF SOCIAL SERVICES

The concept of railways as a 'public service' being far from dead, it follows that there will be a proportion, perhaps large, of deliberately 'unprofitable' output. 'Unprofitable', it should hardly need to be emphasised by now, is not necessarily the same as 'uneconomic'[2].

If there is to be such unprofitable output, someone must judge how much there should be, who should benefit and from whom financial losses should be recouped. Until the 1968 Transport Act, the railways themselves were left to do this job, endeavouring to cover the cost of unremunerative services from profitable ones.

Such practices make it very difficult to judge the efficiency of management. The annual profit and loss figure of the British Railways Board is quite meaningless if it reflects large losses on services that the management cannot discontinue if they wish to. According to the 1968 Act, such a responsibility is one that the state should explicitly assume.

---

* Not *completely*, because a positive role was exercised in such matters as ensuring safety and technical standardisation, e.g. the track gauge.

2. ELSE, P. K., and HOWE, M., 'Cost-Benefit Analysis and the Withdrawal of Railway Services', *Journal of Transport Economics and Policy*, Vol. 3, No. 2, pp. 178–194 (1969). MINISTRY OF TRANSPORT, *Cambrian Coast Line: a cost-benefit analysis of the retention of railway services*, H.M.S.O., London (1969).

This involves the bringing-out into the open of remaining social obligations[3]. Non-paying services should be identified and costed. A conscious decision can then be taken by the state whether or not to 'buy' them. The possibility was left open that some of the costs may be recovered from the beneficiaries—perhaps via their local authorities.

That is not all. Before deciding whether to undertake such subsidisation the government examines the service to be provided in the light of available competitive forms of transport, and reviews the price/output/quality mix suggested by the railways. This may have to be modified to qualify for grants. If such unremunerative services are not thus purchased, then and only then, will the closure procedure come into operation.

THE STATE AS BANKER

The relationship of the state to the railways may be compared to that of a merchant banker to the undertakings he invests in. It might even be developing into something more like a holding company relationship.

As banker and shareholder in an undertaking which in the past found itself in somewhat unfortunate financial circumstances, there is bound to be pressure for more and more detailed government intervention. The performance of the management is certain to be closely scrutinised, though with due regard to the difficulties under which they have had to work. New investment projects are likely to be closely examined. Questions also will arise about fundamental issues of organisation, capital structure and future development.

An important role here was played by the Joint Steering Group appointed by the Chairman of the British Railways Board and the (then) Minister of Transport to review certain aspects of the railway industry. Much of the Group's work was concerned with establishing a basis for identifying and costing non-viable services. Equally important work was done, however, in the analysis of the management structure of the Board and the financial discipline imposed upon the industry.

The government accepted the principle of a smaller policy Board

3. For the next few pages, the following source is an indispensable reference: MINISTRY OF TRANSPORT, *Railway Policy* (Cmnd. 3439), H.M.S.O., London (1967).

whose members will, for the most part, not have executive responsibility for specific aspects of management. This new-style Board
was required to submit to the minister a general scheme of reorganisation; being assisted in this by the removal of the statutory
basis of the regional Boards.

There was a capital reconstruction so that . . . 'the Board's capital
liabilities should be so adjusted that they have a fair and reasonable
prospect of achieving and maintaining a break-even position (after
taking account of the proposed social grants) over the years ahead.
The annual revenue account will then become a fair measure of
the success or failure of the industry's management.'

The values of individual assets were scaled down to correspond
with the revised capital liabilities. This ensures that the performance
of the management may be tested against realistic objectives. Such
performance criteria were not hitherto present.

The need for deficit grants will thus be eliminated. This will have
special importance for the Board's future capital investment policy;
it is intended that the interest and depreciation burden should not
grow out of hand again. Great emphasis has now, therefore, been
placed upon the need for long-term financial planning which, in
turn, must be based upon a realistic appraisal of future prospects
for the industry.

The state already takes a close interest in major investment
projects. To a large extent, this interest has been forced upon it
because of the extreme difficulty in judging the *overall* efficiency
of the railway management in making their global investment
programmes. Scrutiny of individual projects was likely to become
progressively more detailed in a situation of large financial deficit.
How far such a process should go is very difficult to say, and there
are bound to be opposing views. To go into great detail would
involve the use of specialist manpower which is usually not available in sufficient numbers within a government machine. There is
also the problem of avoiding interference in detailed management
affairs.

If the system of judging management by performance is successful, there should be need for discussion only of annual and long-
term programmes, and any tendency to take an interest in detailed
questions of management diminished. As deficit grants are discontinued, the management will be judged by their skill. The 1968
Act financial framework is far more sensitive to financial performance and can bring about physical expansion—or contraction—of
the system as circumstances dictate.

The crucial importance of such long-term planning and of the state being closely involved in this process as a partner cannot, therefore, be over-emphasised.

THE STATE AND LONG-TERM PLANNING

British Railways, like other public enterprises, have carried out a considerable amount of planning, much of it concerned with technical developments and specific investment projects. Now there is to be greater emphasis on *corporate* planning: the development of co-ordinated plans for the achievement of objectives set for the undertaking. This means the forward planning of *all* the organisation's activities and resources in order to make the best possible use of the opportunities in the markets selected, using the approach outlined in Chapter 3.

The state is bound to be closely associated with this process in several different ways. First of all, the Board's over-riding objectives, both financial and otherwise, are established by the government. The statutory financial objectives are supplemented by those set under the provisions of the White Paper *Nationalised Industries. A Review of Economic and Financial Objectives.*

When, within these overall objectives, the Board turn to establishing more detailed objectives for different sectors close collaboration is needed in such matters as overall traffic forecasting. This is, of course, no reflection on the forecasting abilities of British Railways. It is merely a recognition that the government spans a much wider field and, together with other departments, gathers information on practically all forms of inland transport and traffic through ports.

Out of such long-term planning will flow a strategy, i.e. a statement of *how* the objectives for each sector or activity are to be achieved. In a complex organisation with such a large number of interacting factors, major feasibility studies are often required to weigh up possible alternative strategies. Often, the number of factors that can vary and interact may be such that the use of mathematical models is essential. Only after this stage will specific investment projects emerge. These projects then are submitted to the government department concerned for approval.

If it is such a difficult problem to draw up a strategy for the railways in isolation, it is even harder to say whether, and to what extent, the possible railway strategies fit into the overall transport picture.

Consider the cases where investments in road and rail are effective *alternatives*. By this is meant a situation in which the future distribution of traffic between modes of transport will be affected by the investment decisions made.

Incompatible traffic assumptions may perhaps be made on each side. Each decision-maker may assume that new or improved facilities will pull traffic from the other mode of transport plus the greater part of new traffic generated. Any serious inconsistency of traffic forecasts on both sides could obviously lead to wrong decisions.

Even if consistent traffic forecasts were used, both the road and the rail investments might appear to be justified when measured against internal objectives of the kind just discussed. The 'solution' of going ahead with both investments, however, is not necessarily optimal. It might well be best to concentrate investment on one of the two modes, or at least distribute it differently from what is implied by the result of the 'isolated' appraisal exercises.

The greater the scale and the longer the time horizon involved, the more likely are these types of error to arise—and even be compounded. Such problems emphasise the need for the government to play a role in channelling resources. Models such as those discussed in Chapter 6 may help throw light on the subject.

THE STATE AND THE 'RULES OF THE GAME'

Exercises such as the transport costs model are essential to provide a quantitative basis for policy making or planning. Once the facts are known, and the consequences of different state actions predictable, the 'rules of the game'—the framework of regulation within which the transport system must function—can be drawn or redrawn.

'Rules of the game' cover two main areas:

1. The amount and type of road 'track' provided and how the costs of that track are allocated to different users.
2. The regulation of operations and organisation (or, to be more accurate, aspects of them) on both rail and road.

The Department of the Environment is not only concerned with policy and regulation of transport; it is also one of the largest business units in the country. Leaving aside other road categories, its construction and control of motorways and trunk roads would qualify the department for that position. Control of the level and direction of road investment, together with the influence on rail investment is a very powerful planning tool.

The costs of establishing and maintaining the road system have been dealt with in Chapter 7. So has the problem of how those costs should be shared out. This area of policy-making probably has a smaller impact upon the allocation of traffic than others. There are so many factors entering into the choice of transport mode besides that of operating costs (only a proportion of which is affected) that a basic misallocation of resources has yet to be demonstrated—at least between the main competing forms of inter-urban transport.

Probably much more important than road taxation as a means of influencing resource allocation is that of establishing the organisational framework within which the competing modes operate. There are two sets of relationships here: firstly the extent to which the railway system is organisationally linked to other transport undertakings and, secondly, the 'rules of the game' governing the way in which the struggle with other modes is conducted.

In the first respect, the railways have, during the past twenty years, passed through several distinct phases. There was first of all the brief period of the British Transport Commission as established by the 1947 Act, in which the Railway Executive was a subsidiary body to the B.T.C. The 1953 Act abolished the Railway Executive, the B.T.C. retaining general policy and financial control in theory while delegating the running of the system to Area Boards. In practice far more centralisation was found to be necessary than originally envisaged. Then came the 1962 Act which abolished the Commission and converted British Railways into a 'free-standing' organisation.

The 1968 Act reintroduced a form of organisation based upon the concept of integration*. So far as freight is concerned, publicly owned assets were reorganised and a National Freight Corporation formed.

The National Freight Corporation is a 'free-standing' body directly responsible for the 'integration' of publicly owned freight services. It is responsible for all public-sector freight traffic moving

* A widely accepted definition of 'integration' might be a sufficient degree of organisational fusion to allow traffic/economic decisions to be taken on the basis of what is optimal for the transport system *as a whole* rather than the taking of sub-optimal decisions (though rational for the individual undertakings) by isolated, fragmented units.

wholly by road or partly by rail, leaving the British Railways Board responsible for traffic (mainly bulk freight) moving solely by rail*.

This form of organisation, it has been argued[4], will ensure that integration of freight traffic movement will be concentrated on the areas where it is most productive: mass movement of containers and 'small' consignments ('parcels' and 'sundries' which have to be grouped to form wagon-loads).

What does integration seek to achieve? The technical and operational development of long-distance freight transport compels operators to stop viewing road and rail services as separate, competitive elements. The logic of using containers, for one thing, insists that many long-distance transits be regarded as an integral whole, with rail 'trunking' and road 'shunting'. Moreover, before the economies thought to exist by moving large, regular flows of traffic by rail can be realised, that traffic must be collected and grouped; and this is no small organisational task.

If traffic is not thus grouped by some organisation possessing a bird's-eye view of the total freight market, the economies of mass movement by rail cannot be reaped; quality of service may remain at a low level; charges will reflect low utilisation of equipment; traffic suited to rail may thus be lost to its 'small unit' competitor, road haulage. Integration is seen as a means of breaking out of this vicious circle. Indeed, so powerful is its logic that, in countries where there are institutional barriers to road/rail integration, third parties such as the forwarding agent have arisen to span the gulf. The forwarding agent, in effect, carries out the role assigned to the N.F.C.

In pursuance of this kind of objective, the N.F.C. has taken over from the former Transport Holding Company all its specialist and general road haulage services and shipping. It has taken over from B.R.B. the freightliner services and road cartage services. A freightliner company, subsidiary to the N.F.C., now has commercial responsibility for the marketing and management of freightliner services (B.R.B. have a substantial minority shareholding in this company).

The N.F.C. have commercial freedom in determining their

_____

* There is also a substantial amount of traffic moving in wagon-loads for which the N.F.C. acts as an agent providing road collection and delivery services for the British Railways Board.

4. See: MINISTRY OF TRANSPORT, *Transport of Freight* (Cmnd. 3470), H.M.S.O., London (1967).

charging policy and a financial duty of at least breaking even, taking one year with another. There will be a specific, but tapering subsidy, in respect of the present large loss on railway 'sundries'.

Such is the theory. That theory has been successfully carried into practice in other parts of the world. There is, however, one crucial requirement: long-distance rail freight services really have to be competitive with other modes of transport in respect of cost and quality of service for trunk haulage.

Can 'competitive' be defined with analytical rigour? The case for investing in a new freightliner service rests on the extent to which the freightliner long-run average cost curve falls below the corresponding road haulage average cost curve. An investment analysis must also indicate the volume of traffic required to reach the lowest point on the L.R.A.C. curve (as with electric power generation we could regard this point as representing L.R.M.C.); if there is a substantial cost advantage to freightliner operation, there will also be a substantial range of volumes of traffic for which the freightliner offers a more competitive service. This range must also be established.

When investment in new freightliner trains or terminals is being considered the question is whether the long-run marginal costs will be low enough to enable a service, fully competitive with road haulage, to be operated. L.R.M.C. must include an appropriate contribution to railway indirect costs, and, on routes where the freightliner service represents a significant proportion of total traffic, to any new capital expenditures required to increase the effective track capacity.

The justification for a new freightliner service must be that it can offer a fully competitive service with road, when assessed on its full long-run marginal costs. It therefore follows that unless these estimates are optimistic the freightliner service should be able to undercut road traffic rates, while still covering full capital charges, and possibly making some true surplus as well.

Recent developments in high-speed data transmission and 'real-time' computing (pioneered in airline seat reservation systems and derived originally from I.C.B.M. 'early warning' systems) have made possible, at least in principle, the *allocation* of traffic on the basis of S.R.M.C.

Short-run marginal costs can vary enormously on a railway and any information system that can help allocate traffic on that basis could have immense importance. In real life, traffic comes in surges, and it is rarely economic to cater for the high peak so that no traffic is ever turned away. Such an instrument, if adapted by the N.F.C., would enable it to operate an integrated system of trains and road vehicles in which containers would be almost instantaneously allocated on the basis of lowest cost, with charging on the basis of long-term cost. In other words, it is possible in principle to overcome the two most serious obstacles to the use of the cost mechanism in allocating traffic: the inability of any rates book to keep up with hourly (or even more rapid) changes in local cost situations and the difficulties of discriminating between consignors by offering some of them low rates to fill up temporary 'spare' capacity. Thus could be achieved the minimum cost allocation of traffic across the system as a whole.

THE REGULATION OF ROAD HAULAGE

The 'rules of the game' within which the road haulage industry operates were radically changed by the 1968 Act. Some of the changes are of great economic interest. Perhaps the most important change is the abolition of the system of carriers' licensing which lasted for more than 35 years. That system has had the dual purpose of giving an element of protection to the railways and of providing some stability (i.e. absence of 'destructive' competition) within road haulage.

The method used was to restrict entry to the industry by means of control exercised by licensing authorities. Essentially, would-be providers of new services had to prove that their services were physically required. It was not enough to offer lower charges, or improved quality of service; it had to be proved that *additional* traffic was available and that any new capacity offered would not drain carryings away from established operators. Naturally enough, operators 'on the inside', together with the railways, were not slow to object when danger was seen to threaten. Over the years, the system tended to become more restrictive with the growth of 'case-law' and the development of a body of specialist consultants and legal experts.

The 1968 Act, in providing for the almost complete abolition of this system, followed the conclusions of the Geddes Committee which concluded that licensing no longer served its original purpose and was in many respects economically wasteful. After all, such licensing had not prevented a continued erosion of railway traffics. There had also been a great 'uncontrolled' growth of road haulage, primarily the so-called own account fleets*. All that licensing did was to fossilise the industry.

An important argument against such abolition was that removal of entry restrictions would allow large numbers of newcomers, lacking even rudimentary technical and costing ability, to do considerable economic harm.

The safety of road users in general might be threatened by the operation of badly maintained vehicles, driven by men weary from many hours at the wheel. Rates might be progressively driven downwards to such a level that operators in general could not recoup their long-run costs as the newcomers desperately tried to stay in business. When they had been squeezed out of business, their place would almost certainly be taken by others of this kind. After all, the basic equipment is but one vehicle, and that may be financed by means of hire purchase.

The system of operators' licensing is intended to deal with such problems and particularly that of safety†. To obtain such a licence (popularly known as a 'quality' licence) applicants must have a 'clean' record and possess 'adequate' maintenance facilities. (Originally, it was also intended that some responsible person within the undertaking would be required to hold a Transport Manager's Licence. The purpose of the latter was to ensure that the responsibility for keeping to the regulations falls clearly upon one person.)

It is difficult to see any rational objection to measures such as this and the tighter control of drivers' hours. Additional costs are imposed upon road haulage, but it is important also to look at the benefits. Quite apart from the social benefits of the legislation, however, it seems likely that initial outlays on improved maintenance facilities will be at least counterbalanced by the economies from more efficient operation and improved vehicle availability. The long-run gains could well be substantial.

Another important set of provisions concerning road haulage were the powers to introduce a system of special authorisations (popularly known as 'quantity' licensing). At the time of writing

---

* Own account ('C' licence under the former system) vehicles are those operated by organisations whose business is not primarily transport. The acquisition of such a licence has been a formality, subject only to safety provisions.

† In addition to the Transport Act, 1968, the Road Safety Act (1967) has brought about important changes such as the introduction of Plating which will work in the same direction. Plating is the recording on a prominent place on the vehicle of its maximum permitted weight. This procedure makes possible a precise check on gross weight and axle loadings. It is carried out in special testing stations.

these provisions were to be revoked but the economic ideas involved are interesting enough to examine.

Special authorisations concerned freight hauls of more than 100 miles or, for certain bulk commodities such as iron ore or coal, transits of any distance⋆. If the railways could demonstrate that they could offer a lower charge and an equivalent quality of service (speed of transit, reliability, freedom from damage, and so on) the licensing authority would have refused the application for a road licence. (It should be noted that own account transport is included in the system; no longer was it a formality to obtain such a licence as it was under the old system.)

It should be emphasised that the background assumption here was that rail freight services would prove to have such competitive strength that they would inevitably win a large slice of tonnage now going long distances by road, without any help from the 'rules of the game'.

Suppose, however, that the background assumption proved to be wrong. In that case, it would have been difficult to use the licensing system described in the Act to syphon traffic on to the railways. The system was flexible enough to allow a movement of traffic in either direction.

Consider how it would have worked. The British Railways Board or the National Freight Corporation (and nobody else) could object to the granting of special authorisations. There would be an examination of each case by the Licensing Authorities— as under the old system. Both sides would state their case at a hearing.

At this hearing the Licensing Authority would have to decide whether overall, in terms of cost, quality of service and other relevant factors, the road haulage applicant could provide as good a service as rail for the goods concerned, looking carefully at the needs of the consignor. Both applicants and objectors would have the right of appeal to the Transport Tribunal.

In considering all this the Licensing Authority would be required to take a wide view. 'Speed', for instance, would be door-to-door transit times and not merely a comparison of railway timetables with trunk road journey times. 'Reliability' would include such factors as the effect upon the consignor should operators fail to deliver the goods on time. 'Cost' would always be, where possible, 'door-to-door' rates, whichever transport mode was considered.

⋆ The system, it should be noted, applies only to traffics carried by road vehicles of more than 16 tons gross weight.

Where no rates were available (i.e. as with own account vehicle operation), the *costs* rather than rates would be taken for comparison.

If the B.R.B. or N.F.C. objected they would have to put forward a full statement of their arguments, including a description of the alternative service offered with charges. At the same time, the licence applicant—the road haulier or own account operator—would put forward his own statement. The Licensing Authority would, therefore, have two sets of arguments in front of him.

When the applicant was a public haulier he would be able to call in support evidence from his customer. An own account operator would be able to produce details of his costs, defined in the widest possible way.

Some special problems of interpretation arose, such as what to do about 'return' loads, Return loads, like outward loads, would have been judged against the statutory criteria. But where a haulier needed to apply for a special authorisation, he would be able to include in the application all the types of journeys, in any direction, that he wanted to be able to do.

Occasionally, the Licensing Authority might have found that the rival claims of road and rail were evenly balanced. If so, he would then have looked at other factors. One was whether any persons for whom the applicant carried goods—or the applicant himself in the case of an own account operator—would have suffered 'substantial detriment' if the application had been refused. For example, if the refusal of part of an applicant's service were to cause serious loss to customers for *other* parts of his service, this would have been taken into account. If, let us say, one loaded working of a multi-leg schedule was at issue, the economics of the entire schedule could be analysed.

What are the positive advantages of such a system for the economy as a whole? Operators are compelled to do some fundamental thinking about the costs of particular operations and traffics. They are required to translate various 'intangible' factors into cold calculations of benefits and costs.

Increasingly, freight transport is regarded as but one part of a much wider process. 'Reliability' may be far more important to the decision-maker than minimisation of transport operating costs in the narrow sense. Here, consciously or not, the manager is 'trading-off' reliability against operating costs: he may decide to 'buy' reliability at the price of higher operating costs; or vice versa. Special authorisations would encourage him to make *explicit* decisions about this instead of, as at present, largely replying upon 'experience and judgement' or doing 'what we have always done'.

With reliability, the relevant question is: what is the cost of *unreliability*? If it is really true that factory production lines may be held up by failure to deliver one part, then the costs of unreliability may be truly astronomical. But astronomical or not, some estimate must be made of them—even if this takes the form of a range. Under the proposed system, it would have been necessary to produce evidence on the probability of such a failure in relation to each mode of transport.

Another method of tackling such a problem may be to assess the need to hold extra stocks, with all that involves in extra warehousing space, etc. In addition to such effects, higher door-to-door transit times may lead to adverse developments on the demand side. It should be possible to make a calculation of these effects, in however broad terms.

A similar approach may be made to damage and pilferage, the servicing of customers (after delivery) and the changed nature of packaging, the exhibition of advertisements, and so on. Susceptibility to damage, in particular, may have an exceptionally important influence on consumer goodwill. Evidence to this effect could have been produced.

Special Authorisations, at the time of writing, were not to be introduced. The problems of the railways and their role in the economy are likely to be with us for some time, however. This kind of economic analysis is therefore likely to retain its relevance.

LONDON TRANSPORT'S PROBLEMS

The London Passenger Transport Board, as it then was, was first established by Parliament in 1933. In return for a monopoly of public passenger transport (other than surface rail transport) in London, the Board was given certain statutory duties of which the main ones were:

1. To provide an 'adequate' service.
2. To 'pay its way'.

Until recently London Transport were able to carry out these obligations in broad terms. Financial buoyancy made possible a great deal of cross-subsidisation within the undertaking. In recent years, however, changes in social habits and the growth of private motoring have reduced the need for public transport, especially for leisure travel.

Urban public transport has competitive disadvantages because:

1. As already noted, the marginal cost of motoring is relatively low and the motorist's conception of M.C., perhaps lower. There is a strong incentive to use private transport once acquired, except for work journeys when congestion is a deterrent.
2. Public transport can rarely offer a door-to-door service, may involve changes and delays and is often less comfortable.

The result has been a dwindling off-peak traffic, whereas peak demand has remained steady or even grown. This divergence has been accentuated by urban centre employment trends and shortening of working hours. These have resulted in more concentrated peaks[5].

At the same time, as in most labour-intensive service industries, costs tend to rise more quickly than costs generally. London Transport have great difficulty manning their services, particularly on the buses. Road congestion adds to the cost of bus operation and makes their services less reliable and attractive. Declining service quality loses passengers; it is possible to talk of a highly elastic demand *in relation to service*.

THE BOARD'S OBJECTIVES

The basic objectives of the London Transport Board are now very difficult to reconcile. What the travelling public regard as 'adequate' service cannot be provided in such a way that a financial deficit is avoided[6].

The interpretation of adequacy has been that of the Board, and the whole pattern of services in the London area was based on their interpretation. As well as reflecting the Board's view of their public

5. The classic analysis of the peak in urban passenger transport may be found in PONSONBY, G. J., 'The Problem of the Peak with Special Reference to Road Passenger Transport', *Economic Journal*, Vol. 68, No. 269, pp. 74–88 (1958).
6. Much of the analysis that follows is based upon MINISTRY OF TRANSPORT, *Transport in London* (Cmnd. 3686), H.M.S.O., London (1968).

responsibility*, such rules are also very much influenced by pressure from the public and trade unions. We have earlier noted the role of Transport Users' Consultative Committees, but less formal indications of public feeling, such as letters of complaint from individuals, have traditionally been taken very seriously by the L.T.B. It is easy to overlook the importance of these elements of pressure in shaping quite important economic decisions.

Minimum standards are principally questioned when there are proposals for new services, or proposals for withdrawal or modification of existing ones. Withdrawals have become more frequent in recent years against a background of falling traffics. Against such a background, standards have had to be somewhat revised. This applies particularly to off-peak and to week-end services.

So far as financial performance has been concerned, it has been the practice to attempt to break even, subject to certain obligations about reserves, taking one year with another. A policy of covering costs on each individual service has not been followed: services have been provided at standard fares that might or might not cover costs in any particular case. In practice, loss-making services regarded as socially necessary have been operated. In addition, specific 'social' services have been provided at a price which did not cover the additional costs incurred, e.g. all-night buses. This interpretation has made it very difficult to adjust services in the conditions now prevalent so as to meet the Board's financial objective of 'paying its way'.

ADEQUACY OF SERVICE

The concept of adequacy is not easy to define. To a considerable degree, the definition may depend upon public opinion: urban travellers accustomed to very frequent services will have different notions from country dwellers used to very infrequent services, though the latter will still be expected to be regular and reliable. Perhaps no community would be willing to pay for a service so adequate that it gave rise to no complaints.

Can one identify the components of an 'adequate' service? The principal elements may be capacity, frequency and distribution over a close enough network. Others may include reliability;

---

* Outside London this role is played by the Traffic Commissioners, who have statutory powers to authorise, or refuse, applications for particular services.

speed; safety (with perhaps expensive safety provisions on rail-ways); comfort (especially in relation to private car competition); and quality of staff (with its influence upon passenger reaction to services). Clearly, some working rules are required to define 'level of service' standards.

For *capacity* the Board may provide*: sufficient to prevent an unduly long waiting time before boarding a vehicle. Peak waiting time, for example, should be not more than ten minutes after first being unable to board a bus (or twice the time-tabled interval on services where the interval is more than ten minutes).

With *frequency* there must be enough journeys to ensure that the 'reasonable' needs of sufficiently large communities are met even though carrying capacity may not be fully used. In areas of low passenger demand, a service designed to produce economic loads may very well be too infrequent to be regarded as reasonable. Less than two buses per hour in the Monday to Friday off-peak periods would normally be considered inadequate. Less frequent services might be tolerable at the week-ends.

As for *distribution*, the service network must be designed to prevent unduly long walks from passengers' origins or destinations, at least in fully built up areas. In practice this means that no large number of potential passengers should be more than about half a mile from public transport.

FINANCIAL VIABILITY

In recent years the Board have sought to raise sufficient revenue (within the constraints of the fares structure) to cover, as far as possible, their costs while losing as few passengers as possible. What revised fares levels should be is a matter for commercial judgement, i.e. what the market will bear. There have also been ministerial interventions to delay proposals for fares increases, the resulting financial loss being made up by the Exchequer.

Where costs per bus mile are high, the main contributing factors are heavy peaking and low speed; and where receipts per bus mile are low, the main factors are heavy peaking and directionally unbalanced traffic. This is of special interest in showing again the problems created by peak-hour services.

* These are rules that have been applied in respect of L.T.B. Central Buses. Different criteria may be applied to other services, but the principles are similar.

The most significant conclusions that may be drawn from recent studies are that:

1. The bulk of the Board's deficit cannot be attributed to particular loss-making services or groups of services; and
2. The major factor underlying the Board's deficit is the imbalance between peak and off-peak services.

THE PROPOSED REDEFINITION OF OBJECTIVES

From this analysis it is clear that the concepts of viability and adequacy of service are irreconcilable in an environment such as that described. Neither is there any apparent means by which the Board can achieve viability without external help.

It has been concluded[7] that changes were needed in the financial and physical framework in which the Board operate. A Joint Inquiry considered it was essential that London Transport should pay their way. 'Firstly, because in a commercial undertaking viability is desirable for management and operating efficiency, and for the morale of the organisation. Secondly, because viability can be precisely and objectively defined. Thirdly, because it is our view that, if defects in the financial framework and competitive position are remedied, and public transport given the benefit of infrastructure grants (which recognise its value to the community as a whole), the revenue cost of the expensive service provision (in fact the peak service) which Londoners expect can, and in general should, be paid for by the passengers[8].'

As for the level of service, the group thought that the 'adequacy' objective might best be expressed as *carrying as many passengers as possible while continuing to provide a network of services and operating within viability*[9].

It was further considered that any transport planning arrangements should provide for joint decision regarding the shape of the network and levels and types of services the Board would provide at break-even fares. Joint decisions could also be made, the group felt, about specific payments (from sources other than fares) for services, concessions for particular classes of people or

7. Ibid. The Report of the Joint Inquiry mentioned is reproduced in this publication.
8. Ibid., para. 43, p. 38 (1968).
9. Ibid., para. 47, p. 39 (1968).

other facilities which cannot be provided within the limits of viability.

Emphasising the need for clearly defined, achievable objectives, there was a case for setting a short-term break-even period fixed by agreement in advance, i.e. something like the 'target' procedure which other nationalised industries have. Such 'targets' should allow the Board to build up reserves in order to run at a loss, for good reason, for a limited period if this were thought desirable.

FARES LEVELS

The level of resources employed in the Board's operations is governed largely by peak needs. The group thought that the right way of paying for the peaks is through revenue from peak-hour fares. This would mean higher fares in the peaks than in the off-peaks, though with the charges so related to one another as to constitute together a realistic fares structure overall. Highly relevant here is the peak pricing analysis of Chapter 5. The group did not think it realistic to continue the close control over London Transport fares by a Tribunal. If there were to be new arrangements for organisation of transport in London, with strong local authority influence, there should be no need for the Tribunal—even as an appeal Tribunal for the general protection of the public against unreasonable fares. During the transition period until competitive conditions had been equalised, however, the Tribunal might remain for this purpose.

The Inquiry into London Transport gives interesting examples of the influence of modern management thinking. For example, it is emphasised that 'defects in the environment' and lack of realistic objectives have made long-term planning difficult. A new emphasis on such planning was required: co-ordinating capital investment, research and development activities, manpower recruitment and training programmes over five to ten years. This would take place within the wider context of a wider planning organisation for London.

Further points were:

1. Quality of information. In various spheres of activity this was found to be inadequate, or of the wrong kind for management decision-taking. Activities where better information was required included:

(a) forecasting to achieve better resource utilisation. There was a tendency to match supply to *past* demand, rather than to act on present or potential demand;

(b) where, when and in what circumstances have losses of passengers occurred in recent years;

(c) the mid- and long-term effects of fares increases on particular classes of traffic, or in particular places;

(d) the nature and size of demand for off-peak services so that adequate policies for off-peak service provision could be formulated.

2. Investment. The Ministry and the Board should work out together the criteria to be applied to new investment and there should be regular reviews of the results of new projects compared with the assumptions made at the time of their original appraisal.

3. Measurement and control of performance. There were two related needs here: criteria for assessing L.T.B.'s overall success in meeting the new conditions; and developing criteria to apply within the Board's operations. As for internal performance criteria, financial control through budgets and a system relating performance to physical standards were required, as were mathematical models representing the various operations. Control traditionally exercised through revenue budgets could be extended to include targets for progressive operational improvement and cost reduction.

4. Research and development. There was scope for more direction and co-ordination of the Board's research and development programme and closer links with planning objectives. Moreover, cost/benefit criteria should be applied and assessed in terms of benefits to other agents (perhaps thus justifying financial assistance).

5. Manpower. Labour productivity was crucially important because staff shortage has been a persistent problem and because of the need to reduce costs. Equipment-replacement programmes should be reviewed to see whether manpower or other savings would justify accelerated replacement. The possibilities of keeping down peak costs by the employment of part-time workers (men and women) ought to be investigated. A smaller and more flexible labour force on the basis

of high productivity and high earnings should be aimed at. Work study methods should be applied in workshops and at stations and the whole management and working structure in mechanical engineering departments reviewed before making any commitment to new methods of payment.

6. Commercial policies. The 1968 Act removes many of the present restrictions on the Board's manufacturing and trading powers. They are enabled to manufacture and sell spare parts for buses and thus obtain higher prices when disposing of second-hand buses. This could be important in future if buses are withdrawn early from service in order to accelerate the reshaping of the bus services. The Board may also be helped in providing more car parks, including multi-storey ones, if they are free to offer ordinary commercial services to motorists as part of the car park facilities.

CHANGES IN THE ORGANISATION OF
PASSENGER TRANSPORT IN LONDON

Change in the organisation of London's passenger transport is intended to help deal with this situation. The Greater London Council assumes a new role; it will become an overall transport planning authority. It assumes policy responsibility for all public transport operated by London Transport in Greater London, and shares a co-ordinating function with the Department of the Environment and British Railways for rail services over a larger area. The Council also has wider highway responsibilities and strengthened powers as a traffic authority.

The Council now has a statutory responsibility to produce integrated transport plans for Greater London, i.e. 'integrated' in the sense that all major investing agents will be brought within the same decision-making framework. The transfer of L.T.B. is perhaps the most significant development involving transfer to a local authority of responsibility for a nationalised enterprise. A new London Transport Executive with a separate statutory existence has been set up. The Executive is vested with the main assets of the former London Transport Board. Members of the Executive (but not their officers and employees) will be appointed by the Council, much as members of a nationalised industry board are appointed by the relevant minister.

The Executive operate their services in accordance with general policies laid down by the Council; in particular, the Council is responsible for approving the Executive's capital and revenue budgets, and for fares policies. It also has certain powers of direction over the Executive, but not in relation to day-to-day management matters. (Once again the parallel with a nationalised industry is apparent.)

There will be more flexibility with the executive's basic operating powers to reflect new circumstances. For example, there is no formal milage or geographical limits to its powers to operate transport services, though they will be controlled in other ways (e.g. by the Traffic Commissioners for bus services outside Greater London).

THE STEEL INDUSTRY

The iron and steel industry has been subjected to a degree of public supervision for some 40 years. This process culminated in the nationalisation measure of 1951, when a large number of separately owned undertakings were brought together. Denationalisation, in the form of the 1953 Iron and Steel Act, retained an element of supervision by a Board appointed by the Minister of Power. The Board were required 'to exercise a general supervision over the iron and steel industry . . . with a view to promoting the efficient, economic and adequate supply under competitive conditions of iron and steel products'[10]. Production capacity, prices, procurement and distribution of raw materials and fuel were matters the Board were required to keep under review, in addition to certain other activities such as safety, health and welfare of employees.

The Board had the power to determine maximum prices, setting 'reasonable delivered prices'. It also had power (subject to ministerial appeal) to control 'substantial' projects, i.e. capacity expansion. There were powers in reserve allowing the Board to arrange import or distribution of raw materials or the import of steel products and to assist research and training. The minister's powers under the 1953 Iron and Steel Act, were very limited.

10. Quoted in MINISTRY OF POWER, *Steel Nationalisation* (Cmnd. 2651), H.M.S.O., London, para. 8, p. 4 (1965).

THE ARGUMENT FOR PUBLIC OWNERSHIP

Why were these arrangements considered to be inadequate and full public ownership[11] necessary?

Firstly, it was argued the powers of the Iron and Steel Board were essentially negative. They could, within limits, prevent action contrary to the 'public interest'; they could not insist on 'positive developments' in the national economic interest which were not also in the interests of commercial individual companies. Such conflicts, it was argued, were in the nature of things and likely to recur so long as the industry was privately owned.

An example was the controversy about the timing and location of new strip mill capacity. Such capacity was only provided with the help of government intervention and large public funds. With an industry of such importance, an investment failing to secure a commercially acceptable rate of return might be justified when the disbenefits imposed upon steel users and the economy in general by failure to invest (e.g. balance of payments effects) were brought into the calculation. State intervention in such situations would result in 'substantial, and perhaps exclusive, privileges to particular private concerns'.

Secondly, difficulties arose with the financing of expansion programmes. Considerable sums of public money were provided for steel companies in the period after the 1953 denationalisation. With technological progress and the growth in size and complexity of units, the already high cost of major projects in the steel industry was expected to increase further. Private investors (i.e. providers of funds) may be unduly cautious when contemplating projects taking many years to construct and commission. Such difficulties may be compounded when, as with the strip mill expansion programme mentioned above, a social cost/benefit calculation suggests provision of additional capacity on a larger scale and rather earlier than could be justified on a strict commercial view.

Thirdly, the provision in 1953 requiring the Board to promote

11. Ibid. Quotations are all from Cmnd. 2651 (1965). *See also*: DE PEYER, C., *Steel: Public Enterprise or Private Ownership?*, Sunday Citizen Pamphlet, London (1964) (Mr de Peyer was formerly in charge of the Iron and Steel Division at the Ministry of Power), and PRYKE, R., *Why Steel?*, Fabian Research, Series 248, London (1965). The reader should acquaint himself with the case against public ownership, although much of the latter material was ephemeral. BRITISH IRON AND STEEL FEDERATION, *Steel—Leave Well Alone*, provides counter arguments.

the efficient, economic and adequate supply *under competitive conditions* of iron and steel products had not been successful. There had been very little domestic competition on price between British steel companies, although it was recognised that the capital-intensive nature of the industry and the effects of cyclical fluctations in demand were influential in encouraging monopolistic practices. The industry had made arrangements to ensure that actual selling prices should be the *maximum* prices fixed by the Board. Furthermore, they defended this policy before the Restrictive Practices Court, which 'found it contrary to the public interest'*. Agreements of that type were abandoned, but 'effective and wide-spread price competition' was slow to emerge. This was, perhaps, hardly surprising: as in most countries, the steel industry tends towards price leadership.

Such monopoly characteristics in a basic industry, it was considered, strengthened the case for public ownership under which 'price policy would be determined and prices fixed with regard only to the public interest'.

The conclusion flowing out of the analysis was that a public corporation should be established, thus nationalising the main part of the industry. The residual private sector is particularly important in specialist finishing operations on the borderline between the steel and engineering industries. The controls hitherto operated by the Iron and Steel Board were abolished. The government holds in reserve powers to control private development projects in iron- and steel-making alone.

The specific duties of the corporation are to:

1. Promote the efficient and economic supply of iron and steel products in such quantities and at such prices as may seem to them best calculated to meet the reasonable demands of consumers and to further the public interest.
2. Avoid, and ensure that the nationalised companies avoid, undue preference or unfair discrimination between customers but without prejudice to such variations in the terms and conditions on which their iron and steel products are supplied as may arise from ordinary commercial considerations or from the public interest.
3. Promote the safety, health and welfare of their employees and the employees of the nationalised companies, and consult

* In a judgement dated 22 June 1964.

with appropriate organisations about the establishment of machinery for negotiation and joint consultation.

4. Promote the export of iron and steel products and any other products they or the nationalised companies produce.

5. Promote research and development in iron and steel activities and in any other activities which they or a nationalised company carry on[12].

The corporation has to ensure that the industry's revenues are not less than sufficient to meet outgoings properly chargeable to revenue account, taking one year with another, and to establish and maintain a general reserve.

The nationalisation measure provided for the establishment of a Consumers' Council and consumers will be further protected by the specific duties to be imposed on the corporation.

The statutory framework is therefore traditional. Can one supplement the Act by asking what objectives were expected to be achieved from the new arrangements?

OBJECTIVES OF THE NEW ARRANGEMENTS

These largely follow from the analysis of the private industry's deficiencies. Central planning of investment programmes has been introduced. Project decisions will be taken on the basis of economic analysis of what is best for the national economy. Central planning in the public sector will make it possible to concentrate production in the lowest-cost location, achieving scale economies in the process. Marketing for the public sector as a whole and not merely for individual units will help eliminate cross-hauls and improve the industry's service to consumers generally by integrating marketing with production. The improvement in competitive efficiency due to public ownership will assist exports and contribute to those of the engineering and other steel-using industries. Common ownership of the main productive units can help concentrate export steel making on works best placed to meet overseas requirement. The need to develop exports will be taken into account in siting decisions.

To achieve such objectives basic rationalisation of the structure of the industry is required. The finances of the main part of the

12. MINISTRY OF POWER, op. cit., para. 30, pp. 11–12.

industry, could be dealt with as a whole. Central services, particularly in the fields of raw materials and research, could also be improved once the limits of individual company ownership were transcended.

Could such changes have come about as the result of private mergers? This, it was argued, was most unlikely. In any event, there would be strong objections to such a concentration of power in private hands. Furthermore, nationalisation could provide new opportunities for increasing co-operation between management and the trade unions in the sphere of man-power use and the tackling of the human problems resulting from structural and technological changes.

This legislation offers the most recent example of the nationalisation process and it is interesting to look at the principles governing the payment of compensation to shareholders.

COMPENSATION

Compensation was 'paid' in the form of Government Stock which, in the opinion of the Treasury, was currently equal to the valuation of the securities.

This valuation was done as follows. For quoted Stock Exchange securities an average of quotations over an appropriate period was taken. This was held to reflect the stock market's view of the industry's commercial and political prospects. The period selected was October 1959 to October 1964 (inclusive). This included the various phases of the trade cycle and thus capacity utilisation. It was also presumed to reflect movements of opinion about the prospects of renationalisation. As some securities made a better showing towards the end of the period, the period May to October 1964 was taken if it gave a higher valuation.

POWERS OF THE NATIONALISED INDUSTRY

While a company structure has been retained, the powers of the nationalised companies will in general be those in their memoranda of association.

The nationalised steel industry will be able to diversify its activities when this appears commercially advantageous. Diversification is a common practice among private companies, and was discussed in Chapter 3. Such diversification moves would require government consent.

Such are the objectives of public ownership. Whether the objectives are secured or not is a matter for the facts and it is, perhaps, too early to draw any conclusions yet.

THE POST OFFICE

The Post Office[13] is, broadly speaking, a commercial enterprise covering the cost of its services by pricing. In form, the Post Office has been part of a government department and not a nationalised industry. In common with other public enterprises its financial affairs have been conducted in accordance with the principles set out in Cmnd. 1337 (see Chapter 9)[14].

The conclusion was drawn that the form should be changed to correspond to that of a public corporation, with members appointed by and responsible to a minister. Within this corporation the various services now have an opportunity to develop on more independent lines than would be possible in an organisation controlled directly by the government.

Evolution had been tending in this direction for some years. In the past, a contribution to the Exchequer was theoretically fixed but, in practice, all revenue was paid into the Exchequer and all expenditure voted by Parliament. Greater freedom was permitted (by the Post Office Act 1961) when a separate Post Office Fund was set up. Practically all receipts and payments were made into and out of this. The Post Office ceased to present annual estimates to Parliament and its provisions disappeared from the Budget.

Important issues arise, as with London Transport, about service standards, e.g. with postal services, letter box collection times, the number and timing of deliveries and time taken in delivering mail. In particular, should there be reduced standards of service in an attempt to keep prices down, or higher charges to maintain a high standard of service? These issues are complicated by the existence of high peaks of demand for the use of postal services.

13. SELECT COMMITTEE ON NATIONALISED INDUSTRIES, *The Post Office*, Vol. I, H.M.S.O., London (1967).
14. CHANCELLOR OF THE EXCHEQUER, *The Financial and Economic Obligations of the Nationalised Industries* (Cmnd. 1337), H.M.S.O., London (1961).

THE PRICING OF POSTAL SERVICES[15]

Let us begin with the parcel service. This is different from the rest of the postal service in that the Post Office has no monopoly. The demand for parcel traffic is relatively elastic in regard to both price and service quality. Here, charging policy would appear to depend, to a large extent, on what the market will bear, subject to covering escapable costs.

With letter mails, there is more scope for experiment. The traditional uniform basis of charging by weight may thus be rethought. One departure has been the 'two-tier' service under which charges are based on speed of service rather than on the contents of packets.

A 'two-tier' system introduces a flexibility into the postal charging structure. The two streams of mail may be clearly distinguished on the demand side by the sender and on the supply side by the handling practice of the Post Office. It should, therefore, appear to be relatively simple to widen the differential charge between the two types of mail service if thought desirable. It would be possible to raise either the higher or lower charge, or both. The faster service could be charged for according to its value to the sender; the slower according to handling costs.

Traditionally, there has been substantial cross-subsidisation over the Post Office's different services. The first-class letter service, for example, has generated sufficient profit to support the other mail services. (Telecommunication services have also been profitable.) On account of this, a common policy in the past has been to increase the first-class letter charge whenever the service as a whole has run into deficit. This has often been done regardless of the situation in that specific market.

It is not clear that there is a strong case for much of this cross-subsidisation. The parcel service, for example, is an area where it would be inaccurate to equate unremunerative services with social obligations. The service is predominantly used for commercial purposes (e.g. mail order), and commercial road and rail services compete with those of the Post Office.

Attempted cross-subsidisation has led to financial deficits. Accumulated deficits on postal services have increased the borrowing requirements, and thus interest charges. This in turn has led to

15. NATIONAL BOARD FOR PRICES AND INCOMES, *Post Office Charges* (Cmnd. 3574), H.M.S.O., London (1968).

the need for further revenues. The results of all this have been that the Post Office as a whole has found it difficult to achieve their financial objectives.

It will be very interesting to observe what use the Post Office will make of its newly found flexibility.

9

PUBLIC ENTERPRISE AND THE STATE: 2

What should be the purpose of government control of public enterprises? To a considerable extent, the answers one gives to this question will depend upon what one considers the purpose of public enterprises to be. Let us suppose that the following purposes are accepted:

1. To carry out certain social obligations/objectives.
2. To act as a social and economic showcase and/or stimulator of other sectors.
3. To secure the greatest possible degree of 'accountability' to the 'shareholders', i.e. the general public.
4. To ensure maximum possible managerial efficiency.
5. To attain maximum possible economic efficiency.

We have dealt with (1) in the preceding chapter. A conclusion reached was that, in order to avoid conflict with other purposes, it is necessary for such social obligations to be defined carefully and decisions about their scale and incidence to be made, and financed, by the government.

With railways, the introduction of such specific compensation has been noted (Chapter 6). Social obligations of various kinds have, however, been carried by other nationalised industries such as electricity generation and distribution. The nuclear power investment programme (Chapter 5) has, to a considerable extent, been financed by consumers of electricity; the cost differences between nuclear and comparable alternative conventional power stations that would have been installed by the C.E.G.B., if the Board had been simply minimising long-run costs, have been made up out of general electricity prices. So has the Board's contribution to atomic power research and development expenditure. Purchasing policy in the form of priority to British equipment has been intended to help the manufacturing industry. Rural electrification is an example of an activity carried on for purely social reasons; there has been no subsidy from public authorities to cover these costs. There have been different phases of government policy in regard to conversion of stations from coal to oil and vice versa, which have had nothing to do with the minimisation of generation costs.

From the point of view of strategic control, it is desirable that all these 'social' activities should be isolated, costed and specifically treated.

Much of (2) could be carried out without detriment to the other purposes. An enlightened labour relations policy or the enforcement (by the statutory Fair Wages Clause) of minimum rights and conditions for employees in organisations from whom supplies are purchased, could have beneficial effects on (5). Equally, this purpose could well turn out to have a considerable overlap with, if not be identical to (4).

(3) is attempted by such devices as Consumer Councils and Select Committees of Parliament. The problem here is how to allow public pressure to have an important influence upon the practices of nationalised industries without hampering day-to-day management. This problem is still unresolved and we cannot go into it here.

That bring us to (4) and (5). By managerial efficiency we mean the relationship between resources used and quantity (and quality) of output produced. By economic efficiency, we mean the allocative issues discussed in Chapters 1 and 2, though the systematic application of investment appraisal techniques will have a strong influence on managerial efficiency. The management techniques of Chapter 3 were concerned to a considerable degree with managerial efficiency, though they have long-run allocative implications also. Reorganisations of the kind discussed in the previous chapter may have as their rationale increases in both these kinds of efficiency. The introduction of a 'competitive' rather than a 'monopolistic' framework may, for instance, be advocated as a method for stimulating efficiency, of both kinds, from outside. The setting of a financial target might be regarded as an attempt to secure managerial efficiency. Where the financial calculation is complicated by the existence of 'non-commercial' factors, managerial efficiency may be measured by productivity comparisons. For instance, the rate of increase of productivity in specific public sectors may be compared with those in comparable private firms or industries. The evidence to date indicates an impressive performance by most public enterprises[1].

The advocacy of a general pricing rule might be regarded as being primarily aimed at improving allocative efficiency. Have there been examples of broad pricing rules (e.g. marginal cost pricing) being advocated even though a financial loss might ensue? A National Board for Prices and Incomes study of the Orkney and Shetland Islands' transport links to the mainland of Scotland offers an excellent case study[1a].

Operating costs of the shipping services are continually increasing but there seems to be little scope for substantial cost savings. The price structure is, to a large extent, based upon charging 'what the traffic will bear', i.e. it attempts to charge as much as possible without 'killing' or 'driving away' the traffic.

Obviously, the exact level of price will depend upon the relevant demand elasticities. This is a type of profit maximisation though, paradoxically perhaps, it has often been justified in the name of equity, and systems of charging control by quasi-judicial bodies (as with railways and the Transport Tribunal) have been based upon the system.

In the view of the National Board for Prices and Incomes, freight charges should be related to loading and unloading costs as well as space required, and both passenger fares and freight charges should reflect seasonal and directional patterns of cost.

Such changes, the Board felt, 'would facilitate the adaptation of the economic activity of the islands to changes in the real costs of its shipping services and, at the same time, make for greater economic efficiency in the operation of the company's services by providing an incentive to utilising the carrying capacity as fully as possible'[1b]. Adoption of the policy, however, would lead to a financial deficit.

1. PRYKE, R., 'Are Nationalised Industries Becoming More Efficient?', *Moorgate and Wall Street*, pp. 55–72 (Spring 1970).
1a. NATIONAL BOARD FOR PRICES AND INCOMES, *Passenger Fares and Freight Charges of the North of Scotland, Orkney & Shetland Shipping Co. Ltd.*, Report 67 (Cmnd. 3631), H.M.S.O., London (1968).
1b. Ibid.

How would the deficit be made up? The local authorities should contract with the shipping company to provide the service and make up the difference between the revenue from the revised pricing system and the full revenue needed to operate the service and provide the company with a 'reasonable' profit. The finance should be drawn from the rates. Revenue would then be a mixture of collective payments by the islanders and charges to individual users. The collective payment element would be justified by the communal need for such a service.

One question it will be necessary to weigh up is the relative gains from stimulating each kind of efficiency. An organisation that is highly inefficient from the managerial point of view might fulfil the marginal conditions with great subtlety; society might gain substantially, if it was compelled to make the choice, by opting for managerial efficiency at the price of some resource misallocation; and, conceivably, vice versa.

FINANCIAL AND ECONOMIC GUIDELINES

Several kinds of guideline[2] can be employed to steer nationalised industries in the desired direction. These guidelines determine prices charged and, hence, the volume of goods or services sold. They therefore influence to a great extent the amount of new productive investment and thus the scale of the undertaking. The relationship of prices to costs also determines the net revenue surplus generated and the ability to provide internal finance.

Such guidelines can be expressed in a number of different ways. Emphasis can be placed on the financial *end result* to be achieved either annually or over a period. This can be expressed as a target rate of return on capital, or in other ways.

Alternatively, pricing or investment *criteria* could be formally or informally prescribed. More rigidly, industries could be subjected to specific constraints regarding prices or investment decisions, directly determined by ministers. Or direct controls

2. *See*: SELECT COMMITTEE ON NATIONALISED INDUSTRIES, *Ministerial Control of the Nationalised Industries*, H.M.S.O., London (1968), particularly Chs V and VI. Vol. III, Appendices and Index, contains a number of very useful papers. The government's response to this report is contained in *Ministerial Control of the Nationalised Industries* (Cmnd. 4027), H.M.S.O., London. *See also*: FOSTER, C. D., *Politics, Finance and the Role of Economics*, Allen & Unwin, London (1971).

could be placed on decisions affecting the costs of the industry, e.g. wage rates or purchasing practices. These methods, of course, are not mutually exclusive. An industry could be required to follow certain rules of pricing and investment, which would result in a certain financial objective, while subject to a variety of specific constraints on its activities.

As we have noted, most of the nationalisation statutes required 'not less than sufficient' revenue to be raised so that, 'taking one year with another', 'all items properly chargeable to revenue including interest, depreciation, the redemption of capital and the provision of reserves' could be met. The phrase 'not less than' implied a minimum acceptable performance and not a maximum. It was, however, generally accepted that nationalised industries should merely be expected to 'pay their way' and not try to generate, at least regularly, large financial surpluses.

This has been the only statutory economic guidance that public enterprises have received. In particular, there is no statutory definition of 'proper provision for the depreciation and renewal of assets' or what are 'proper allocations to general reserve'. A variety of different pricing and investment policies may be legally compatible with the wording of the nationalisation Acts. There is, moreover, no indication of the extent to which capital investment should be financed from accumulated surpluses.

In the absence of fuller economic guidance, different boards pursued different policies. Some aimed simply to pay their way; others aimed to secure surpluses. There seemed to be no generally adopted policy.

The White Paper of 1961[3] embodied the results of a basic re-thinking of nationalised industries policy by the government on the subject of financial and economic obligations.

It was accepted that many of the nationalised industries operated in spheres where a low return on capital was traditional. This was partly because of the absence of risk and partly because of public regulation owing to the monopoly advantages supposedly enjoyed. Moreover, the public expected the products and services of nationalised industries to be provided cheaply, and the boards were subject to continuous pressure to keep prices down. Their financial performance was thus bound to suffer.

The existence of onerous national and non-commercial obligations was also noted. Recognised also was the boards' inability, for

3. CHANCELLOR OF THE EXCHEQUER, *The Financial and Economic Obligations of the Nationalised Industries* (Cmnd. 1337), H.M.S.O., London (1961).

a variety of reasons, to adjust their expenditures as rapidly to economic conditions as other industries. The White Paper considered that if investments were assessed on different (and easier) financial criteria from those used elsewhere, there was a risk of too much capital development in the nationalised industries. Also, if the prices of the goods and services were uneconomically low, demand (and, consequently, investment) might be artificially stimulated. Such phenomena would result either in higher taxation or greater Exchequer borrowing.

The following reforms were therefore introduced.

THE REVENUE ACCOUNT

Financial provisions of the respective Statutes should henceforth be generally interpreted as follows:

1. Surpluses on Revenue Account should be at least sufficient to cover deficits on Revenue Account *over a 5-year period*; in arriving at the surpluses and deficits for each year there should be charged against revenue the items normally so chargeable (including interest, and depreciation on the historic cost basis).

2. Provision should also be made from revenue for:
   (a) Such an amount as may be necessary to cover the excess of depreciation calculated on replacement cost basis over depreciation calculated on historic costs as in (1) above.
   (b) Adequate allocations to general reserves which will be available *inter alia* as a contribution towards their capital development and as a safeguard against premature obsolescence and similar contingencies[4].

It was thought that, in general, anything more than a five-year balancing period would be too long. The undertakings would not be required, however, to make up any under-provision (i.e. on account of the difference between the historic cost basis and the replacement cost basis) which had already occurred.

Experience had shown, it was felt, a general need for nationalised industries to build up 'adequate' reserves to deal with contingencies. In addition, there were '. . . powerful grounds in the national interest for requiring these undertakings to make a substantial contribution towards the cost of their capital development out of

4. Ibid., para 19, p. 7.

their own earnings, and so reduce their claims upon the nation's savings and the burden on the Exchequer: this is particularly so for those undertakings which are expanding fast and which have relatively large capital needs'[5].

The objective for each undertaking would be determined in the light of its own circumstances, needs and capabilities in relation to the criteria outlined above.

CAPITAL ACCOUNT

Existing procedures for discussion and authorisation of investment and borrowing were tidied up as follows:

1. The government will each year discuss with the undertaking and approve the general lines of its plans for development and capital expenditure for the next five years ahead and be ready to agree to long-term commitments as appropriate.
2. In the light of (1), the government will each year fix an upper limit on the amounts to be spent on investment by the undertaking during the two years ahead.
3. The government will approve proposed borrowings on the basis of an annual reasoned estimate submitted by the undertaking.
4. The government will require to be kept informed of the extent to which the undertaking is proposing to invest new capital in projects which are expected to yield a relatively low return[6].

While accepting that there was an argument in favour of nationalised bodies raising money from the market on their own credit, it was felt that the amounts of money needed were too large to make this feasible. This could only be considered after an improvement in the financial record.

PRICES AND COSTS

As for pricing policy, '. . . while recognising the case for greater freedom and flexibility . . .' it was necessary for the government to

5. Ibid., para 22, p. 8.
6. Ibid., para 24, p. 8.

continue to '. . . interest themselves in the prices of these goods and services which are basic to the life of the community and some of which contain a monopolistic element'[7].

It was accepted that costs might be 'significantly affected' by commercially unprofitable activities undertaken on account of public obligations. The method of dealing with these was, 'so far as practicable', to take them '. . . into account in fixing the financial standard for each undertaking. To the extent that commercially unprofitable activities are subsequently imposed from outside, a board would be entitled to ask for an adjustment of its financial objectives.'[8]

It was concluded that nationalised industries could not '. . . be judged mainly on their commercial results: all have, although in varying degrees, wider obligations than commercial concerns in the private sector. The object of these proposals is to find for each industry or board a reasonable balance between these two concepts. The government believe that the closer definition now proposed for the financial and economic obligations of the industries should help improve their performance and morale. It should also reduce the occasion and need for outside intervention in the affairs of the industries and enable them to make the maximum contribution towards their own development and the well-being of the community as a whole.'[9]

Some much-needed precision was therefore injected into the activities of the nationalised industries. Perhaps the two most important developments were (i) the move towards the doctrine that compensation for activities carried out in 'the national interest' or as part of social obligation should be provided and (ii) the system of financial 'targetry'.

The existence of a financial performance test, it could be claimed, would be a strong pressure towards managerial efficiency. Furthermore, as pointed out earlier, such financial targets deal only with desired end results. In principle, they do not infringe the freedom of public enterprise management to decide *how* to achieve the targets. Another important advantage is that the targets provide a simple, easily understood test against which industry's performance can be measured.

The financial performance of nationalised industries since the 1961 White Paper has shown a significant increase in the overall

7. Ibid., para 31, p. 10.
8. Ibid., para 32, p. 10.
9. Ibid., para 33, p. 10.

rate of return on capital. In several industries, moreover, a greater contribution towards financing investment has been made from internal resources.

An important difficulty, though, is that there are ambiguities in the concept of a financial target. For example, the air corporations and the railways possess little or no control over their prices. Financial objectives might provide some incentive to reduce costs, but their main function would be as measures of performance based on what such enterprises could expect to achieve. Targets could not effectively serve as instruments of ministerial control. 'Control' would primarily be exercised by market forces.

For other industries a financial target may be an effective instrument of control. This applies particularly to industries which are, to some extent, able to determine their own prices. With electricity for instance, a financial target, indicating precisely what kind of surplus should be earned, clearly conditions overall pricing policy. Vary the objective, and the policies of the industry also have to be varied.

Is it a bad thing that a concentration upon end results should give little guidance on how such results are to be achieved? The answer might be 'yes', particularly in regard to pricing and investment policy. Industries with considerable unexploited monopoly power can achieve their financial targets simply by raising prices, as opposed to reducing costs or improving resource use. A large amount of cross-subsidisation might be continued. There is no guidance about pricing in such situations as when there is spare capacity in the short run. Prices based (e.g.) on average costs, set so as to achieve a financial surplus, can lead either to excess demand or to failure to exploit resources to the full.

Financial targets also give inadequate guidance on investment policies. An overall surplus or a return on *total* net assets gives no quantitative indication of the return that *new* assets should earn. It has been argued that this could have some odd results. Suppose, for example, that a target rate of return was being exceeded because past investment had been so successful. In that case, an investment with a low or even negative return might be welcome to the management simply because it would help adjust the industries' actual return *downward* in the direction of the target. Commentary here is superfluous.

Another point is that it is difficult to see how an investment discount rate can be derived from an average rate of return on capital. A marginal rate of return on capital is required. (Assuming that, in line with current policy trends, it is desired to reflect the opportunity cost of capital.) The discount rate applicable to new investment has to be determined separately from the average rate of return flowing from *all* assets in the industry, ancient and modern. Such an overall return in any one year may have no relationship whatever to the lifetime return on any specific investment project.

THE 1967 WHITE PAPER

This White Paper[10] changes the relative emphasis between control by end results in the form of targets as opposed to the setting of pricing policies and investment criteria. These are methods of achieving desired results and not ends in themselves.

Financial objectives, it is argued, are 'economically justifiable' only to the extent that they reflect sound investment and pricing policies. If the right pricing and investment policies are used, the right economic results will be achieved. The financial expression of these will be reflected in the financial objective. In a sense, the White Paper clearly separates the economic and financial aspects of the industries' obligations for the first time.

Less emphasis is placed on how investment should be financed, e.g. to what extent should enterprises earn a surplus to finance part of new investment, thus reducing borrowing? We return to the rationale of marginal cost pricing and to practical arguments of implementation. Marginal cost pricing, in the White Paper, is based upon long-run marginal costs (which include provision for replacement of fixed assets, together with a 'satisfactory' rate of return on capital). Capital is supplied to all public enterprises at the same economic price, i.e. the same discount rate is used in investment decision-making. Complications are admitted. For example, social costs and benefits must be brought into account.

The laying down of broad pricing and investment policies adds up to a new emphasis on *strategic* control. There should consequently be less need for ministers to exercise *ad hoc tactical* control. The enterprises themselves will implement the policies. The flow of detailed communication from enterprises to government departments should diminish.

The White Paper summarises all this as follows: 'It is therefore

10. CHANCELLOR OF THE EXCHEQUER, *Nationalised Industries: a Review of Economic and Financial Objectives* (Cmnd. 3437), H.M.S.O., London (1967).

important that, while covering accounting costs wherever possible, pricing policies should be devised with reference to the costs of the particular goods and services provided. Unless this is done, there is a risk of undesirable cross-subsidisation and consequent mis-allocation of resources. The aim of pricing policy should be that the consumer should pay the true costs of providing the goods and services he consumes [11]. Prices therefore needed to be "reasonably related" to costs at the margin. Sometimes, as where there is spare capacity, short-run marginal costs may be relevant. But the main consideration is the long-run cost of supplying additional output on a continuing basis, i.e. the long-run marginal costs.'[12]

There is much scope for controversy about the measurement and significance of marginal costs and how prices should normally 'be related to', 'reflect', 'be based on' or 'be equated with' short-run or long-run marginal costs. 'Pricing policies' are perhaps too complex to be codified in terms of a simple criterion, such as 'long-run marginal costs'. It is not an easy task to express a pricing policy in one simple rule as was demonstrated in Chapter 1.

There is, for example, the possibility of variations in price to meet short-run demand variation clashing with long-run pricing and financial objectives. This problem was not dealt with in the 1961 White Paper, although the 1967 White Paper recognises the existence of the problem.

THE TEST RATE OF DISCOUNT

The test rate of discount is, of course, not at all the same thing as a financial target. Such targets, expressed as returns on net assets, relate to all investment, past and present, and they vary from industry to industry. The test rate of discount applies to *new* investment only. A common public sector rate is adopted, as outlined in Chapter 2. We also noted that discount rate is not the same as the rate of interest paid on capital borrowings. Furthermore, we noted all the difficulties associated with the forecasting of benefits and costs, the assessment of risk and so on.

Here we come to a crucially important issue. There are three possible 'levers' of economic control: pricing policies, investment criteria and financial targets. These levers are closely interrelated.

11. Ibid., para 18, p. 8.
12. Ibid., para 21, p. 9.

Any one of them could be given priority with the remaining ones thus being determined. Until recently, the practice has been to give priority to the financial target so that pricing and investment policies had to be geared so that the targets were achieved.

It is possible to lay down two of these criteria independently; together they would determine the remaining one. A test discount rate for investment and a specific financial target would together determine the prices necessary to achieve these ends. On the other hand, a particular pricing policy plus a particular discount rate must lead to a certain financial result. This end result will become the financial 'target'. The target would thus not be a target at all but a residuum.

Problems arise in real life where criteria such as these can give little help. In particular, there is nothing in the long-run marginal cost pricing rule to indicate the appropriate rate of adjustment of prices to *changes* in costs. In making such adjustments, the effect on the financial surplus would probably have to be considered. The existence of a financial target might thus influence short-run prices 'although in the long-run you would want to be guided by the movement of long-run marginal costs'. Financial targets could also make enterprises 'a little bit keener . . . to get down to a level of costs which achieve the surplus set'. There is, therefore, 'an element of play in the three factors, and it would be a mistake to regard any two of them as sufficient for present purposes'[13].

What would government policy be if confronted with the possible choice between a marginal cost pricing policy with adverse financial results in the short run, or a policy of covering total costs that included the abandonment of M.C. pricing? As pointed out in Chapter 4, such a dilemma exists in the gas industry, where long-run marginal costs may for some time fall below the level of average costs.

It has been argued in transport because of competition 'a pragmatic rather than a theoretical approach to pricing policies is . . . often dictated by circumstance'. With this qualification, the (then) Ministry of Transport encourages public enterprises to price 'on a basis which has close regard to the full long-run cost of the provision of the services which they offer'[14].

On account of railway financial deficits 'a pragmatic pricing policy' had been adopted, i.e. charging what the market would bear, rather than one based on marginal costs. 'Marginal cost

13. *See*: SELECT COMMITTEE ON NATIONALISED INDUSTRIES, op. cit., para 224, p. 53.
14. Ibid., para 230, p. 55.

pricing might result in pricing a service out of the market; regard had to be paid to competition. With these qualifications, however, the concept of making prices proportional to marginal costs was meaningful and could help an industry to clarify its objectives.'[15]

It has been pointed out that the policies laid down in the 1967 White Paper are not as clear as they might be[16]. It is not, for instance, clear to what extent the Treasury will accept marginal cost pricing where such a policy is incompatible with a financial target or, at least, the covering of accounting costs. Here we may refer back to quotations made earlier to the effect that 'nationalised industries' revenues should normally cover their accounting costs in full' but also engage in marginal cost pricing.

If a policy of directly relating prices to marginal costs was adopted, prices would no longer be so directly controlled by ministers but would be much more influenced by industries' actual costs. Whatever the detailed effects upon prices, the scope for ministerial management of the economy by manipulating nationalised industry prices would be reduced.

It would probably be unrealistic, therefore, not to expect ministers to depart from the use of pricing rules for wider policy reasons. They might wish, for example, to limit (or prohibit) price increases in the interests of a prices and incomes policy. Similarly, there may be specific interventions based upon the supposed macro-economic effects of different financial policies. Moreover, we must keep in mind some of the other possible reasons discussed earlier in the book: social, financial, balance of payments, and so on.

For reasons such as these, public policy may depart from marginal cost pricing policies in the strict sense. In line with recent economic thinking, there would be wide agreement about the proposition that such intervention, for non-allocative reasons (which is *not* to say that it is unjustified) must be fully attributed to the Minister concerned.

The test discount rate may be changed under various circumstances. If the comparable rate employed in the non-public sector diverges markedly with that required of public enterprise, the public sector rate should be reconsidered so as to avoid a misallocation of resources. On the other hand, taxation variations could be used to bring private industry into line with the public sector. There is a particularly strong case for raising the test discount rate where there are prospects of a long-term shortage of capital

15. Ibid., para 231, p. 55.
16. Ibid., para 232, p. 55.

or pressure on resources. Similarly it might be lowered in opposite circumstances (although the changed circumstances would probably also affect the return on marginal capital in the private sector).

Adjustment to the test discount rate would not appear to be a suitable weapon for exercising short-term control over nationalised industry investment. It can only influence long-term investment, and the effects would thus probably be experienced when they were no longer wanted. It could also have adverse long-run effects, e.g. perhaps introducing a bias towards labour-intensive projects.

Neither actual investment nor the volume of Exchequer lending to public enterprises is controlled by the government in the same way as 'ordinary' public expenditure. The Treasury have apparently rejected the idea of setting an annual limit on the total of Exchequer borrowing available for all the nationalised industries. Such an idea would be inconsistent with the commercial nature of the industries. Instead public enterprises are allowed to spend, and borrow from ministers, the capital required to provide equipment and services to meet demand created at current charges. The test of whether this investment is needed depends upon the economic return it can generate.

Two departures from these principles are recognised. The first is that some investment projects, incapable of passing the test discount rate test, may yet be permitted if they can be justified by the inclusion of further social costs and benefits involved. We have seen, in Chapter 7, that this is already done with certain kinds of project, although there arises a 'rate of exchange' problem.

Public policy, it is clear, is becoming increasingly influenced by economic thinking. The contents of the last two chapters have made that clear. Further progress will almost certainly be made in the future. One may note, for example, the idea that public sector investment cuts should primarily be made by Nationalised Industry Boards themselves. This could be done within allotted totals with perhaps a hypothetical adjustment to the test discount rate applied to marginal projects to indicate the total cuts required from each industry. On the other hand, it could be carried out according to some rationing system based on investment analysis. The necessary cuts made up to required totals could then simply be reported to ministers for information[17].

The Select Committee were convinced that adoption of the economic framework outlined in the 1967 White Paper and advocated in their Report would enable ministers to concentrate on

17. Ibid., para 274, p. 66.

PUBLIC ENTERPRISE AND THE STATE: 2

a proper exercise of broad strategic and policy control, and leave the boards more managerial freedom. But, they held, this would depend upon clarity of purposes, policies and responsibilities.

CONCLUSIONS

What conclusions can we draw from this discussion? First of all, we may note the broad agreement that 'control' exerted by the government should be strategic and not tactical in nature. It should not, for example, be the business of ministers and civil servants to probe into individual, minor investment projects. Hence the arguments for broad criteria as outlined earlier.

We have noted the movement of opinion towards the establishment of broad pricing rules. A conclusion that may be drawn from much of the analysis in this book, however, is that 'marginal costs', of whatever variety, are difficult to define and often highly specific to individual industries. The practical problems of laying down such rules are likely to be very substantial.

An alternative approach might be to begin with discussion of long-term plans. Those plans, and the strategies and investment programmes flowing out of them, could form the basis for discussion of the public enterprises' development over, say, five-yearly periods. Alternative courses of action could be considered with sensitivity analysis of forecasts and assumptions, objectives and goals perhaps reviewed (financial targets and, in effect, goals in terms of Chapter 3) and past *general* performance monitored. Perhaps only a small sample of investment projects could be taken for systematic evaluation, attention being focused on the size and nature of total investment programmes[18].

Clearly, we may expect some very interesting policy debate around this subject in the future.

18. FOSTER, C. D., op. cit.

INDEX